FISCHE

LIVING WITH NATURE

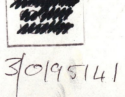

Living with Nature

Environmental Politics as Cultural Discourse

Edited by

FRANK FISCHER
and
MAARTEN A. HAJER

OXFORD
UNIVERSITY PRESS

OXFORD
UNIVERSITY PRESS

Great Clarendon Street, Oxford OX2 6DP

Oxford University Press is a department of the University of Oxford.
It furthers the University's objective of excellence in research, scholarship,
and education by publishing worldwide in

Oxford New York

Athens Auckland Bangkok Bogotá Buenos Aires Calcutta
Cape Town Chennai Dar es Salaam Delhi Florence Hong Kong Istanbul
Karachi Kuala Lumpur Madrid Melbourne Mexico City Mumbai
Nairobi Paris São Paulo Singapore Taipei Tokyo Toronto Warsaw

with associated companies in Berlin Ibadan

Oxford is a registered trade mark of Oxford University Press
in the UK and in certain other countries

Published in the United States
by Oxford University Press Inc., New York

© Frank Fischer and Maarten A. Hajer 1999

The moral rights of the author have been asserted
Database right Oxford University Press (maker)

First published 1999

British Library Cataloguing in Publication Data

Data available

Library of Congress Cataloging in Publication Data

Data available

ISBN 0–19–829226–0
ISBN 0–19–829509–X (Pbk.)

1 3 5 7 9 10 8 6 4 2

Typeset in Dante MT by Best-set Typesetter Limited
Printed in Great Britain
on acid-free paper by
Biddles Ltd, Guildford and King's Lynn

To Hanna and Thea Trautmann

Frank Fischer

To Minke and Louke Hajer

Maarten Hajer

Preface and Acknowledgements

Somewhere in a forest in Southern Finland stands a car wreck with a tree growing out of its hood. It is a strong and intriguing image. At first glance, it appears as a metaphor about the relation between nature and society. Contradicting our usual perception of the relationship, it suggests a contest in which nature has *reconquered* space it had lost to the culture of automobility. In actual fact, the photo depicts a work of art by the Finish artist Ossi Somma. Titled *Optimistic Nature*, the irony of the picture is the play on the *culture of progress* and the way in which we tend to conceive of the natural environment: as something *out there*. Somma manipulated both nature and culture and constructed a new image of the relation between society and environment. The image helps us to appreciate the ways in which we culturally interpret rather than objectively reflect the relationship of society to nature. It opens the questions: what alternative ways of seeing we can envisage; how do we analyse environmental problems?; and how do we want to live both in and with nature?

Today sustainable development has become an established way of conceptualizing the challenge for environmental politics. As such, environmental politics is increasingly mediated through scientific presentations of the state of nature, which in turn, supply the technocratic basis for so-called *win-win* solutions for environmental renewal. The essays presented here are written out of the conviction that we need to step back and reconsider the assumption and premises that underpin present-day environmental discourse. Even though sustainable development has become an established policy concern, the sorts of institutional approaches that have emerged in its wake are often problematic and exclude other ways of approaching environmental politics.

Approaching the question from a variety of backgrounds, the authors in this book not only elucidate the problematic social and cultural assumptions underlying the dominant environmental discourse, they also suggest alternative ways of deliberating about the meaning of nature and environmental politics. Moreover, from a cultural conceptual vantage-point they suggest a rethinking of basic practices that are by now institutionalised ways of conducting environmental politics.

We are grateful to all of those that have made the publication of this book possible. In addition to the authors, we should also like to extend special thanks to Dominic Byatt and Amanda Watkins of Oxford University Press for their steady support and helpful editorial assistance. We would further-more like to thank the Pori Art Museum, Finland for granting us permission to reproduce the picture of *Optimistic Nature* on the cover.

Some of the chapters in this book are elaborations of earlier papers. Chapter 3 is a strongly revised version of 'Spiritual Connections with the Natural Environment: Pathways for Global Change' which appeared in *Organization & Environment* Vol. 10, Number 4, pp 407-431. An earlier version of Chapter 7 appeared as 'Security and Solidarity: an anti-reductionist frame-work for thinking about the relationship between us and the rest of nature' in Vol. 163, (2) of *The Geographical Journal* July 1997, pp.141-149. It appears in this volume with kind permission of *The Geographical Journal*. Chapter 8 'The Environment of Justice' is reprinted from *Justice, Nature and the Geography of Difference* with the permission of Basil Blackwell, Oxford. Finally, Chapter 4,'Engineering the Environment' was translated from the Dutch original by Rob Kuitenbrouwer with financial support by the Royal Nether-lands Academy of Arts and Sciences.

Contents

List of Abbreviations

AAEC	Association of African Earthkeeping Churches
CFC	chlorofluorocarbon
CNN	Cable Network News
CPT	Commisao Pastoral da Terra
EC	European Community
EPA	Environmental Protection Agency
GAD	Gender and Development
GATT	General Agreement on Tariffs and Trade
GDP	Gross Domestic Product
IBM	International Business Machines
IPAC	[Women's] International Policy Action Committee
IUCN	International Union for the Conservation of Nature
LDC	Less Developed Country
MIBE	Management Institute for Business and Environment
MIT	Massachusetts Institute of Technology
NATO	North Atlantic Treaty Organization
NGO	Non-Governmental Organization
OECD	Organization for Economic Co-operation and Development
OPEC	Organization of Petroleum Exporting Countries
PCB	polychlorinated biphenyl
SEATO	South-East Asia Treaty Organization
TNC	Trans-National Corporation
UN	United Nations
UNEP	United Nations Environmental Programme
UNCED	United Nations Commission on Environmental Development
USAID	United States Agency for International Development
WEDO	Women's Environmental and Development Organization
WHA	World Heritage Area
WTO	World Trade Organization
WWF	World Wide Fund for Nature (prev. World Wildlife Fund)
ZIRRCON	Zimbabwean Institute of Religious Research and Ecological Conservation

Contributors to this Volume

CAROLYN P. EGRI is at the Faculty of Business Administration, Simon Fraser University, Burnaby, Canada. She is author of numerous articles on organization, work, and the environment, including essays on organic farming and other forms of resistance to industrialized agriculture.

FRANK FISCHER is professor of Political Science at Rutgers University in New Jersey at Newark. He is author of the forthcoming *Citizens, Experts and the Environment: The Politics of Local Knowledge*, and co-editor of *Greening Environmental Policy: The Politics of a Sustainable Future* (New York: St Martin's Press, 1995).

YRJÖ HAILA is professor at the Department of Regional Studies and Environmental Policy of the University of Tampere, Finland. He is author (with Richard Levins), of *Humanity and Nature. Ecology, Science and Society* (London: Pluto Press, 1992).

MAARTEN A. HAJER is professor of Political Science at the University of Amsterdam. He is the author of *The Politics of Environmental Discourse—Ecological Modernization and the Policy Process* (Oxford: Oxford University Press, 1995).

DAVID HARVEY is professor of Geography at the Department of Geography and Environmental Engineering of the Johns Hopkins University, Baltimore. His most recent book is *Justice, Nature and the Geography of Difference* (Oxford: Blackwell 1997).

JOSEF KEULARTZ is associate professor at the Department of Applied Philosophy of the Agricultural University at Wageningen, the Netherlands. His latest book is *Struggle for Nature—A Critique of Radical Ecology* (London: Routledge, 1998).

TIMOTHY W. LUKE is professor of political science at Virginia Polytechnic Institute and State University, Blacksburg, Va. His most recent books are *Capitalism, Democracy, and Ecology: Departing from Marx* (University of Illinois Press, 1999) and *Ecocritique: Contesting the Politics of Nature, Economy, and Culture* (University of Minnesota Press, 1997).

CAROLYN MERCHANT is Professor of Environmental History, Philosophy, and Ethics in the Department of Environmental Science, Policy, and Management at the University of California, Berkeley. Among her many books are *The Death of Nature: Women, Ecology, and the Scientific Revolution* (1980); *Radical Ecology: The Search for a Livable World* (1992); and *Earthcare: Women and the Environment* (1995).

WOLFGANG SACHS is at the Wuppertal Institute for Climate, Environment and Energy at Wuppertal, Germany. His most recent book with R. Loske and M. Linz, is *Greening the North: A Postindustrial Blueprint for Ecology and Equity* (London: Zed Books, 1997).

PETER J. TAYLOR teaches in the Graduate Program on Critical and Creative Thinking at the University of Massachusetts, Boston. He is author of 'How Does the Commons Become Tragic? Simple Models as Complex Socio-Political Constructions', *Science as Culture* 7(4), 1988, and co-editor of *Changing Life: Genomes Ecologies, Bodies, Commodities* (University of Minnesota Press, 1997).

MICHAEL THOMPSON is at The Musgrave Institute, London, UK and the University of Bergen and The Norwegian Research Centre in Organization and Management, Bergen, Norway. He is the author, with R. Ellis and A. Wildavsky, of *Cultural Theory* (Boulder, Colo.: Westview Press, 1990) and, with Michiel Schwarz, *Divided We Stand: Re-defining Politics, Technology and Social Choice* (Philadelphia: University of Pennsylvania Press 1990).

DOUGLAS TORGERSON is professor of Political Science at Trent University, Peterborough, Canada. His new book *The Promise of Green Politics: Environmentalism and the Public Sphere* is forthcoming at Duke University Press in 1999.

EDITORS' INTRODUCTION

Beyond Global Discourse: The Rediscovery of Culture in Environmental Politics

MAARTEN HAJER AND FRANK FISCHER

In many analyses of contemporary environmental politics, the 1992 Earth Summit in Rio de Janeiro marks the moment in which the awareness of the global dimension of the ecological crisis was 'finally' accepted and confronted politically around the world. This global turn facilitated a new way of seeing and apprehending the world. It portrayed environmental problems in terms of a major 'ecological crisis' and, paradoxically, hinted at a solution. All environmental problems should, we learned, be understood in terms of a broader all-encompassing ecological 'problematique'. This new way of seeing created the basis for the new political strategy of 'sustainable development', delineated in the 1987 United Nations' Brundtland Commission report *Our Common Future*. With Brundtland and Rio an era of persuasion and learning came to a close as the world finally seemed to appreciate that when it comes to the environment, 'we are all in the same boat'.

Rio certainly spelled out some massive problems: the need to reduce carbon dioxide emissions, the limited sustainable pathways to development in the South, the need to fight poverty and stop deforestation, as well as the need to develop new strategies for water resources management and the protection of biodiversity. What is more, Rio established 'Agenda 21', a package of long-term goals that were to form the basis of a concerted effort to address these problems. In the spirit of the common bonds acknowledgement at the 'Earth Summit' it was also agreed to reconvene after five years to 'renew the spirit' and 'keep the momentum'. Environmental discourse had turned global and the time had come for serious policy making.

The 'Rio-plus-Five' conference held in New York in 1997 was, above all, a wake up call. It offered a very disturbing finding—none of the important commitments made at Rio had been kept. In spite of the agreement to bring down carbon dioxide emissions to the 1990 levels by the year 2000, emissions in 1997 were higher than ever before. Furthermore, the intention to raise northern aid for the 'sustainable development' of the southern countries to 0.7 per cent of GDP in 1992, went entirely unheeded. A mere five years after Rio even less foreign aid was available than at the time of the Rio summit itself. Equally troubling, the forest cover continued to decline, the management of water resources was seen to have failed, and the commitment to defend biodiversity had been neglected. The ironical—embarrassing—explanation for this lack of progress was the argument that many countries had experienced growth over this five-year period. More economic growth had simply led to more pollution.

What to make of all of this? The failure of Rio, of course, reflects a lack of political determination. But just as problematic, the framing of the problem that emerged substantially limits the space for a meaningful response. Indeed, the Rio agreements should be seen as the climax of a *particular* take on environmental politics and policy that has in itself contributed to the slow and disappointing results. Hence, the 'global turn' of Rio and its Agenda 21 is, we argue, not to be interpreted as the 'climax' of environmental discourse *per se*. Although a key moment in the determination of environmental problems as they are now being addressed, the terms that it sets out remain incomplete and problematic. It is now time to reframe environmental politics in an effort to find new ways of dealing with the politics of environmental change.

Reconsidering Sustainable Development

The concept of sustainable development should be credited with providing the 'generative metaphor'—or story line—around which different key economic and environmental interests could converge. As such, it initially proved to be a very functional concept for setting out a common way of talking about environmental issues. Yet its conceptual basis has been weak from the outset (cf. Torgerson 1995). Essentially, the concept suggests that we 'can have it all', both further growth and a cleaner environment (Dryzek 1997). Still, it would be wrong only to conceive of sustainable development as an evident non-starter, designed mainly to divert environmentalism from a more radical course of action, in particular more stringent limits on economic growth (Fischer and Black 1995). Sustainable development, as a project, evolved out of a progressive discourse inside the UN which was, in the best social-democratic spirit, concerned with making the world environment a safer, fairer and more prosperous place (Hajer 1995: 99 ff.).

Unfortunately, however, it is clear that sustainable development has not produced the sort of institutional restructuring that appear to be necessary. To the extent that sustainable development has come to have meaning, it has—following the shape of the coalition that promoted the notion— primarily served as a vehicle for a form of 'eco-managerialism' (see Luke, Chapter 5 and Harvey, Chapter 8). In its most sophisticated form it has facilitated elements of what has been called 'ecological modernization'.

In both cases important critical messages contained in much of environmental discourse before Brundtland and Rio are lost. Missing is the critique of industrial progress, in paricular the question about the viability of endless material growth and consumption. The principal problem is, sustainable development remains caught in what the British novelist John Berger has called the 'culture of progress'. Basic to this culture is an insistent reliance on the idea that problems, once recognized and publicly acknowledged, can be handled by the institutions of science, technology, and management. Lost to this approach is the deeper cultural critique of modern society itself. We should not forget that the contemporary environmental movement emerged in significant part as a counter-cultural challenge (Roszak 1969). The pollution incidents and reports on damage done to the natural environment led to a critique of the industrial and social arrangements that made these things possible. Yet in the end, sustainable development has facilitated a project of 'institutional learning' according to which the existing institutions internalized the ecological dimension into their thinking but without addressing this cultural critique.

The failure of sustainable development to give rise to a new era of green politics suggests the need to re-examine the discursive frame in which it sought to define strategies for change and renewal. From a discursive perspective, sustainable development quickly illuminates a remarkable but problematic continuity in terms of the conceptual frame and specific actors through which environmental discourse gets reproduced. The problem with sustainable development, then, seems to be lodged in the global 'discourse-coalition' that shaped up around the notion. It comprises a variety of actors, including the environmental policy makers of various nation-states and international organizations, such as the UNEP, OECD, and World Bank, the institutionalized environmental sciences, and increasingly professional reform-oriented environmental NGOs. This discourse-coalition frame has given shape to and promoted a set of institutionalized practices through which the particular interpretation of sustainable development is produced, reproduced, and transformed (Hajer 1995). The political meaning and implications of the environmental 'problematique' are predetermined in an ongoing conversation among these actors. Between them, the key actors of this discourse-coalition—although obviously not all with equal weight—have basically framed the issues, determined the language in which the environmental debate is conducted, and pre-defined the direction in which solutions are to be sought. In order to be heard, one needs to comply with the terms of this pre-given discourse and, at least as important, engage in a debate with the aforementioned actors.

Our argument here is that nowadays it is not the metaphor of 'sustainable development' in itself that leads environmental politics astray. Rather, it is with the interpretation of its meaning, in particular the fact that it does not compel existing institutions to reconsider the normative and cultural assumptions and premises underlying their operational practices. To the contrary, such institutions have created new sets of mutual interlinkages, around an understanding of sustainable development that refers at least as much to the perpetuation of modern techno-industrial arrangements as it does to our basic socio-cultural relationships with the nature environment *per se*. Indeed, sustainable development is a perspective that offers these economic and social institutions a new lease on life, a new perspective in which there is still a clear role for them to play more or less on their own terms.

How did this happen? Here it is important to appreciate that, sustainable development always was a reform-oriented *inclusionary* discourse. As such, it has sought to facilitate a non-adversarial approach to environmental politics. Since there is now a general consensus around sustainable development—so this argument goes—there is no longer need for conflict, only for collaboration. Yet every consensus has its price. After all, in this perspective, sustainable development is framed in terms not so much of fundamental social change as of adjustment of basic institutional practices. The dominant discourse that shaped up around the notion of sustainable development was one that suggested that the major institutions could learn, had learned and would be able to reinvent themselves so as to become co-producers of a new sort of development that would be more environmentally sustainable.

Unfortunately, this discourse has led to a reduction of the reflexive potential of environmental politics. Andrew Jamison (1996), for instance, has shown how the globally operating NGOs such as the International Union for the Conservation of Nature (IUCN), the World Wide Fund for Nature (WWF), or Greenpeace adopted a firm inclusionary orientation, thinking with and for policy-makers at inter- and supranational governmental meetings and councils. To the extent that this modernizing discourse has prevailed, it has hindered the emergence and development of more temporarily and spatially focused attempts to reconstruct institutional routines and socio-natural relationships. Jamison provocatively argues that the institutional successes of particular environmental NGOs can now also be interpreted as a *constraining* force on environmental discourse.

Sociologists and political scientists have pointed out that the conceptual bridge between the recognition of the environmental problem and the insistence that the (existing) system could adapt glosses over important characteristics of a globalized modern capitalist society (see U. Beck 1992; Lash, Szerszynski, and Wynne 1996). After all, the ecological crisis is the (unintended) consequence of some of capitalism's essential features, such as the continued reliance on economic growth and its insatiable desire to create new markets, as well as its use of such growth to create space for political interventions (thus avoiding active redistribution of resources). Behind this, we see various key practices of modernity working to further this political–economic dynamic: the dominance of scientific rationality and expert knowledge, the strong reliance on—and belief in—technological innovation as the agent of progress, the implicit legitimization of the use of violence, and the central tendency to see nature as an exploitable resource or as an externality. For instance, the approach of sustainable development suggests that sustainability and economic growth can go hand in hand because it presumes that our knowledge is sophisticated enough to reveal the limits of nature, thus permitting us to exploit resources safely up to that limit. As Taylor (Chapter 6) makes clear, everything to date about environmental science raises serious questions about the validity of this assumption.

Seen in this light, present institutional efforts seem to be based on a very partial analysis of the societal forces that produced the crisis in the first place. Rather than seeking to adjust these key practices, the discourse-coalition of sustainable development has indeed 'bracketed' the essence of the socio-political order. Indeed, its efforts have advanced the typical modernist features of big science and co-ordinated management with all the institutional arrangements that come with it: policy planning, concerted action, scientific management, monitoring, risk assessment. As an institutional approach that purports to deal with the challenges of environmental degradation, while leaving aside basic cultural and political questions about the institutions implicated in producing the crisis in the first place, as well as more generally questions about the kind of society we want, sustainable development has become very vulnerable to radical critique.

Environmental Politics and Culture

It is our conviction that the discourse on environmental policy is plagued by the fact that it has been cut off from the cultural dimension of environmental politics. Given that environmental discourse emerged in large part as a cultural critique of modern society, this is more than a little ironic (see Hays 1987, Worster 1988). Consider, for example, one of the initial documents of modern environmental discourse, Rachel Carson's *Silent Spring* (1962). Carson, a scientist who turned to writing more popularly about the environment, primarily aimed to illuminate the extent to which new toxic chemical substances such as pesticides, fungicides, and herbicides, had not only penetrated the ecosystem, but also our way of life. To be sure, Carson had a purpose: she wanted to show that the usage of pesticides was a danger-ous mistake. Against the idea that we could 'control' nature by such scientific–industrial means, she argued for a return to a more biologically grounded appreciation of nature and its cycles of decline and renewal. This was in itself already a critique of a particular way of relating to nature. What really captured the public's imagination, however, was the discursive construct of a possible 'silent spring' and the examples of how the proliferation of chemicals actually had penetrated our cherished life-worlds already. It was through these examples that people came to realize that nature as they valued it—again, a cultural notion—was at stake. People were disturbed by the prospect that something that one would take for granted—that singing birds mark the coming of springtime—might be a fragile experience. What is more, they were horrified to discover that pesticides had already been found in the breast milk of mothers nursing their children. *Silent Spring* thus confronted society with the things we value without ever having had to argue for them. It put on the agenda the need to find a new way of living with nature.

Because culture is a difficult term, it is therefore important to be clear about what we mean by it. In *The Long Revolution* Raymond Williams (1961) distinguished three definitions of culture: an aesthetic definition of culture as 'art', the Latin definition of 'Cultura' as cultivation of mind and spirit, and the anthropological conception of culture as a 'way of life'. Throughout this book we use culture in the latter anthropological sense. We talk about culture as the implicit systems of meaning and frames of reference that underpin the various institutional practices through which we conduct environmental politics. We reintroduce culture to further the appreciation of the *particularity* of the way societies relate to the natural environment, to explore the different ways in which the social order is implicated in environmental politics, and the particular approaches to environmental policy.

We aim to explore the various practices through which particular ways of relating to nature get reproduced and, by so doing, we hope to politicize the cultural underpinnings of present strategies.

One thing that has become clear over the last decade is that even though sustainable development has created joint global discourses on environmental politics, we cannot assume that this will in itself produce better outcomes. Behind all the consensus are different frames of reference that inspire the way in which different cultures take up the challenges implicit in sustainable development. Such differences in cultural frames of reference now lead to new sorts of conflict in environmental politics, for instance cases where the cultural bias in sustainable development is denied and sustainable development is seen as being imposed on people. Similarly, we might now need to pay more attention to the cultural embeddedness of policy-making, of our social life, and of the way of governing economic activity.

This is of course, not completely new territory. Culture has been reintroduced into the study of politics by the pioneering work of Mary Douglas and Aaron Wildavsky (1982). Important as the 'cultural theory' was for opening up the debate, the work unfortunately remained overly focused on the cultural ideal-types. What is more, it was hampered by an obvious anti-environmentalist bias. Here we seek to step beyond that frame to more specifically investigate the observable practices that shape the course of events in present day environmental politics.

To get a grip on culture we distinguish 'cultural critique' from 'cultural politics'. *Cultural critique* refers to the various utterances within environmental discourse that problematize existing arrangements and suggest alternative ways of living with nature. The public resonance of *Silent Spring*, for example, was not merely related to the usage of pesticides but pointed to a more general unease with the 'effluents of affluence'. In this respect, cultural critique, has always accompanied modern environmental discourse. It has been the recurring confrontation with 'incidents'—from oil spillages and industrial contamination to explosions in nuclear power plants—that produced and intensified a particular and persistent form of cultural critique within the discourse of the environmental movement and eventually society more generally. The way in which society related to nature was up for reconsideration. Yet with the uptake of environmental discourse in the established sphere of institutional politics this dimension of cultural critique has lost much of its impact.

However, over the past decade the need to return to an analysis of the broader cultural implications of environmental discourse has become increasingly clear. What the social sciences have started to appreciate much

more over the last decade is how environmental discourse, often uninten-
tionally, can itself be a cultural force. Indeed, it can be analysed as a form
of *cultural politics*. Cultural politics is about the way in which different
systems of ordering are either maintained or imposed on others, how questions of identity feature within environmental discourse, how social relationships get redefined, or how particular ways of doing things either get
reproduced or are changed. To examine environmental discourse as cultural
politics is to reconstruct the ways in which these cultural power effects occur,
as well as their broader social implications. It thus becomes possible to
recognize that the institutional response to the cultural critique has its own
cultural power effects.

This idea of analysing environmental discourse as cultural politics is partly
based in the empirical findings of the effects of environmental policy-
making over the last decade, as various essays in this book indicate. Elsewhere Hajer has argued that culture is always fundamentally implicated in
environmental politics, not only as cultural critique but also in a much more
implicit form. Pointing to Mary Douglas's classic definition of pollution as
'matter out of place', he underlines how debates on pollution or environmental 'degradation' are always also debates about preferred social orders
(Hajer 1995, 1996, cf. also Harvey, Chapter 8). Analysing both the particular
practices in environmental politics and the discourse in which environmental issues are addressed allows us to come to grips with this hidden or implicit
cultural dimension of environmental politics.

Sustainable development, then, can be approached as a policy-discourse
with strong cultural–political underpinnings (Fischer and Black 1995). Of
course, the concept of sustainable development officially acknowledges the
cultural diversity and complexity of the global sphere. Yet it does so in a way
that misses the point: culture is all too quickly relegated to a care for the
diversity of folklore. Absent here is the more pressing cultural politics of sustainable development, namely the need to address the issues of growth and
consumption, the narrow framing of the environmental crisis as a scientific
problem, and the resultant reliance on techniques such as risk assessment
and its orientation on technological and managerial solutions (Fischer 1995).
Interpreting culture, in other words, is not limited to the understanding of
'other' cultures as is the case with indigenous cultures, but rather is a
reflexive exercise relating to the project of sustainable development as well:
culture is also brought to bear in its very own conceptualizations and policy
technologies.

The analysis of environmental discourse offered in this book suggests
the need for a formulation of a new cultural critique. What we see is how
sustainable development is in danger of becoming a replay of earlier tech-

nocratic efforts to redress the relationship of man and nature in the contemporary era. As with the US conservationist movement in the early 1900s sustainable development has given birth to technocratic cadres of sustainable development experts, who, as Luke argues in Chapter 4, seek to disassemble, recombine, and subject the natural environment to the needs of contemporary economic strategies. Such experts are to calculate and plan the 'carrying capacities' of local and regional ecosystems, i.e., the very kind of technocratic institutional orientation that counter-cultural environmental movement of the 1970s and 1980s argued against. Now the discourse of sustainable development has become a central vehicle for the continued reliance on these very policy practices and technologies.

Interestingly, we can see how this cultural dimension of environmental discourses has itself been acted upon already. This appears in the rediscovery of various cultural predispositions in the wake of the endorsement of sustainable development. Indeed, it now becomes clear that the global turn in environmental politics is in fact a reduction of the complexity of the problem. This new awareness, as Milton (1996) has shown, has led to a *reappreciation* of the many local particularities. Global environmental discourse has suggested much more unity and shared understanding than can be legitimately assumed. Those who thought that once a shared understanding was established, ameliorative environmental action would only grow and spread are now proven clearly wrong (cf. Yearley 1996).

Beyond understanding this cultural dimension as a reason for the failure of sustainable development, it is also essential for the identification of new perspectives. The confrontation with sustainable development as a global policy regime brought to the fore the 'whole complex of social and natural relationships' that Raymond Williams describes as 'at once our product and our activity' (see Taylor, Chapter 6). Through this perspective we come to see that the relationship between ways of life and the concern over environmental change is far more complicated than generally portrayed. In fact, as Martinez-Allier (1990, 1995) has pointed out, there are clearly different 'environmentalisms'. Environmentalism cannot only be seen as a product of post-material values of middle classes of the industrialized North. There is now as well a new 'environmentalisms of the poor' that has grown out of the distributive conflicts over the use of ecological resources. Rather than luxury consumption, as in the case of the middle classes, such resource conflicts for the poor typically concern their basic means of subsistence (e.g. deforestation); or erupt over the unequal distribution of environmental risks (e.g. the US environmental justice movement).

The complexity of these relationships between society and nature deserves a more prominent position in our thinking about environmental politics. Acting on this recognition, we begin to move beyond the dominant global techno-managerial discourse and its recommendations. Towards this end, we seek an approach capable of including the contemporary emphasis on global environmental problems while at the same time moving beyond it. As Haila emphasizes (Chapter 2), it is a matter of finding a new balance between our capacity for abstract reasoning and the local manifestations and appreciations of environmental politics. Herein lies a tremendous task for social science. It is to this task that our cultural–analytic focus seeks to contribute. Such a social science will not only make us aware of the diversity of the global environment, but also help us to deal with the questions of social justice, political economy, and democratic legitimation needed to implement this more inclusive cultural understanding of sustainable development. As a social science that more explicitly recognizes the importance of cultural identity in environmental politics, in particular our own relationship to nature, it seeks to uncover possibilities for alternative trajectories that are both more explicitly socially sustainable and culturally attractive.

The Essays

Part I of the book, 'The Natural Environment as Cultural Construct', opens with, 'Sustainable Development and the Crisis of Nature: On the Political Anatomy of an Oxymoron' by Wolfgang Sachs, focusing on the politics of global sustainability. Pointing to the long tradition of northern industrial exploitation of the southern hemisphere's natural resources, Sachs argues that these activities have boomeranged back on the North in the form of a 'crisis of nature'. Today, problems such as global warming and the widening of the ozone hole affect the globe as a whole.

'Sustainable development', he argues, fails to address directly the difficult questions concerned with levels of growth, what kinds of needs should be satisfied, and how available resources should be distributed. Side-stepping the problems of social justice associated with further development, sustainable development skirts a much-needed discourse of the implicit assumptions embedded in the concept. To illustrate his argument, Sachs outlines three primary discourses currently framing the debate on sustainability—the 'contest perspective', the 'astronaut's perspective' and the 'home perspective', each resting on different political and cultural assumptions. Whereas the contest perspective works on the silent assumption that the development can still be made durable for the richer parts of the world, the astronaut's perspective recognizes the degree to which the range of harmful effects produced by the North now cover the entire planet and sees the need for global adjustments. In contrast to the contest perspective, the home perspective accepts the finiteness of growth but questions the astronaut's emphasis on global adjustments. From the home perspective, sustainable development is an oxymoron: it tries to reconcile two fundamentally opposing elements.

Sachs argues that all three discourses are at best partial. What is needed is an effort to move beyond a managerial emphasis on more efficient—and thus presumably cleaner—forms of development to what he calls the 'sufficiency' revolution. A revolution that can neither be engineered nor programmed, as it depends on a mix of cultural and institutional changes in society more generally. Rather than emphasizing use of energy and resources, a discourse truly capable of guiding us toward a sustainable future has to be grounded in a critical discussion of the socio-cultural values and institutional patterns of modern societies. For Sachs, this requires a new way of measuring prosperity that does not depend on permanent growth. His discussion thus poses the cultural challenge of finding other ways of living together well with less.

Extending the North/South theme, in Chapter 2 Yrjö Haila examines the contemporary global definition of the environmental problem in the light of previous colonial struggles. While the astronaut's image of the 'shrinking earth' has played an important role in making us aware of responsibility to take care of our 'fragile spaceship', the image of the earth as a whole viewed from afar is, ultimately, impossible to sustain. The perspective, Haila argues, loses the earth as setting for real human life-worlds; the world emerges in terms of abstractions concerned with rarefied networks of interconnections. In the prevailing view of the global environment, human history is reduced to a unilinear, law-like progression toward an inevitable catastrophe. As he puts it, 'the conquest of nature through human ingenuity is replaced with the destruction of nature through human stupidity and avarice, but the *hubris* remains'. The challenge for environmental politics, he maintains, is how to hang on to an awareness of the earth as a whole without losing our sensitivity to the cultural particularity of entities, processes and situations.

Toward this end, he offers an insightful discussion of earlier conquests— in particular, the Russian conquest of the capital of the Republic of Yakutia in eastern Siberia and the Spanish take-over of large empires of Central and South America to illustrate the consequences of such objectifications. In the case of the Spanish, for example, success is seen in significant part to have resulted from their ability to objectify the Indians as 'others', and to integrate this understanding of the Indian culture into their global world-view. This made it possible to turn the Spaniards' Christian, universalized world-view into a purposeful belief system for legitimating the manipulation of the locally constructed Indian cultures. Moreover, he shows the ways in which such processes of systematic objectification have been extended to the conquest of nature. Through the invention of scientific taxonomies of nature, a new mode of thought emerged in European scientific centres to order the vast amount of new material acquired in the aftermath of the conquest. An important result was the gradual shift away from a pre-determined divine order of things to an emphasis on the belief that nature is governed by laws that need to be explained in terms of analytical classifications of natural processes. As nature was both externalized and objectified as an object of knowledge, it easily became the object of exploitation.

Beyond the scientific effort to come to grips with the present-day destruction of nature is the need to uncover the specific socio-natural relationships that relate man to nature in particular cultural situations. Here we need to regain the capacity of 'listening to' and 'learning from' both nature and other human beings. Respect for both nature and cultures that understand nature provide a fertile soil for the basis of developing a new social solidarity. Insofar as mutual help and solidarity have been basic prerequisites of human existence for tens of thousands of years, a rediscovery of respect for and care of the particularities of both nature and cultures can provide us with a way to learn to live together with nature in particular circumstances.

This need to reflect on different cultural relations to nature is illustrated in quite a different way by Carolyn Egri in her discussion of how nature has been understood in alternative spiritual world-views: Chapter 3, 'Nature in Spiritual Traditions: Social and Cultural Implications for Environmental Change', demonstrates the ways in which nature-centred religions and philosophies in other cultures have constructed distinct understandings of the relationships of humankind to nature. Focusing on humankind's need to find modes of social organization that allow it to survive with nature, she shows how different cultures have searched out and constructed different meanings and purposes for nature. Through archaeological evidence of prehistoric hunter-gathering societies that depicts long eras in which humankind lived relatively harmoniously with nature, she makes clear how very recent is the modern economic and scientific emphasis in western societies on the ascent of man over nature.

Drawing on environmental philosophers such as Berry, Spretnak, and Merchant, all pointing to the urgent need for transformations that extend beyond the biophysical environment to the deeper realm of values and beliefs, Egri argues that spiritual traditions can help to create less mechanistic, more harmonious cultural relationships with nature, that will be more appropriate to meet the environmental challenges of the twenty-first century. They relate to the question of identity politics that has played a central role in cultural critique more generally. She asks how this framing might inform both contemporary environmental discourse and action strategies adopted by environmental organizations. Egri concludes by emphasizing the importance of difference and identity. There is no one universal environmental system or one single best way to relate to or identify with nature. Rather we have to move beyond the mechanistic views that have informed modern society to become more cognizant and respectful of the many significant and fundamental differences among orientations to nature. Local contexts do not automatically fit into a global discourse. Just as there is a need for biodiversity on the planet, there is also a need for diversity in human expression and action that reflects the unique historical, cultural, and biophysical realities that have evolved separately throughout the world.

Part II, 'Cultural Discourse in Environmental Expertise and Policy Making', turns from general considerations concerning the social construction and understandings of the natural environment to the more pragmatic applications in scientific expertise, management and policy making. Chapter 4 by Jozef Keulartz, 'Engineering the Environment: The Politics of Nature Development' opens the discussion. Narrating a remarkable development in nature conservation, he illuminates how nature conservation policy discourse in the Netherlands has shifted from protecting and conserving existing nature to the actual *production* of 'new nature'. In what has come to be called 'nature development', conservationists have entered a new age of environmental engineering geared to the creation and stabilization of preferred natural environments. Nature development, which is most commonly used to refer to the development of nature into cultivated land, thus gets a new, reflexive meaning. 'New nature' reopens the debate on what 'nature' and 'cultivated' mean. Keulartz points to the fact that the discourse of nature conservation has entered the era of 'technical reproducibility' (cf. also Böhme 1992), stepping beyond the constraining construct of Bill McKibben's idea of an 'end of nature', it thus opens a new perspectives for a politics of nature.

By focusing on nature development's cognitive roots, as well as its main sources of social authority, Keulartz shows that the principles of Dutch nature development involve a dubious form of cultural politics in which science is used to impose a particular cultural view of nature upon local communities. Ironically, the approach seeks to return the environment to its untouched natural state through technological manipulations. By turning a blind eye to rival visions of nature, it binds certain social groups together while excluding others.

What does this analysis tell us? Much of the debate around nature development, as Keulartz shows, has centred around the question of who has the correct image or definition of nature. Nature developers have tried to dominate the debate by presenting their image as *the* one and only objective and scientifically legitimate representation of nature. But from the perspective of evolutionary ecology, as Keulartz shows, this argument depends on a highly selective use of ecological findings. Alternatively, evolutionary ecology shows that nature changes, i.e. that 'naturalness' is a constant process of transformation rather than control and stability. Because undisturbed nature should not be conceived of as constant, bringing back the 'original situation' through nature development has no privileged position from which to make its claims. Science, in short, is in no position unilaterally to lay down the criteria for nature policy. What is needed, argues Keulartz, is an openess to other genres and vocabularies more in tune with a democratic culture of nature. More concretely, this means establishing more argumentative planning procedures (cf. also Fischer and Forester 1993). Such an approach to planning is open to a variety of solutions and scenarios that give more weight to social priorities and local potentials, as well as allowing for a redefinition of the cultural relations to nature. Suggesting an alternative to the controversy between nature conservation and development discourse, Keulartz ends his chapter with a plea for what he calls a 'democratic landscape'. Here environmental politics would again turn on the question what sort of relationship to nature we really want.

Chapter 5 by Tim Luke, 'Eco-managerialism: Environmental Studies as a Power/Knowledge Formation', examines the impact of the sustainable development discourse on the academic curriculum. More particularly, he conveys the ways this ecological emphasis on technical rationality is transmitted in schools dedicated to the training of professional ecologists and foresters. Like Keulartz, Luke is concerned with the fact that nature is an interpreted construct whose meaning is always contestable. His basic purpose is to show the ways in which the contemporary graduate ecology programmes in major universities in the United States are vital sites for constructing understandings of, and policy approaches to, the environment and nature. But not just any approach, as he shows. In accordance with the prevailing regimes of truth in techno-science, academic centres of environmental studies reproduce those bodies of practices and types of discourses which the top executive management of contemporary economic and political institutions regard as 'objective', 'valid', and 'useful'.

During the past decade, countries such as the United States and Britain have witnessed an explosion of such environmental programmes designed to produce professional–technical analysts and administrators. Offering training to deal with the environmental crisis on 'sound scientific and technical grounds', the curriculums of these programmes typically focus on the theories and practices of resource, risk, and recreational managerialism. Luke coins the term 'infrastructuralization' of nature to refer to the use of tools such as risk–benefit analysis for making judgements on dos and don'ts. In the process, Luke argues, students learn to rationalize the performative norms embedded at the core of capitalist theory and practice. Although Luke is aware of the limits of his empirical sample, his analysis nonetheless poses an important concern: the academy is deeply implicated in the discourse-coalition that exorcized the cultural critique from environmental debate. Students who enter these professional schools of environmental studies in search of the wisdom of Aldo Leopold or John Muir run the risk of leaving as technocratic practitioners of ecological risk analysis and environmental management in the tradition of Gifford Pinchot.

In Chapter 6, 'Mapping Complex Socio-Natural Relationships: Cases from Mexico and Africa', Peter Taylor focuses on the levels of complexity underlying the construction of environmental issues. Pointing to the fact that accounts of environmental change rarely include more than a few of the complexities that constitute a particular situation, Taylor illustrates the ways in which scientific techniques simplify reality in an effort to control the multiple manifestations of complex phenomena. To demonstrate how we might begin to uncover the processes through which such simplifications occur, as well as their socio-cultural implications, he explores the cultural politics involved in constructing scientific knowledge. We see that the underlying social and cultural relationships that give meaning to particular phenomena are primary casualties of conventional scientific practices.

To convey more clearly the degree of complexity that we are dealing with in ecological projects, Taylor presents a political–ecological outline of an analysis of a study of soil erosion in a mountainous agricultural region of Oaxaca, Mexico. The socio-historical evolution of the problem is seen to interweave a multiplicity of heterogenious, interacting, and inseparable social and natural elements operating at both micro and macro levels of explanation. An adequate explanation of such a phenomenon, Taylor argues, requires trans-disciplinary modes of enquiry grounded not only in the particular site, but in the practices of the investigators themselves.

In the second half of the chapter, he focuses on the problematic consequences of the abstractions basic to computer modelling and systems dynamics, key techniques in contemporary environmental policy-making. Specifically, he draws on an analysis of an MIT computer-based systems-dynamic model of ecological and social arrangements in nomadic pastoral sub-Saharan Africa. The example makes clear how the logic of the model works to supply simplicity and economy of explanation by screening out important concepts at the expense of others. In the concluding section of the chapter, Taylor introduces the techniques of mapping workshops to illustrate how a multi-dimensional perspective he calls 'heterogenious construction' might be employed to change the ways that society and nature are scientifically represented. By encouraging participants to be more explicit about their assumptions and choices concerning boundaries, empirical categories, levels of analysis, normative generalizations, he shows that mapping procedures can be used by analysts to develop the kind of richer, more textured understanding of the socio-natural phenomena called for by the central themes of the book as a whole.

The need for an alternative approach to environmental analysis and management is also taken up by Michael Thompson. In Chapter 7, 'Security and Solidarity: An Anti-Reductionist Analysis of Environmental Policy', Thompson engages the topic through the contemporary concern with 'environmental security'. Opening up security concerns to environmental discourse, environmental security has enlarged the circle of actors discussing the implications of ecological crisis. Whereas environmental policy-makers have discovered the ways in which security issues impacted on environmental degradation, security policy-makers have become aware of how environmental degradation has led to 'environmental refugees' and the potential for social unrest in various regions of the world. For Thompson, this discourse on environmental security draws too extensively on traditional state-level responses—admirals are commanded to ready their ships for battle. If we look more closely at what 'environmental security' should be about, however, we come to realize that in matters of security the local level is every bit as important, if not more so.

At the local level, as anthropological research shows, security is best understood in terms of social and cultural solidarities. From experiences of mountain villagers, as Thompson shows, we learn that security depends on the ability of locals to respond flexibly to nature. Drawing on the cultural theory of Mary Douglas, to which he himself has made important contributions over the last decade, Thompson identifies four types of cultural responses: hierarchist, individualist, egalitarian, and fatalist in style. Defining environmental security as the ability of the actors to move flexibly within this reportoire of styles as the situation requires, with scale or size constituting the critical dimensions of the situation. We need, in this respect, to learn to move beyond the kinds of one-dimensional thought associated with eco-managerialism. Beyond the 'one-best-way' of scientific management, we need to move to an anti-reductionist approach to the environment. As each new response to the environmental problem brings new conditions, the challenge is not 'getting it right' as much as it is 'covering all of the bases'. Elaborating on the four behavioural repertoires, he offers a number of principles to guide an anti-reductionist approach to environmental policy.

Moving from policy and expertise to the issues of environmental politics and cultural difference, Part III opens with Chapter 8 by David Harvey, on 'The Environment of Justice'. Harvey takes up the issues of social class raised by the environmental justice movement in the United States. The discussion begins with the primary issue that has given rise to the movement, namely the dumping of toxic wastes in poor communities or countries. Since most of the poor and the disempowered are people of colour, the negative health consequences are visited on those least able to deal with them. These impacts are thus racially discriminating; Harvey suggests that it might be likened to a form of 'cultural imperialism'.

In the early 1990s, however, the struggle against this practice gave rise to one of the most vigorous components of the contemporary environmental movement in the US, the environmental justice movement, organized by poor communities themselves. This bottom-up grassroots movement, described by many as the most progressive force in contemporary environmental politics, aggressively organizes around the issues of race, class, and gender. In response, the Clinton administration felt compelled to enact an executive order designed to ensure that no federal programme would unfairly inflict environmental harm on the poor and minorities. The executive order declares that the environmental needs of low-income and minority communities must be fairly addressed and that environmental issues can be adjudicated in terms of civil rights laws. Although the order has to date largely been more symbolic than substantive, its existence testifies to the force of the movement.

Taking the issue beyond the specific case, Harvey argues that all environmental arguments are arguments about society in general and thus 'complex refractions of all sorts of struggles being waged in other realms'. To illustrate this point, he examines three major environmental discourses—environmental management, ecological modernization, and wise use—to show how their positions are grounded in the existing society and the ways that these positions have compelled the environmental justice movement to articulate its oppositional arguments in very particular ways. Emphasizing inequalities in protection against environmental hazards, suspicion toward reliance on expert and professional discourses, the need for a biocentric focus on the fate of nature, and the need for local empowerment, the environmental justice movement seeks nothing less than a redefinition of the environment. In this view, 'the totality of life conditions in . . . communities—air and water, safe jobs for all at decent wages, housing education, health care, humane prisons, equity, [and] justice emerge as the concerns through which environmental pollution has to be understood and considered'. In short, environmental pollution is understood as an expression of social and cultural problems manifested in other sectors of society.

Harvey closes with a comparison of these environmental discourses in terms of the principles of social justice. It is on this terrain, he argues, that we now find an essentially unresolvable debate on the proper form of environmental ethics unfolding, especially as each discourse attaches itself to long-standing, respected philosophical traditions. There is, he argues, no way to define a philosophical or discursive answer to the intense questions of social relations, power, beliefs, and institutions that underlie the environmental problem. In the final analysis, we must recognize the truth of Marx's argument: 'Between equal rights, force decides.' Against this understanding, writes Harvey, the struggle for environmental justice will thus remain a struggle embedded in experiences of particular local places but driven by larger, more encompassing struggles for recognition, respect, and empowerment.

Douglas Torgerson, in Chapter 9, 'Images of Place in Green Politics: The Cultural Mirror of Indigenous Traditions', continues this discussion of place with an examination of a specific cultural problem that surfaces in environmental discourse, namely the relation of indigenous cultures to the dominant culture of the North. In particular, he analyses a tension between the green movement's defence of place and its promotion of environmental democracy as open discourse. On the one hand, the defence of place counters the abstract notion of neutral space that has guided western efforts to conquer nature through colonial expansion and industrial development. Place, valued in its particularity, is infused with meaning as a part of ways of life. On the other hand, the open discursive ethos of green politics challenges the dominant practices of technocratic decision-making and related efforts towards narrow framing of policy argumentation. Generally assumed to be mutually compatible, Torgerson reveals a troublesome tension between open discourse and indigenous places through a case study of an alliance between greens and indigenous people.

Drawing on an environmental struggle over logging practices in British Columbia, he shows that the defence of place for indigenous peoples means something more than offering public arguments. Toward this end, Torgerson introduces what he calls 'the paradox of open discourse'. The paradox is employed to demonstrate the need for greater cultural sensitivity by greens involved in indigenous struggles. Not only do greens need to be more sensitive to the complexities of indigenous cultures, they must avoid allowing their own cultural development to be constricted by the demands of open argument in the public forum.

Carolyn Merchant's concluding chapter, 'Partnership Ethics and Cultural Discourse: Women and the Earth Summit', points to the fact that the conference at Rio shifted environmental discourse beyond mere recognition of the environmental crisis to the basic issue of restructuring society to create an enduring relationship with nature and the non-human world.

One of the important products of the Rio conference has been the emergence of a new democratic praxis that encompasses feminism, environmental justice, multicultural concerns, and North–South conflicts. Underscoring the intertwining of nature and women's interests, Merchant argues that a new cultural politics arising out of women's experiences can provide a new environmental ethics for sustainability, or what she calls a sustainable partnership with the natural world. 'Partnership', she writes, 'is a word experiencing a renaissance in the discourse of the business and environmental communities'. Offering a new approach to environmental collaboration, an ethics of partnership in the new discourse refers not only to humans and social processes, but also to natural entities and natural processes. As such, it holds out the possibility of moving us beyond the rhetoric of environmental conflict toward a discourse of ecological co-operation.

Whereas other major approaches to environmental ethics reflect conflicts inherent in modernist institutions, a partnership ethics, she argues, can draw on their strengths while rejecting the egocentric ethics associated with capitalist exploitation of people and nature. Toward this end, she outlines a code of ethics that recognizes the need to reorient economic production away from its narrow emphasis on endless growth and corporate profits to the sustainable fulfilment of basic human needs. By so doing, she illustrates how environmental discourse could again become a basis for a cultural politics of rethinking the way in which we live with nature.

The Cultural Embeddedness of Environmental Politics

Where does this leave us? This book argues that by bringing out the cultural in environmental discourse we can an get a new handle on environmental politics, both in terms of understanding its dynamics and for creating new options for political action. By so doing, the global turn of environmental politics no longer emerges as the final or definitive frame. Quite the contrary, it turns out to be a—perhaps necessary—stop on the way to a reappreciation of the importance of cultural diversity, both in terms of the search for meaningful approaches to environmental politics and in terms of analytical perspective.

Recognition of the physical manifestations of the environmental crisis, as well as consciousness of its various social implications, are now so widespread that the call for an environmentally responsible socio-economic system will scarcely fade away. To successfully deal with it, however, we need to rethink the way in which socio-natural relationships are conceptualized. As Manuel Castells puts it, 'throughout the globe, the old, simplistic opposition between development for the poor and conservation for the rich has been transformed into a multi-layered debate over the actual context of sustainable development for each country, city, and region' (Castells 1997: 110–11). Such problems, moreover, will remain with us until our institutional discourses and cultural practices succeed in transforming our 'modes of production and consumption as well as our social organization and personal lives'. Towards this end, our policy-making models must be reoriented around more sophisticated socio-cultural assumptions that recognize the great variety of experiences involved in an effort to find different ways to achieve the same goals. In short: one size cannot fit all. A new environmental politics, in this respect, has as much to do with a well-considered choice of alternative futures as with the reduction of emissions *per se*. Haila's call to recapture our understanding of the earth as a 'scene of real human life-worlds' without giving up the modern ability to analyse abstractly from a distance, speaks to this challenge. The next phase in environmental politics, requires a repositioning of environmental issues to recapture the task of cultural critique transcending the search for efficient solutions.

PART I

The Natural Environment as Cultural Construct

PART 1

1

Sustainable Development and the Crisis of Nature: On the Political Anatomy of an Oxymoron

WOLFGANG SACHS

At the Dawn of the Security Age

It appears as if today, near the end of the century, a cycle is coming to a close. It was opened by Columbus, as he set out on his journey across the Atlantic Ocean, more than 500 years ago. With his departure from Palos in search of a direct route to Asia—thinking of God, spices, and gold—he unknowingly set the sails for the expansion of Europe to the ends of the world. First, ships discovered ever more remote coastlines, then expeditions penetrated into the innermost regions of countries, and, bit by bit, the Europeans progressed, until barely any white spot was left on the map. Missions and trading posts established early global interconnections, the hunger for raw materials later spurred colonial empires, while CNN and Mondovision now finally create the global experiential space. Many departures followed the one from Palos; as a result, innumerable separate living spaces have been integrated into a single world. European civilization has circumnavigated the globe in the wake of Columbus.

Until recently, the burden of the unification of the world had to be carried almost exclusively by the peoples of the southern hemisphere, starting with the plague killing millions of Aztecs and Mayas immediately after the white man's arrival, passing through the deportation of generations of blacks as slaves to America, right down to the slums and favelas in today's mega-cities in the 'Third World'. And those who have been saved from these kinds of consequences, have often had to struggle with political dependence, economic disadvantage, and cultural degradation. Whatever achievements have been brought to the most remote regious of the globe by the gradual integration of the world shrink into insignificance in the face of the bitter consequences which have come along with it. By comparison, the countries of the North were able to corner the gains that accrued from the unification of the world for themselves. Notwithstanding financial drain or humiliating retreat at times, it is sufficiently obvious that the rise of the North has in part been fuelled by the riches drawn from the South through the network of global interconnections. By and large, the unification of the world seemed to be governed by some kind of magnetic law according to which the advantages concentrate in the North and the disadvantages in the South.

But this law, after 500 years, cannot be relied upon any longer. Now, for the first time after Columbus' departure, the bitter consequences of the unification of the world begin to reach the North as well. Though these events stand no comparison with those in the South, the tide is nevertheless turning. Consider for example the increasing economic strength of some countries in what used to be called the 'Third World'. Over the last twenty years the competitive edge of some of those countries has sharpened, putting considerable pressure on jobs and entire branches of the economy in the North, as the pupils of yesterday are about to outdistance their masters. Later, a similar configuration emerged in an entirely different area. Ever since Saddam Hussein's attack on Kuwait, if not before, the North has become aware that the many years of arming the South threaten to backfire on the North; since then governments nervously watch the accumulation of mega-arms in several countries of the South. Moreover, the population in the North feels alarmed, since a flow of immigrants and refugees legally and illegally arrive in the northern belt of prosperity. The fear of migration and population pressure rising from the South has firmly taken root in the subconsciousness of the rich countries. And last but not least, environmental dangers are also building up in the South, dangers that threaten in the long run to engulf and to destabilize even the North. After all, the rainforests in the tropics act as 'lungs' for the global (and, by implication, the northern) climate, the loss of biodiversity impinges upon the high hopes placed on a bio-technological future in the wealthy countries, and an unfettered motorization in China and India would finally transform the entire globe into a greenhouse.

Taking everything together, the boomerang seems to be a suitable metaphor for understanding the novel features of a rising epoch in North–South relations. The increasing integration of the world engenders consequences that, like a boomerang, threaten to rebound upon the North.[1] Although the reasons for this turnaround reach far back into the history of colonialism, two principal chronic conflicts have built up in the fifty years of accelerated world integration after World War II, whose effects increasingly spread around the globe.

The Crisis of Justice

Epochs rise slowly, but the opening of the development era happened at a
certain date and hour. On 20 January 1949, President Harry Truman, in his
inauguration speech before Congress, drawing the attention of his audience
to the conditions in poorer countries, for the first time defined them as
'underdeveloped areas'.[2] Suddenly, a concept which has become indispensable since, was established, cramming the immeasurable diversity of the
globe's South into one single category—the underdeveloped. That Truman
coined a new word was not a matter of accident but the precise expression
of a world-view: for him all the peoples of the world were moving along the
same track, some faster, some slower, but all in the same direction. He saw
the northern countries, in particular the US, running ahead, while the rest
of the world— with its ridiculously low per-capita income—were lagging far
behind. An image the economic societies of the North had increasingly
acquired about themselves was thus projected upon the rest of the world:
the degree of civilization in a country is indicated by the level of its production. Starting from that premise, Truman conceived of the world as an
economic arena where nations compete for a better position on the GNP
scale. No matter what ideals inspired Kikuyus, Peruvians, or Filipinos,
Truman recognized them only as stragglers whose historical task it was to
partake in the development race and catch up with the lead runners. Consequently, it was the objective of development policy to bring all nations into
the arena and to enable them to run the race.

After forty years of development, the state of affairs is dismal. The gap
between frontrunners and stragglers has not been bridged; on the contrary
it has widened to the extent that it has become unimaginable that it could
ever be closed. The aspiration of catching up has ended in a blunder of planetary proportions. Since 1960, according to the 1996 Human Development
Report, the distance between industrial and developing countries with
regard to per capita income has tripled. To be sure, upon closer inspection
the picture is far from homogeneous, but neither the South-East Asian
showcases nor the oil-producing countries change the result that the development race has ended in disarray. The world might have developed—but
in two opposite directions.

This is even more true if one considers the destiny of large majorities of
people within most countries; the polarization between nations repeats itself
within each country. On the global as well as on the national level, there is
a polarizing dynamics at work, which creates an economically ambitious
middle-class on one side and large sections of socially excluded populations
on the other. The best one can say is that development has created a global

middle-class of those with cars, bank accounts, and career aspirations. It is made up of the majority in the North and small elites in the South and its size equals roughly that 8 per cent of the world population which owns an automobile. They are, beyond all national boundaries, increasingly integrated into the worldwide circuit of goods, communication, and travel. An invisible border separates in all nations, in the North as well as in the South, the rich from the poor; entire categories of people in the North, like the unemployed, the elderly, and the economically weak, and entire regions in the South, like rural areas, tribal zones, and urban settlements find themselves increasingly excluded from the circuits of the world economy. 'North' and 'South' are therefore less and less geographical categories but rather socio-economic ones, referring to the line which divides the strong world-market sectors from the competitively weak, economically superfluous sectors in society.[3] A new bipolarism pervades the globe and reaches into every nation; it is no longer the East–West division which leaves its imprint on every society but the North–South division.

The Crisis of Nature

A second result of the development era has dramatically come to the fore in recent years. It has become evident that the racetrack leads in the wrong direction. While Truman could still take for granted that the North was at the head of social evolution, this premise of superiority has today been completely shaken—if not shattered—by the ecological predicament. For instance, much of the glorious rise in productivity is fuelled by a gigantic throughput of fossil energy which requires mining the earth on the one hand and covering her with waste on the other. By now, however, the global economy has outgrown the capacity of the earth to serve as mine and dumping ground. After all, the world economy increases every two years by about the size ($ 60 billion) which it had reached by 1900 after centuries of growth. Although only a small part of the world's regions has experienced economic expansion on a large scale, the world economy already weighs down nature to an extent that she has in part to give in. If all countries followed the industrial example, five or six planets would be needed to serve as 'sources' for the inputs and 'sinks' for the waste of economic progress. Therefore, a situation has emerged where the certainty which ruled two centuries has been exposed as a serious illusion: that growth is a play with an open end. Economic expansion has already come up against its biophysical limits; recognizing the finiteness of the earth is a fatal blow to the idea of development as envisaged by Truman.

500 years of protected status of the North seem to be drawing to an end. Europe's journey to the ends of the earth, initiated in the fifteenth century and completed in the twentieth, has lifted history to new heights, but has at the same time produced a configuration of conflicts which will inevitably shape the face of the twenty-first century. A world divided and a nature ill-treated is the heritage which casts its shadow forward. It is not that the conflicts as such are new, but their impact potentially spreads worldwide, as the pace of globalization is accelerating. For the unification of the world increasingly shows its seamy side; the globalization of goodies is accompanied by the globalization of nasties. What is new, in fact, is that the North is less and less protected by spatial and temporal distances from the unpleasant long-term consequences of its actions.

For several centuries the North could avoid dealing with the reality of a divided world, since the suffering occurred far away. Long distances separated the places of exploitation from the places of accumulation. However, as distances shrink, also the distance between victims and winners shortens, exposing the North to the threats of a divided world. Globalization not only joins the haughty North with the South, but also the chaotic South with the North. Likewise, the bitter consequences of the ill-treatment of nature make themselves felt without delay. Many generations could afford to neglect the limits of nature as a source and as a sink; the costs of the present have always been transferred to the future. The more, however, the rate of exploitation increases, the faster the finiteness of nature makes itself felt on a global scale. Since the distance in time, which for so long bolstered industrialism against its effects, is shrinking, the biophysical limits of nature have forcefully emerged in the present. For these reasons, time and space, delay and distance, have ceased to provide a protective shell for the world's rich; as globalization promises the simultaneity and ubiquity of goodies and of troubles. The departure of Columbus, after a long cyle, is followed by the return of menace.

The Horns of the Dilemma

'Development', as a way of thinking, is on its way out. It is slowly becoming common sense that the two founding assumptions of the development promise have lost their validity. For the promise rested on the belief, first, that development could be universalized in space and, second, that it would be durable in time. In both senses, however, development has revealed itself as finite, and it is precisely this insight which constitutes the dilemma that pervades many international debates since the UN Conference on the Environment in Stockholm in 1972. The crisis of justice and the crisis of nature stand, with the received notion of development, in an inverse relationship to each other. In other words, any attempt to ease the crisis of justice threatens to aggravate the crisis of nature, and vice versa: any attempt to ease the crisis of nature threatens to aggravate the crisis of justice. Whoever demands more agricultural land, energy, housing, services or, in general, more purchasing power for the poor, finds himself in conflict with those who would like to protect the soils, animals, forests, human health or the atmosphere. And whoever calls for less energy or less transport and opposes 'clear-cutting' or input-intensive agriculture for the sake of nature, finds himself in conflict with those who insist on their equal right to the fruits of progress. It is easy, however, to see that the base from which the dilemma rises is the conventional notion of development; for if there were development which used less nature and included more people, a way out of the dilemma would open up. Small wonder, therefore, that in the last two decades committed minds from all corners of the world have been calling for an 'alternative model of development'.

The comet-like rise of the concept 'sustainable development' is to be understood against that background. It promises nothing less than to square the circle: to identify a type of development that promotes both ecological sustainability and international justice. Since the times of the Club-of-Rome study 'Limits to Growth', two camps of political discourse had emerged, one under the banner of 'environment' and the other under the banner of 'development'. The voices from the North mostly emphasized the rights of nature, while the voices from the South tended to bring the claims for justice to the fore.[4] In 1987, the World Commission for Environment and Development (Brundtland Commission) appeared to have succeeded in building a conceptual bridge between the two camps, offering the definition which has become canonical: sustainable development is development 'that meets the needs of the present without compromising the ability of future generations to meet their own needs'.[5]

Already a quick glance, however, reveals that the formula is designed to maximize consensus rather than clarity. As with any compromise, that is no small achievement, because the definition works like an all-purpose cement which glues all parties together, friends and foes alike. The opponents of the 1970s and 1980s find themselves pinned down to a common ground, and since then everything revolves around the notion of 'sustainable development'. Nevertheless, the price for this consensus was considerable. Dozens of definitions are being passed around among experts and politicians, because many and diverse interests and visions hide behind the common key-idea. As so often happens, deep political and ethical controversies make the definition of the concept a contested area.

The formula is based upon the notion of time. It invites the reader to raise his eyes, to look at the future, and to pay due consideration to the generations of tomorrow. The definition officially confirms that the continuity of development in time has become a world problem. The egoism of the present is under accusation, an egoism which sells off nature for short-term gain. In a way, the phrase reminds one of the words by which Gifford Pinchot, the steward of Theodore Roosevelt's conservation programme, sought to bring utilitarianism up to date: 'conservation means the greatest good for the greatest number for the longest time.' But upon closer inspection, one will note that the definition of the Brundtland Commision shows no reference to 'the greatest number', but focuses instead on the 'needs of the present' and those of 'future generations'. While the crisis of nature has been constitutive for the concept of 'sustainable development', the crisis of justice finds only a faint echo in the notions of 'development' and 'needs'. In the definition, the attention to the dimension of time is not counterbalanced by an equal attention to the dimension of space. It is therefore not an exaggeration to say that the canonical definition has resolved the dilemma 'nature versus justice' in favour of nature. For two crucial questions remain open. 'What needs?' and 'Whose needs?' (*The Ecologist* 1992). To leave these questions pending in the face of a divided world means to sidestep the crisis of justice. Is sustainable development supposed to meet the needs for water, land, and economic security or the needs for air travel and bank deposits? Is it concerned with survival needs or with luxury needs? Are the needs in question those of the global consumer class or those of the enormous numbers of have-nots? The Brundtland report remains undecided throughout and therefore avoids facing up to the crisis of justice.

Environmental action and environmental discourse, when carried on in the name of 'sustainable development', implicitly or explicitly position themselves with respect to the crisis of justice and the crisis of nature. Different actors produce different types of knowledge, they highlight certain issues and underplay others. How attention is focused, what implicit assumptions are cultivated, which hopes are entertained, and what agents are privileged, depends on the way the debate on sustainability is framed. What is common to all these discourses, I would submit, is the hunch that the era of infinite development hopes has passed, giving way to an era in which the finiteness of development becomes an accepted truth. What renders them deeply different, however, is the way they understand finiteness; either they emphasize the finiteness of development in the global space and disregard its finiteness in terms of time or they emphasize the finiteness of development with regard to time and consider irrelevant its finiteness in terms of global space. In the following sections, I would like to sketch out three different perspectives of 'sustainable development' which differ in the way they implicitly understand finiteness. The *contest perspective* works with the silent assumption that development, unfortunately, will have to remain spatially restricted, but can be made durable for the richer parts of the world. It neglects the fact that the range of harmful effects produced by the North now covers the entire globe and limits the responsibility of the North for its own affairs. The *astronaut's perspective* takes a different view. It recognizes that development is precarious in time and seeks global adjustment to deal with the crisis of nature and the crisis of justice. As a response to the global reach of harmful effects, it favours the extension of the range of responsibility, until it covers the entire globe. The *home perspective*, in turn, accepts the finiteness of development in time and suggests delinking the question of justice from the pursuit of development. It draws a different conclusion from the fact that the range of effects produced by the North has vastly outgrown the radius of northern responsibility, and advocates reducing the effects, until they remain within the given radius of responsibility. It is quite possible that the relative strengths of these perspectives will shape the future of North–South relations.

The Contest Perspective

Some years ago, the French author Jean Christophe Rufin, in a book titled *The Empire and the New Barbarians*, proposed a telling metaphor for describing the changing mood in rich societies which face the globalization of threats. Dipping deep into European memory, he evoked the archetype of all frontiers, the *limes* (Latin, 'frontier'), for describing the new perception of North–South relations. Much as the Romans erected the *limes* to separate themselves from the barbarians beyond their empire, present powers, he suggests, are busy drawing a perceptual wall between the market-integrated parts of the world and the rest. Indeed, large parts of the southern countries now are no longer considered laboratories of the future, but zones of potential turbulence, and a source of all kinds of danger: the eruption of violence, the threat of immigration, the flooding of markets with cheap products, the population time-bomb, hurricanes. As the finiteness of development in terms of space moves into the consciousness, the perception changes: the countries of the South change from places where hope resides to places where threats arise.

Having been for a long time the economic masters of the world, the northern elites feel the pressure rising, as the newly industrialized countries become players on the world market. For these reasons, the attention of economic actors is firmly focused on international competitiveness; to counter globalized threats by the particular weapon of 'competitive strength' is their primary concern. Given the obsession to get ahead in the competitive struggle between the USA, Europe, and East Asia, achieving some ecological modernization along the way is all that seems conceivable. As a consequence, concepts and strategies of sustainability cannot be allowed to interfere in the medium and long term with the struggle for economic power; on the contrary, they are framed in such a way as to become part and parcel of that effort. How to bring the concern for the environment in line with the concern for economic efficiency and accumulation is the question squarely on the agenda of the contest perspective.

Growing for the Environmnent

First of all, in the light of the contest perspective environmental concern emerges as a force propelling economic growth. Shifting consumer demand spurs innovation, trimming down resource use lowers production costs, and environmental technology opens up new markets. Ecology and economics appear to be compatible; and the pursuit of both promises to be, as the magic formula goes, a positive-sum game. Growth is regarded as part of the solution, no longer as part of the problem (e.g. Reilly 1990, Fritsch *et al.* 1993). Indeed, it was perhaps this conceptual innovation which has done most to propel environmentalism into mainstream thought. Ever since the OECD in the early 1980s (advocating a new mix of resources, a changed structure of growth, and an emphasis on prevention) raised the prospects of an ecological modernization of industrial economies (Hajer 1995), a language linking business and environmental concerns has been developing. It centres around the redefinition of the environmental predicament as a problem of efficient resource allocation. Natural resources are considered grossly undervalued and therefore wastefully allocated, while human resources along with technology are underutilized; redressing the balance would basically do the job. Thus, achieving 'eco-efficiency' (Schmidheiny 1992) is proposed as the key-strategy for business, a strategy of considerable innovative power. The contest perspective goes further, however; by transferring the principle from the micro-economic to the macro-political level, it looks at society as if it were a corporation. In this view, political regulations which do not aim at efficiency are regarded as pointless or even wrongheaded. Issues such as legislation controlling multinationals, the evaluation of technologies in the public interest, or a sustainable WTO (World Trade Organization) are pushed off the agenda. Through the Business Council on Sustainable Development, for instance, whose membership list reads like the 'Who's Who' of the chemical, steel, and automobile industry, this perspective largely shaped the results of the UN Conference at Rio de Janeiro in 1992. Public authority in the realm of business activities remained a taboo; an outcome which, however, fits nicely in the neo-liberal utopia of those years which pretends that a society can be built bypassing collective human decisions (Hobsbawm 1994: 565).

But even the contest perspective needs to look beyond the arena of competition. After all, the rich economies require more land and natural resources than are available for them within their own boundaries. Plugging into the 'syntropy islands' (Altvater 1992) of the South had for centuries fuelled accumulation in the North, a scheme which is increasingly threatened as biophysical limits to exploitation come to the fore. As natural resources become scarce, some new regime, based either on the price mechanism or on political agreements, is mandated in order to cool down exploitation and to keep it at an manageable level. Moreover, in the 1980s the concern for nature as a resource was complemented by the concern for nature as a sink. The absorptive capacity of the biosphere for CFCs and CO_2 seemed to be exhausted, suggesting that the scarcity of sinks is even more pressing than the scarcity of sources. Whereas, however, access to sources could classically be secured bilaterally through occupation or trade, securing the access to sinks required limiting the emissions of a large number of countries. Making all utilize less can only be achieved multilaterally. For that reason, a new domain of international politics has emerged, in which international conventions are negotiated with the purpose of containing the claims to the biosphere. As a consequence, multilateral negotiations no longer centre on the redistribution of growth, as in the negotiations about the New Economic Order in the 1970s, but on the redistribution of reductions. However, given that all governments feel obliged to maximize their space for economic development, any reduction is seen as a loss. As a consequence, the ensuing conflicts are usually heated, up to a point that the environmental objectives fall by the wayside, as has happened with most of the Rio agreements.

From the Conservation of Nature to the Conservation of Growth

Likewise, the concept of nature changed. The conservation movement up until the 1970s was shaped by biocentric values; forests, waters, soils, and wildlife were deemed worthy of preservation in their own right. In a certain way, nature was regarded as the opposite of development, embodying values of otherness and permanence to be safeguarded against the pressures of economic growth. With the 1980 'World Conservation Strategy' of the IUCN, WWF, and UNEP, however, a shift in perception took place at the global level which had already occurred among US-American protectionists after the turn of the century. Nature turned from a treasure to be preserved to a resource whose yield had to be sustained (Hays 1959). The emphasis thus shifted from the protection of nature to the protection of the productivity of natural resources for economic use. It was in the 'World Conservation Strategy' that the concept of 'sustainable development' appeared for the first time. By linking 'sustainable' to 'development', however, a terrain of semantic ambiguity was created. The new concept subtlly shifted the locus of sustainability from nature to development; while 'sustainable' previously referred to natural yields, it now refers to development. With that shift, the perceptual frame changes; instead of nature, development becomes the object of concern, and instead of development, nature becomes the critical factor to be watched. In short, the meaning of sustainability slides from conservation of nature to conservation of development. Moreover, since 'development' is conceptually an empty shell which may cover anything from the rate of capital accumulation to the number of latrines, it becomes eternally unclear and contestable just what exactly should be kept sustainable. This is the reason why all sorts of political actors, even fervent protagonists of economic growth, are today able to couch their intentions in terms of 'sustainable development'. The term has become inherently self-referential, as a definition offered by the World Bank neatly confirms: 'What is sustainable? Sustainable development is development that lasts' (World Bank 1992: 34).

On the theoretical level, this change in perspective led to the reinterpretation of nature as capital (El Serafy 1991). With this conceptual operation, it becomes possible to compare natural capital with economic capital, to assess the costs and benefits of substituting one with the other, and to combine the two in an optimal fashion. In the light of the all-pervasive cost-benefit logic, anything—not only nature, but also human life—turns into a variable which can in principle be traded off against something else. As a consequence, supporters of this view may consider climate protection, for instance, suboptimal in comparison to future adjustment to adverse climate effects, which appears to be more a lesson in the sustainability of money than of the environment.

The South as Arena for Ecological Adjustment

The search for competitive strength can live with the insight about the finiteness of development in space, but cannot go along with the notion of finiteness of development in time. In this view, therefore, the growth civilization, and its further diffusion through 'free trade', remains unquestioned in terms of time, while its limitation in geographical space is quietly accepted. Though the bitter environmental effects produced in the North reach the far corners of the globe, the radius of responsibility remains restricted.

As is generally the case in the contest perspective, it is the South which emerges as the major arena for environmental adjustment. The South is urged to act responsibly, while the North is considered to be the home of reason, stability, and—why not?—cleanliness. A story-line is being developed in which effects are reinterpreted as causes; one reads environmental dangers, poverty, and destabilization not as part of the global effects of the North, but locates their origins in the Third World. Responsibility thus can be repressed, expecting from the South the initiative for urgent action. Logically, the population question figures prominently on the global agenda of the contest perspective. After all, no issue lends itself so easily to taking the South to task, no issue grants the status of innocence so clearly to the North like this one. The exploding number of people, indeed, serves as a convenient pattern of explanation for the two most important threats facing the North: environmental insecurity and migration. The former is understood as the result of rising numbers of claimants to the biosphere, while the latter is understood as the result of rising population pressure in the countries of origin. In both cases, the reaction follows straight from the explanation: one rushes to call for strategies to contain population growth.

The inclination to define environmental problems in the South in such a way that their solution can only come from the North is a benign variant of the tendency to project responsibility onto the South. For example, the bulky 'Agenda 21'—the plan of action resulting from the United Nations Conference on Environment and Development (UNCED)—has been largely drafted in this spirit. It divides the world ecologically into deficit countries and high-performance countries. Environmental problems in the South are framed as the result of insufficient capital, outdated technology, lack of expertise, and slackening economic growth. And the definition of the problem already implies its solution: the North has to increase its investments in the South, to provide technology transfer, to bring competence in eco-engineering, and to act as a locomotive of growth for the South

(Hildyard 1993). It is easy to see how the conventions of development think-ing shape this outlook; once again the South is pictured as the home of incompetence and the North as the stronghold of excellence.

The Astronaut's Perspective

At the foot of the Santa Catarina mountains, about forty miles north-east from Tucson in Arizona, a huge edifice of glass sends sparkles of sunlight across the plane. Noah's ark in a modern spirit. For the long, pyramid-like hall contains the world in miniature: a rain forest, grasslands, a desert, swamps, and even an ocean. Moreover, there are gardens and fields for the eight people who lived there along with a number of animals, altogether 3,800 species of plants and animals. The experiment was called 'Biosphere 2', and the name reveals the intention; the scientists attempted nothing less than creating a model of 'Biosphere 1'—the earth—under the glass roof. John Allen, the research director of 'Biosphere 2' sums up his intentions in the following words: 'Biosphere 2 presented the opportunity to develop a comprehensive biospheric monitoring and management system on a scale more approachable than earth's. The successful development of such a model would be a large stride towards developing a more accurate model for Earth'(Allen 1991: 125).

The Planet as an Management Object

The scientists in Arizona exemplify a thought-style which often colours the discussions on the real earth of 'Biosphere 1'. Environmentalism is being framed through an astronaut's perspective. Many of these environmental-ists proclaim to save nothing less than the planet. For them, the blue earth, that suggestive globe, suspended in the dark universe, delicately furnished with clouds, oceans, and continents, has become the reality that ultimately matters. Since the 1970s the world has been increasingly perceived as a physical body maintained by a variety of biogeochemical processes rather than as a collection of states and cultures. As did the world models which led to 'Limits to Growth', so too does the biophysical conception of the earth as a system[6] project a transnational space where the existence of nations, the aspirations of communities or other human realities fade into irrelevance when compared to the overwhelming presence of the natural earth. In this way, especially within an epistemic community of scientists around the globe (Haas 1990), a discourse has developed which constructs the planet as a scientific and political object. This community thinks in planetary terms; they frame 'sustainable development' through an astronaut's perspective.

Without the photographs of the earth it would scarcely have been possible to view the planet as an object of management (Sachs 1994). But there are political, scientific, and technological reasons as well. Only in the course of the 1980s—with the ozone hole, acid rain, and the greenhouse effect—did the border-crossing, global impact of pollution by industrial societies force itself into the foreground. Furthermore, scientists have made enormous headway in representing the biosphere as an all-embracing ecosystem, linking biota with processes in the atmosphere, oceans, and the earth's crust. And finally, as happens so frequently in the history of science, a new generation of instruments and equipment created the possibility of measuring global processes. During the past decade, satellites, sensors, and computers provided the means for calibrating the biosphere and displaying it in models. In fact, research on the biosphere is rapidly becoming big science; spurred by a number of international programmes (Malone 1986), 'planetary sciences', including satellite observation, deep-sea expeditions, and worldwide data processing, are being institutionalized in many countries. With this trend, sustainability is increasingly conceived as a challenge for global management. Experts set out to identify on a planetary scale the balance between human extractions/emissions on the one hand, and the regenerative capacities of nature on the other, mapping and monitoring, measuring and calculating resource flows and biogeochemical cycles around the globe. 'This is essential', says Agenda 21, 'if a more accurate estimate is to be provided of the carrying capacity of the planet Earth and of its resilience under the many stresses placed upon it by human activities' (chapter 5.1). Feeling the pulse of the earth seems to be the unstated objective of a new geoscience, the planet is put under sophisticated observation like a patient in an intensive care unit. The management of resource budgets has become a matter of world politics.

Global Co-operation

The image of the circular earth underscores the assumption, fundamental to this perspective, that since the effects of industrial civilization spread globally, the range of responsibility of the North also should embrace the entire globe. As a consequence, the entire globe is considered the proper arena for environmental adjustment, and not mainly the South, as in the contest perspective. Security against global threats is sought primarily in the rational planning of planetary conditions, not in the defence of the empires of wealth. The fragility of the biosphere under stress by human action, is the storyline of this approach. It is recognized that economic development is threatened along the dimension of time. Since, however, the rational design of global conditions can never be achieved without the co-operation of many political actors, some new balance between North and South has to be found. To put it more delicately, at least some of the expectations of the less privileged parts of the global middle class have to be met if a new global order is to be achieved. In this perspective, the commitment to countering the crisis of nature does not allow neglecting the crisis of justice.

However, the worldwide crisis of nature puts into the limelight the impotence of the world society in creating a global framework for sustainability. Had not the image of the planet shown that the unity of mankind is not just a dream of the Enlightenment but a biophysical fact? What is required, in the eyes of global ecologists, is to translate the biophysical reality into political fact. Therefore, numerous environmentalists belong to the most outspoken promoters of global institutions and ground-rules. Like Al Gore, at least in his earlier life: 'Merely addressing one dimension or another or trying to implement solutions only in one region of the world or another will, in the end, guarantee frustration, failure, and a weakening of the resolve needed to address the whole of the problem. . . . But if world government is neither feasible nor desirable, how then can we establish a successful cooperative effort to save the environment? There is only one answer: we must negotiate international agreements that establish global constraints on acceptable behaviour . . .' (Gore 1992: 295, 302).

The strategic objective of such a plea is for multilateral regulations through common obligations across many areas of politics. Other protagonists are ready to go further; they call for new schemes of global governance, from global expert commissions to regulatory frameworks for nations and their economies, and eventually some sort of global mutilateral government. Since the inclusion of the South is imperative for such a strategy, Al Gore proceeds and calls for a 'global Marshall Plan'. It would aim at concentrating all efforts on stabilizing the world population, developing environmentally sound technologies, modifying the economic rules of the game, concluding collective treaties, and launching an information campaign for the citizens of the globe. On the horizon is the noble vision to make ecology the centrepiece of a domestic world politics which would carry out the rational organization of global affairs.

The Home Perspective

'Sustainable development' in this perspective is neither about economic excellence nor about biospherical stability but about local livelihoods. From this angle, the environment suffers in the first place from overdevelopment and not from an inefficient allocation of resources or the proliferation of the human species. At the centre of attention is the goal and structure of development, which in the South is seen as disempowering communities, in the North as diminishing well-being, and in both as environmentally disruptive. 'Sustainable development' is therefore suspected to be an oxymoron; in one way or the other, practical and theoretical efforts aim at alternatives to economic development. What is more, it is only in this perspective that the crisis of justice figures prominently in the debate. Internationally, conserver societies in the North are expected to expand the room for southern societies to flourish, while nationally sustainable lifestyles for the urban middle classes would leave for peasant and tribal communities more control over their resources. Consequently, the question of whose needs and what needs sustainable development is addressing is looming large in this perspective; most inquiries in the last analysis turn around the question: how much is enough? (Durning 1992).

Two years ago, the world was surprised and looked at Mexico with irritation, as hundreds of armed Indios all of a sudden occupied the city of San Cristóbal de Las Casas. The Chiapas rebellion was a sudden signal. It pulled back the veil of oblivion from those indigenous and rural populations in the hinterland of the global middle classes, which are largely excluded from the fruits of the unification of the world. They are to be found everywhere, in innumerable villages and on all continents, peasants and landless workers, migrants and tribals, the periphery of the world market. Despite all their differences, they generally share the common fate of being threatened by the claims urban-industrial developers lay on their resources. The crisis of nature and the crisis of justice coincide for large parts of the world population in the experience of being marginalized by expansionist 'development'. For when water sources dry up, fields get lost, animals vanish, forests dwindle, and harvests decrease, the very basis of their livelihood is undermined, pushing them onto the market, for which they have insufficient purchasing power. Misery is frequently the result of enclosed or destroyed commons. Wherever communities base their subsistence on the renewable resources of soil, water, plant and animal life, the growth economy threatens nature and justice at the same time; the environment and the people's life-support are equally degraded (Gadgil and Guha 1992). In that context, for many communities, sustainability means nothing less than resistance against development (Tandon 1993). To protect both the rights of nature and the rights of people, the enclosure of extractive development, a federal state with village democracy (Agarwal and Narain 1989) and an affirmation of people's 'moral economies' are called for. Searching for sustainable livelihoods in this sense means searching for decentralized, and not accumulation-centred, forms of society.

The North as Arena for Ecological Adjustment

Non-official NGOs, social movements, and dissident intellectuals comprise most of the social base of the home perspective. What links the efforts of southern groups with dissidents in rich countries is that both expect the North to retreat from utilizing other people's nature and to reduce the amount of global environmental space it occupies. After all, most of the northern countries leave an 'ecological footprint' (Wackernagel and Rees 1995) on the world which is considerably larger than their territories. They occupy foreign soils to provide themselves with tomatoes, rice, feedstuff, or cattle; they carry away raw materials of any kind; and they utilize the global commons—like the oceans and the atmosphere—far beyond their share. The Northern use of the globally available environmental space is blown out of proportion; the style of affluence in the North cannot be generalized around the globe, it is oligarchic in its very structure. From the home perspective, the North is called upon to reduce the environmental burden it places on other countries and to repay the ecological debt accumulated from the excessive use of the biosphere over decades and centuries. The principal arena for ecological adjustment is thus neither the southern hemisphere nor the entire globe, but the North itself. It is the reduction of the global effects of the North to the reach of domestic responsibility which is at the centre of attention, not the extension of northern responsibility to coincide with the radius of the effects, as from the astronaut's perspective. The home perspective believes in making room for others by means of an orderly retreat; it proposes a new kind of rationality, which could be called 'the rationality of shortened chains of effect' for meeting the crises of justice and of nature. Good global neighbourhood, in this view, requires above all the reform of home out of a cosmopolitan spirit.

Efficiency and Sufficiency

But the reform of home is a major challenge, particularly in industrial countries. According to the current rule of thumb, only a cutback of between 70 and 90 per cent in the throughput of energy and materials over the next 40 to 50 years would live up to the challenge (Schmidt-Bleek 1992). Therefore, the home perspective hesitates to overemphasize efficient resource management and attempts to focus the social imagination on the revision of goals rather than on the revision of means. For over the longer term saving effects are invariably swallowed up by the quantity effects involved, if the overall dynamics of growth are not slowed down. Consider the example of the fuel-efficient car. Today's automobile engines are definitely more efficient than in the past; yet the relentless growth in the number of cars and miles driven has cancelled out that gain. And the same logic holds across the board, from energy saving to pollution abatement and recycling. In fact, what really matters is the overall physical scale of the economy with respect to nature, not simply the efficient allocation of resources (Daly and Cobb 1989). Herman Daly has offered a telling comparison: even if the cargo on a boat is distributed efficiently, the boat will inevitably sink under too much weight— even though it might sink optimally! Therefore, efficiency without sufficiency is counterproductive; the latter has to define the boundaries of the former.

A society in balance with nature, according to this view, can only be approximated through a twin-track approach: both through intelligent rationalization of means and prudent moderation of ends. In other words, an 'efficiency revolution' remains without direction if not accompanied by a 'sufficiency revolution'. Nothing is ultimately as irrational as rushing with maximum efficiency in the wrong direction. A 'sufficiency revolution', however, can neither be programmed nor engineered; it involves a mixture of subtle and rapid changes in the cultural outlook and the institutional set-up of society. Therefore, this sustainability discourse tends to focus more on values and institutional patterns, in short, on the symbolic universe of society, while both the contest and the astronaut perspectives rather highlight the energetic–material processes, in short the world of material quantities.

New Models of Prosperity

Fortunately for the home perspective, wealth is not anymore what it used to be. Meanwhile, there are a number of indications that many industrial societies passed a threshold in the 1970s, after which growth in GNP does not relate any longer to a growth in quality of life. (Cobb and Cobb 1994). This is good news for the home perspective, because it encourages these voices to assume that even a shrinking volume of production would not necessarily lead to a shrinking well-being; on the contrary, even a growth in well-being can be imagined.

Given that the negative consequences of economic growth seem to have increased faster than the positive consequences for the last twenty years, the home perspective view counts on the emergence of counter motives to the growth philosophy of the ever 'faster, farther and more'(Sachs, Loske, and Linz 1997). Consider, for instance, the energy-intensive urge for acceleration. If pursued thoroughly enough, acceleration demonstrates the unfortunate tendency to cancel itself out. One arrives faster and faster at places at which one stays for ever shorter periods of time. Acceleration shows, beyond a certain level, a counter-productive tendency; it is therefore not so surprising that a renewed interest in slowness advances beneath the veneer of enforced acceleration. What would an advanced transportation system look like that is not shaped by the imperative of acceleration? As with time, so with space: after a distance-intensive lifestyle has spread widely, a new appreciation for one's place and community is forming. What would a politics look like that centred on the regeneration of places? A similar sensibility might be growing with respect to the possession of things. The resource-intensive accumulation of goods, the thousand brands and fashions, increasingly congest everyday life, making it difficult to keep up. As a consequence, the ideal of lean consumption becomes more attractive, because a wealth of goods is at odds with a wealth of time. What would things that were designed with a view to quality, durability, and uniqueness look like?

Such questions are being raised; all of them reveal a fundamental concern of the home perspective: the search for a society which is capable of remaining on an intermediary level of performance. In other words, a society which is able not to want what it would be capable of providing. Self-limitation always implies a loss of power, even if it is sought in the name of a new prosperity. However, in what way a renunciation of power for the sake of the common good could be reconciled with the quest for individual liberty, remains the conundrum of the home perspective. At any rate, both the crisis of justice and the crisis of nature suggest looking for forms of prosperity that would not require permanent growth. For the problem of poverty lies not in poverty but in wealth. And equally, the problem of nature lies not in nature but in over-development. It is likely that Aristotle was well aware of these interconnections, as he wrote the following: ' The greatest crimes are committed not for the sake of necessities, but for the sake of superfluities. Men do not become tyrants in order to avoid exposure to the cold' (*Politics* 1267a).

2

The North as/and the Other:
Ecology, Domination, Solidarity

YRJÖ HAILA

One World or Many?

'Globalization' has become a term often used to characterize the spirit of our times. No doubt there are good reasons. The globe seems to be shrinking. It is difficult not to be constantly, and painfully, aware that our actions here and now can have a great impact on other peoples' lives elsewhere, and vice versa. As has often been noticed, the feel of a shrinking globe gets support from the powerful image of the earth photographed from Apollo spaceships in the 1960s which, by a metaphoric transformation, made the earth look like another spaceship. The globe circling forward through an empty space became an emblem symbolizing the responsibility of humans to take good care of this fragile spaceship which is their abode.[1]

Despite the metaphoric power of such images it is not quite clear what 'globalization' actually implies. One implication certainly is unification: everything seems to be connected to everything else on the spaceship earth. But, as a paradoxical side-effect, such unification produces abstraction: the earth begins to appear as a rarefied network of connections assumed important on theoretical grounds. To the extent that this happens, the earth as a scene of real human life-worlds is lost (Ingold 1993). If, indeed, we can scrutinize conditions on the earth from a distance, as it were, and construct rules that human passengers on their earthly spaceship have to obey, then the lived, tiny but world-constituting affairs that fill up human lives vanish. In other words, viewing the earth as one whole from afar implies alienation from the earth.

A particularly disturbing implication of this vision, and a difficult one to challenge, is that global environmental thinking strengthens such alienation from the earth. Global environmentalism is readily commensurate with a reduction of human history to a unilinear, law-like progression toward an inevitable catastrophe. A number of versions of this metanarrative are on offer in environmentalist literature. The conquest of nature through human ingenuity is replaced with the destruction of nature through human stupidity and avarice, but the *hubris* remains (Haila and Heininen 1995).

Global environmentalist visions get additional support from arguments grounded in neo-Malthusianism (Taylor and García-Barrios 1997). Paul Ehrlich, as a characteristic example, has promulgated a view that human use of ecological resources of the earth is a 'zero-sum game': whatever humans have ever done has diminished the space available for other forms of life. According to Ehrlich, human impact on the environment can be summarized by the formula *Impact = Population × Affluence × Technology* (I = PAT) (Ehrlich and Ehrlich 1990: 58). The formula hides three critical assumptions. First, each one of the terms on the right-hand side is assumed to be quantifiable in a straightforward manner. For this to be true, they should be composed of indivisible basic elements which can be added up to get the total value of each variable. Second, the terms are assumed to connect together in a linear way without interaction terms; for instance, the possibility that increasing affluence facilitates new technologies which have a diminishing impact on the environment is excluded. Third, the earth is assumed to be a unified and *uniform* whole: the impact is the same irrespective of whether the person in question lives in Greenland or in the Amazon. It is very difficult to imagine that any of these assumptions could be true. The formula reveals a strong metaphysical commitment to unification: both the 'volume' of the earth and the total human impact on the earth can be calculated, and an assessment of the interaction is a simple matter of subtracting the totals.

However, the image of the earth as one whole viewed from afar is ultimately impossible to maintain, except as a poetic vision. After all, an Archimedean point is unattainable, every viewer is tied to his/her point of view. A perception of unity requires strong ontological assumptions.[2] As a matter of fact, uniformity breaks down also when looking closely at the Apollo images. They show the surface of the earth covered alternatively by ocean or land, the land being distributed in discontinuous clumps, thus raising the question: Are these separate lands similar, or different? Is the land on the earth one, or several? Does this question matter?[3] Furthermore, the image of discontinuous continents brings forth, in the modern mind, consciousness about a temporal sequence. We know that the continents had a different configuration in the past, and the trajectories of their geological and biological evolution have diverged from each other depending on their separations and mergers. In historical thinking, pluralism broke through in the nineteenth century (Braudel 1980: 181).

How big a difference makes a difference? How much heterogeneity is needed within a whole for it no more to be a whole? In traditional metaphysics similarity and difference were negotiated through the doctrine of 'natural kinds', but this does not work any more as a guideline for dividing up the world, one of the reasons being that 'kinds' recognized by humans are interest-relative (Hacking 1991). Once an interest is articulated, it can define a perspective for distinguishing kinds, but not the other way round. Uniform entities cannot be constituted just by assuming that they must be there, for instance, by assuming that a planet such as the earth must be a dynamically unified whole.

Thus, there are good reasons to be suspicious about the totalizing global perspective which so automatically seems to grow out of environmental concerns. However, it would also be foolish to reject out of hand our modern ability to take distance, evaluate particular situations from afar, and detect connections invisible to the 'naked eye'. Ernest Gellner (1992) defends consistently and elaborately the view that the capacity for systematic accumulation of knowledge and for consistent action on the basis of such knowledge is a precious and by no means historically inevitable resource made available to us by the process of modernization.[4] Gellner's point cannot be rejected out of hand. By analogy, objectifying science does provide us with an understanding of issues that we overlook at our peril. The effect of our activity on the environment, potentially on the global scale, is such an issue.

The question is, how to retain sensitivity to the particularity of entities, processes, and situations while also being aware of the earth as a whole? This is not an either/or choice. Instead, we need to cope with both. This requires an ability to define priorities in every particular context in which humans lead their lives. In concrete contexts human activity and natural processes interpenetrate one with another (Haila and Levins 1992; Haila 1998). A genuinely ethical choice is involved because every context is permeated by human interests and actions. We cannot pretend that 'science' makes decisions on our behalf as to what is important.

Where, then, can we find resources for achieving a balanced and flexible synthesis between local and global, particular and general, situatedness and evaluation-from-a-distance? These questions define the theme of this essay. I believe a synthesis can be reached through acknowledging and respecting the richness of particulars in the historical interpenetration of human culture and nature. This emphasis on particulars may be an aesthetic preference, in the sense that Richard Levins once defined aesthetic preference as a determinant of scientific problems.[5] I also lean on the 'working hypothesis' of Levins (1996): 'all theories are wrong which promote, justify, or tolerate injustice.' In the following sections I use the North as an example, drawing upon both literary sources and personal experiences.[6] However, the region used as an example is not critical for the conclusions.

The Conquest

In an illustrated guide of Yakutsk, the capital of the Republic of Yakutia in eastern Siberia, the chapter on the history of the city opens with the following passage: 'The XVII century. Russia was looking for new lands, new riches. Now it turned to the North-East. Detachments of daring people ventured to its far reaches along unbeaten tracks.' This sounds familiar: the powerful ones went and took what they wanted from others who hardly existed, and afterwards this is described as natural course of history. In the seventeenth century Siberia was, of course, inhabited by a large number of peoples; there were no 'unbeaten tracks' to be trodden by the Russians. But the expansion took place. At the same time, or perhaps a little bit earlier or a little bit later, other powers turned to northern Atlantic islands, the Americas, and the great Antipodean lands and archipelagos in their search for new lands and new riches.

Riches, indeed, is what the colonists were after, in Siberia as well as elsewhere. The colonial history of Siberia was, from the beginning, closely connected with the colonial history of other parts of the world (Forsyth 1994; Slezkine 1994; Vaughan 1994). This is understandable: after all, the European colonial expansion was the decisive historical process which brought all continents within the same sphere of influence and power. Once the expansion began it continued like an avalanche. Economic incentives inspired state powers. Collecting tributes was an important incentive in Siberia, first in the form of fur, later on also in ivory (i.e. mammoth tusk). Russian Cossacks used force whenever needed and, for instance, took hostages among natives and thus got them to comply with the exaction of tribute. There was also opposition, but the Chukchees in the far north-east were the only ones successful in resisting Russian armed forces, no doubt because of the inaccessibility of the terrain and scarcity of valuable game and, hence, lack of motivation on the Russian side. However, the colonization was also furthered in a more peaceful and gradual manner by traders and merchants who had to be on good terms with native peoples. An important group of settlers in Siberia were religious dissenters, the 'old believers', who escaped from the grip of established authorities of the Russian Orthodox Church after a religious split in 1658 and spread throughout Siberia.

The European conquest created a novel type of confrontation between peoples. The conquest of America was crucial in this regard: never before and never after have the conquerors and the conquered been as unprepared for meeting each other as in Central America in the 1490s. The result of this confrontation marked the opening of a new era, as characterized by Zvetan Todorov (1984: 5).

The history of the globe is of course made up of conquests and defeats, of colonizations and discoveries of others; but, as I shall try to show, it is in fact the conquest of America that heralds and establishes our present identity; even if every date that permits us to separate any two periods is arbitrary, none is more suitable, in order to mark the beginning of the modern era, than the year 1492, the year Columbus crosses the Atlantic Ocean.

Todorov claims that the surprisingly easy conquest of the large empires of Central and South America by a handful of Spanish conquistadors was due to the superiority of the Spanish side in adapting to the terms of communication in this new conflict of cultures. The Spaniards were backed by a universalizing zeal and ethos provided by Christianity whereas the Indians were bound to their locally constructed cultural universes. The whole idea of a total conquest was alien to the Indians. The Spaniards subordinated the means they used to the end of conquest and were able to deploy a wide variety of tactical tricks such as betrayals, lies, threats, and manipulation of conflicts among Indian states whereas the Indians were tied to a ritualistic and symbolic (and, hence, extremely rigid) way of dealing with the opponent. The inability of Montezuma, the ruler of the Aztecs imprisoned by the Spaniards, to raise his mighty army to defence bears evidence for this contrast.

Todorov concludes that the Spaniards were able to incorporate the existence of an 'other' into their world-view, to objectify the 'other', and to turn this ability into a purposeful manipulation of the 'other'. This was a new, and thoroughly modern invention, albeit facilitated by earlier European history. Thus, Columbus himself, although much more traditional in his cast of mind than the conquistadors who came later such as Cortés, used naming and mapping as a means of submitting the new lands to the Spanish crown.[7] The Indians, in contrast, lacked this ability to grasp and manipulate the 'other'. They tried to understand the arrival of the Spaniards from within their own traditional culture but this proved tragically impossible.

Todorov regards the lack of phonemic writing among the Indians as very significant in this respect. Cultural characteristics of the Aztecs 'imply a predominance of presence over absence, of the immediate over the mediatized. It is precisely here that the theme of the perception of the other and that of symbolic (or semiotic) behavior intersect . . .' (Todorov 1984: 157). However, there were differences among the Spaniards: Cortés was a more modern manipulator of the 'other' than Columbus. The Indians also learned, of course, but too late.

The novel relationship with 'otherness', complete objectification, was to become a lasting consequence of the conquest for the Europeans: 'By winning on one side, the Europeans lost on the other; by imposing their superiority upon the entire country, they destroyed their own capacity to integrate themselves into the world' (Todorov 1984: 97).

A similar objectifying attitude has constantly been evoked—in addition to the duty of spreading Christianity—as a legitimization of colonization: whatever there is in the world, the Europeans are justified in finding it, (re)naming it, mapping it, and taking it into their possession. It was always from the centre that explorations began: never in history did, say, the peoples of the North send expeditions to rename and map Moscow, Helsinki, Copenhagen, or London.

In other words, the colonial expansion brought the colonizers into a systematic relationship to other peoples as 'others' who had one absolute common denominator: they were not 'us'. This level of consistency and systematism in the relationship toward strangers was never reached in the classical world. All civilizations have located themselves in the centre of the world, but in premodern cosmologies strangers were outsiders. In the modern world strangers came to be 'others' against whom the identity of the centre was shaped; the modern sciences of anthropology and ethnography are offshoots of this gradual transition (McGrane 1989).[8]

Cortés, apparently, was a pathbreaker in this regard; for example, in a memorandum addressed to Charles V in 1537 he wrote that before conquering a country 'it must be determined whether it is inhabited, and if so by what kind of peoples, and what religion or rite they have, and upon what they live, and what there is in the land' (Todorov 1984: 175). Diego Durán, a Dominican who lived in Mexico all his life from the age of five or six and compiled some of the most valuable descriptions of pre-conquest Indian society was driven by the conviction that paganism can be successfully eliminated only if it is thoroughly known: 'If we are trying earnestly to remove the memory of Amalech, we shall never succeed until we fully understand the ancient religion' (Todorov 1984: 202–3). This ethos, 'know in order to eliminate', was later transported by innumerable Christian missionaries to other parts of the world.

Objectification and Domination: Nature as the 'Other'

Systematic objectification was not restricted to people the colonists came across in other parts of the world. As has often been noted, the experience of the conquest strengthened also the objectification of nature (Glacken 1967; Grove 1994). The first reaction among European scholars at the time was to reconcile the discoveries with the belief in a designed earth, accepted as a commonplace in the Renaissance: 'What greater proof of the wisdom, the power, and the creativity of God, then, could one ask than these unexpected findings from the new Lands?' (Glacken 1967: 358). However, this proved increasingly difficult as observations accumulated. A new style of scientific thinking, taxonomy, took shape as a method of ordering the vast amount of new material acquired in European scientific centres in the aftermath of the conquest (Crombie 1988). Gradually a shift occurred from a belief in a predetermined Divine order to an emphasis that nature is governed by laws and processes that need to be explained by natural reasons. Taxonomy, in classical episteme, was an element in a general science of order (Foucault 1970: 72).

The conquest had another consequence for the modern world-view, namely, the vision of the earth as a 'closed space' (Glacken 1967: 623 ff.). This corresponded with the experience that the European powers had reached all the continents of the earth. The vision gave rise to a controversy over the possibility of historical progress. The main proponents of the idea of unlimited progress and perfectibility of man were, as is well known, Marquis Condorcet and William Godwin, and the main critic was Thomas Malthus. The controversy of the 1790s can be viewed as a 'bifurcation' of historical thinking into two horns, namely, unquestioning faith in progress and doubt of unlimited progress. Similar bifurcations in the cultural vision of the future of humanity have occurred repeatedly ever since, the latest example being the moral protest of the 1960s against post-World War II faith in economic growth.

This invites the following hypothesis: the vision of the earth as a 'closed space' has become an essential determinant of modern human identity. Accordingly, global nature appears increasingly as the 'other' of human culture. It has become impossible to think of the human condition without taking 'limits' into account. The force of the idea has two sources. First, that the earth, indeed, is limited is clearly a physical fact. Second, the conclusion follows that unlimited growth is impossible in the limited space of the earth. This deduction can be applied to any phenomenon that might by appearance be due to limited space or resources—as, for instance, Malthus applied it to pauperism in eighteenth-century Britain.[9]

Historically the recognition that the earth is limited is literally due to the conquest of the earth. Maybe the metaphoric force of this historical fact strengthens the grip of Malthusian fears in modern imagination? Once a closed space is conquered to the final border, nothing more is left. Maybe this strengthens the fear that 'nature' can become emptied in a similar way, and then inevitably collapse?

Be that as it may, a break occurred in the early modern period in the view of nature. Nature became externalized and objectified, both as an object of knowledge and an object of exploitation. The concept of nature gradually acquired the connotation of external reality (Williams 1980), and the perception of nature as primarily a collection of 'natural resources' became generalized (Spoehr 1956). Bacon and Descartes are regarded as paradigmatic representatives of this transition.

However, the evaluation of the break requires more analytic rigour than is often the case. In particular, the claim that modern science is intrinsically connected with domination of nature should be reconcilable with what is known about changes in scientific thinking in the early modern era. I doubt whether domination of nature can be extracted as a major trend from this process (see e.g. Foucault 1970; Dear 1995), despite the existence of eloquent propagandists such as Bacon; but even Bacon's texts allow a more nuanced interpretation than is usually admitted (Keller 1985). On the other hand, important shifts in the concept of nature were stimulated not only by the sciences but also by changes in social and political thinking: both the English 'natural rights' tradition and Rousseau's 'social contract' were attempts to define in a coherent way human culture and society as distinct from nature (Spaemann 1967). This was not domination of nature either but rather search for human social and cultural identity.

Overall, it seems safer to locate the main source of 'otherness' in modern culture on the subjective level, namely, in the relationship of the modern subject to his/her 'other'. This was realized by Hegel; in the following I cite Charles Taylor's characterization of Hegel's basic idea (C. Taylor 1975: 156).

[T]he core problem is that the subject is always 'outside himself', he always depends on a surrounding universe; he must therefore come to recognize himself in this surrounding. This is why the principal path to integrity lies through recognition by another; in the human environment a man can recognize himself in others. But we see another important path; man can come to see himself in the natural environment by making it over in conformity with his project. For in doing this we achieve another standing negation, a reflection of ourselves which endures.

The Hegelian concept is based on necessary interactions between every individual with other individuals. The position of the individual in the modern society is characterized by freedom. This freedom 'means the ability to move from a state of indetermination—to determine myself' (Kolb 1986: 29). Such a determination cannot, however, occur in the absence of other individuals; in contrast, it depends on 'structures of mutual recognition that are prior to the achieved selfhood of the individuals involved' (Kolb 1986: 25). This necessary relationship between mutual recognition of individuals and individual freedom brings forth the structure of 'otherness': the other person is an 'other' against whom I can achieve my subjectivity. Implicit in this structure is objectification of other persons. This also applies to nature which is externally available to be moulded by the modern individual and, thus, to be used as a template against which the modern individual can mould him/herself.

Does the external, material reality, that is 'nature', play any role in this process? Hegel did not acknowledge such a possibility because for him nature was just a passive although inevitable stage in the development of mind (Collingwood 1945).[10] Nature was pure externality, a realm of outwardness, a mere stage in the development of mind and, by implication, could not possibly have any constitutive role in the unfolding of human freedom.

However, when we reject Hegel's idealism as regards the evolution of mind from nature we also have to reject the view of nature as 'pure externality' and allow for the possibility that nature does have a constitutive role in human identity. Indeed, examples abound on the positioning of nature as the 'other' of modern cultural identity. Richard Grove (1994) gives material on the multiple faces of the colonial experience in this regard. First of all, the potential of the colonists to destroy environments they occupied by inadvertent behaviour was noticed early on, which gave rise to idealization of island 'Edens' and the origin of what Grove dubbed 'colonial environmentalism'. Later on, in the nineteenth and twentieth centuries, conservation in British colonies was driven by old pastoral ideals of the English landed gentry. 'Virgin' landscapes, assumably untouched by humans, had an important role in the shaping of nationalism in North America (Nash 1982) and in northern Europe (e.g. Denmark, Olwig 1996; Norway, Witoszek 1997; and Finland, Lehtinen 1991). Usually the most admired 'virgin' landscapes were in actual fact shaped by human influence reaching centuries back in time, but this only emphasizes the symbolic significance of nature in shaping modern nationalistic identity.[11]

The domination of nature has got its symbolic images in modern imagination, too. One of these is 'conquest', for instance, the 'conquest' of the

North Pole. But what is there to 'conquer' at the North Pole? Magnificent blocks of ice? Not at all, the point, of course, is completely different. What was at stake was a much more figurative goal of gaining support for the idea that the whole globe, including its most remote and hostile corners, is 'by its nature' subjected to human (European) domination. A proof of this principle by actually visiting the Pole was perceived as a source of enormous prestige. It is almost impossible to imagine the strength of the cultural dynamics produced by the competition for this prestige. The actual history of the conquest presents us with several amazing features. First of all is the very fact that someone actually was determined enough to make it to the Pole (Robert Peary in 1909). Equally striking is the number of participants in the race who had, one can safely judge with hindsight, no chance of success but could, nevertheless, raise financial support for their endeavours which expectedly ended in tragedy; the Swedish engineer Salomon August Andrée's ballooning from the Spitzbergen with two companions to their deaths is an example. Or perhaps the most amazing feature is that when a verdict was reached, despite some doubts, that Peary actually had visited the Pole, it was almost sixty years before further expeditions were undertaken (Vaughan 1994, 198).[12]

Ambivalence

The logic of 'otherness' used as an analytic device is to a certain extent vulnerable to excessive totalization. Once a parlance based on the 'other' is adopted, he/she seems to be present everywhere. It is deceptively easy to use the 'other' as a label for almost anything. For this reason I have the impression that the 'other' has not really had his/her history written. The 'other', in the Hegelian conception, is almost like a logical operation, that is, a necessary consequence of the development of human consciousness and thought (Kolb 1986). As we saw, the 'other' is tied to the origin of modern subjectivity, albeit with precursors that date back to the origin of civilization. According to Hegel, '(t)he modern self is the achievement of a long process, and modern individualism as such is something new in history. Civil society is not the final recognition of a permanent condition; it is the creation of a new condition. This is true because the structures of mutual recognition, and the consequent selfhood of the individuals involved, change at different stages in history' (Kolb 1986: 28).

How does one write the history of a logical operation? By making its constitutive conditions transparent. In this sense also basic mathematical operations have a history: they have been adopted in some particular social conditions in the past. All civilizations developed numerical operations, but there is interesting and significant variation among them in this regard.[13] Similarly with logical operations. In particular, logical operations of the Hegelian type, being tied to conceptual thinking, are closely bound up with social history; this is the point of saying that Hegel was a 'philosopher of modernity' (Kolb 1986).

The logic of the 'other' as a mechanism in identity formation is tied to the modern world. But the modern world itself is bound to history. Consequently, 'otherness' is bound to history as well. Zvetan Todorov has succeeded in unveiling crucial features in the early development of 'otherness' in the modern world. It seems to me that the far north might provide possibilities for further unveiling. In comparison with other parts of the world, the far north is a recently and, perhaps, only half-way colonized area. The destruction of native cultures was never as complete in the far north as in, say, Spanish America or Australia. Maybe this is because the natives have been the only ones who really have been able to live in far northern conditions.[14]

This has, from the very beginning, created a necessity of communication between the colonists and the natives: in order to get help and advice from the local peoples, the colonists had to recognize them. The dependence of southern colonists on the skills of northern aboriginals culminated, in a sense, during Peary's trip to the North Pole: it was the help of Innuit Eskimos that made the feat possible. A similar element was germinating in the sixteenth-century encounters between Spaniards and Indians in Mexico. An effort to know the other, even 'to know in order to eliminate', initiates changes in the knower as well. After all, the tormented compassion of a Bartholomé de Las Casas with the Indians was also a product of the conquest.

This necessity of contact and communication, however vague and contradictory in detail, might help to establish what Todorov (1984: 250) calls a 'new exotopy', that is:

[A]n affirmation of the other's exteriority which goes hand in hand with the recognition of the other as subject. Here perhaps is not only a new way of experiencing alterity, but also a characteristic feature of our time, as individualism (or autotelism) was for the period whose end we are now beginning to discern.

However, for this to succeed an open-minded assessment is needed on the status of the far north in the world today. The times when the far north was an unreachable 'Ultima Thule' are long past. The far north has been subjected to the plundering of exploitable resources which has advanced in pace with new technologies to get at them. Whaling reached a mass scale in the northern Atlantic from the sixteenth century onwards, driven by the demand for oil for lighting and whalebone for decoration in European urban centres. Mineral riches were an attraction for many of the early explorers, but the gold rush to Klondike River, a tributary of Yukon in north-western Canada, in the 1890s was the first mass invasion of prospectors to the Arctic. In our century mineral and coal mining and oil boring have grown into huge industries. In the second half of the century the military forces of the superpowers have been heavily involved all over the circumpolar Arctic.

As everywhere else in the world, the traders and hunters drove into local and regional extinction many of the game animals they were after. The list includes the sable in Siberia, beaver in western North America, fur seal in the northern Pacific and bowhead whale in the northern Atlantic. An emblematic example among the victims of European colonization is the flightless great auk which originally bred in large numbers on northern Atlantic islands from Norway to New Foundland, Maine, and Massachusetts as well as on Iceland and Greenland. The last specimens were taken at Eldey Rock off the coast of Iceland on 3 June 1844. An analogous species in the northern Pacific was the spectacled cormorant which bred on islands off the coast of Kamchatka and Chukotka. Similar to many other island species, the spectacled cormorant was famous for being a 'stupid bird', i.e. not afraid of humans and easily killed (Greenway 1967).

Despite such histories and innumerable other similar ones, I feel the situation in the far north deserves additional consideration. 'Taming' and 'cultivation' are metaphors seldom applied to northern nature. You cannot tame winter storms, and gardening is hardly a feasible endeavour in the Arctic. A Utopian project to graze cattle on the tundra meadows in Vorkuta, northern Urals, that ended in an expected failure during the Khrushchev era in the Soviet Union underlines the point. The extinction of Norse colonies from Greenland by the end of the fifteenth century is another revealing history. It seems the vulnerability of the Norse colonies was primarily due to their social and cultural rigidity. While cooling of the climate following the onset of the 'Little Ice Age' made agriculture gradually less and less feasible, the Norse were unable to adopt elementary hunting skills such as the use of kayak or harpoon from the Eskimos who had no place in their cosmology. Thus, the Norse colonies literally starved in the middle of abundant resources which they were unable to use. Conditions in Greenland by no means turned uninhabitable for humans. Eskimo settlements colonized the areas left empty after the Norse (McGovern 1994).

This inspires an interesting question that relates to ecological theory: are northern ecological conditions 'fragile' or 'robust'? Intuition might support

either of these alternatives. One might conclude that the harsh physical conditions make all forms of life in the far north so vulnerable that any additional human disturbance will cause irreversible damage. Or, the other way
round, one might conclude that the life forms adapted to the far north are
so well buffered against extreme environmental conditions that there is little
humans can do to threaten them.

Both of these extreme views are certainly wrong, but a proper balance is
difficult to achieve. I would lean more toward the second alternative. Huge
variations in environmental conditions have characterized conditions in the
far north during the whole Ice Age, the last two million years (Delcourt and
Delcourt 1991), and variation is the rule at present as well (Chernov 1985).
Hence, organisms living in the far north are probably well adapted to environmental fluctuations (Haila 1994).[15] However, this conclusion is certainly
not a dogma: there is certainly variation across animal and plant species in
this regard which should be recognized and respected.

In a way the peculiar features and seeming contradictions of northern
nature bring into sharp focus an aspect of the 'otherness' of nature that is
worth keeping in mind, namely, what John Passmore (1980: 214) calls
nature's 'strangeness': that 'natural processes are entirely indifferent to our
existence and welfare'. We humans need to be interested in the affairs of
nature, but nature is not interested in us. It is our own task to arrange our
existence in the best way we can, there is nobody else around to do this
for us.

A Chance for Solidarity?

Nature is strange everywhere, but northern nature brings into focus a particularly important aspect of this strangeness: it invites respect. Such respect
does not contradict objectivism, rather, objectivism can provide invaluable
assistance toward conscious respect. What is needed is a communicative
dimension to scientific objectivism: not *impose upon* and *conquer*, but *listen to*
and *learn from*.

However, 'listening to' and 'learning from' are not such straightforward
activities as they may appear. It is not possible to derive criteria for dealing
with nature directly from nature. Natural change relativizes all observable
criteria: there is no litmus test for definitively distinguishing human-induced
and natural change from each other (Haila and Levins 1992: 182–3; Haila
1995). This conclusion has a historical dimension, too: there is no 'starting
point' in the past that could offer straightforward criteria for evaluating

present conditions. For instance, the sites of cities such as Helsinki, Stockholm, Oslo, Montreal, Toronto, and Vancouver were covered by continental ice merely 18,000 years ago. There may be much deplorable in the ecological conditions of these urban centres today, but a wish to return to 'good old times' on a temporal scale of 20,000 years is a non-starter.

Finding out what 'listening to' and 'learning from' nature means is a problem we have to solve ourselves. There is good evidence that some native cultures have adopted views of nature that could help (Callicott 1989), but learning from other cultures must be on the level of attitudes, not of imitation. The Hegelian idea might give us a lead on how to proceed: as Charles Taylor noted in the citation given above, 'the principal path to integrity lies through recognition by another; in the human environment a man can recognize himself in others'.

From this perspective the native peoples of the far north might, indeed, offer us a model of listening to and learning from.[16] The northern aborigines have, of course, come from somewhere else. But they have had time to find ways to relate to particular environments in particular ways. This long evolution and adaptation has followed several pathways. For example, the present reindeer herding peoples of northern Eurasia are descendants of ancient big-game hunters whereas the present cultures of the North-American high Arctic derive from Arctic small tool tradition which was probably brought by a migration from Siberia to Alaska around 4,000 years ago (Fagan 1991).

Some of the peoples living in the north today have arrived more recently. The Yakuts present an interesting problem: how is it that a cattle-rearing, grassland people[17] has successfully colonized northern forests in the harsh climatic conditions of a permafrost country? They owe this to favourable ecological conditions, namely, the natural occurrence of rich grassland habitats in the river valleys (the Lena, in particular), and in geological formations called by the Yakutian word *alas*. These are circular meadows with a lake in the middle, scattered all over the otherwise continuous lowland forests, varying in size from tens of hectares to tens of square kilometres. The *alas* patches are produced by thermokarstic processes (i.e. by thawing of permafrost) which cause the forest to sink down into the permafrost on sites where the upper horizons begin to melt because of some natural disturbance. The formation of an *alas* takes only a few decades, but once formed it may remain unchanged for hundreds, possibly thousands of years.

There never have been closed cultures in the far north. In contrast, the northern peoples have had lively trade connections among each other over huge distances. The great river systems of Siberia have served as natural channels of communication, but also what are nowadays regarded as 'borders' such as the Bering Strait or the Ural Mountains could with better justification be called crossroads. Trade and cultural contact has been particularly important for the northern peoples. It was across the Bering Strait that peoples of the old and the new world maintained mutual contacts throughout the centuries, and the reindeer hunters and herders of the Pechora basin and western Siberia had regular routes across the Urals.

My preliminary hypothesis is that a process of 'learning from' and 'listening to' both nature and other human beings is actually going on all the time. We humans are biological organisms and actively involved in interactions with the world. Results of the interactions are materialized in artefacts in a broad sense, that is, in both material things and cultural habits, customs and conventions (Grene 1974; Dyke 1988). Without continuous interpenetration with the environment, human culture would, of course, be unimaginable. This, as a matter of fact, is true of other animals as well, but the difference is that the structures of human culture and artefacts create continuity across generations. Through such continuity, culture and artefacts make historical change possible on a vastly shorter timescale than is possible for other animals.

If this is valid, then we might find a basis for human solidarity with other natural beings in the shared conditions of existence. Human organisms live in culture 'by their nature' (Grene 1974), consequently, awareness of the preconditions of human existence grows out of cultural experience. This perspective helps to give a more precise formulation to the ethical problem of 'otherness'. Ultimately, recognizing the 'other' is necessary for us to recognize the 'same', that is, ourselves. According to Jean-Pierre Vernant (1991: 205–6), the ancient Greeks left valuable hints as to how to proceed:

If the Same remains enclosed on itself, thought is not possible—and, let us add, neither is civilization. In making the goddess of the margins into a power of integration and assimilation . . . the Greeks pass on an important lesson. They invite us . . . to construe the idea of civilization as giving each his or her place. They invite us to an attitude of mind that not only has moral and political value, but that is properly intellectual and is called tolerance.

If this gives a plausible perspective for the future, how about the crimes and injustices that have been committed in the past? It is not possible to undo any of the crimes. The only thing to do is to find out the sources of the injustices, to support the empowerment of the victims, and prevent the crimes from being repeated. In this effort, both people and nature count. We have no way of getting it right with nature without getting it right with other human beings, no way of reaching solidarity with nature without reaching solidarity with other human beings. Therefore, ultimately, the relationship to human beings is primary. As D. I. Berman once said about Kolyma, one of the worst regions of the Gulag: 'It is no wonder that nobody cares about nature at Kolyma, as nobody has ever cared about human beings at Kolyma' (Haila and Seppälä 1995: 217).

Respect for nature, and for people who understand nature, has a fertile soil in the north. Might this be true of solidarity as well? The harsh conditions mean that mutual help and solidarity has been an absolute prerequisite for human existence ever since the first hunters and nomads arrived here tens of thousands of years ago.[18]

Through respect for and care of the particularities of northern nature, both fragile and robust in its own specific, extraordinary ways, we humans, collectively, might learn to live together with nature. The far north is peculiar, but so are all other regions of the earth, in their own ways. Consequently, I believe this conclusion would arise, *mutatis mutandis*, from a consideration of any other part of the world as well.

3

Nature in Spiritual Traditions: Social and Cultural Implications for Environmental Change

CAROLYN P. EGRI

Throughout the centuries, humans have had a love-hate relationship with the natural environment within which we live. We depend on nature for the air we breathe, the water we drink, the food we eat, the materials and resources to clothe and shelter our bodies. From the natural environment, we obtain the resources to be transformed to meet our material needs. In turn, the natural environment serves as the repository for our waste products. The aesthetic beauty of nature in all its forms is a source of spiritual and cultural inspiration as well as emotional sustenance. The powerful forces of nature are also the harbingers of destruction and death. A less benevolent nature brings the droughts, floods, fires, hurricanes, and earthquakes against which humanity is virtually powerless. There are aspects of nature, living and non-living, with which contact is dangerous for humans. Nature reminds us in innumerable ways of our mortality, that individual lives are but preciously brief journeys in time.

And God said, Let us make man in our image, after our likeness: and let them have dominion over the fish of the sea, and over the fowl of the air, and over the cattle, and over all the earth, and over every creeping thing that creepeth upon the earth. (Genesis 1: 26.)

While this biblical passage has often been used to justify human beings' right to dominate and exploit the natural world, history has taught us much about the complex and intricate 'web of life' that humankind has woven with the natural environment (Wall 1994; Worster 1994). It has been a tale, in one respect, of humankind's struggle to survive with nature; in another, of humankind's search to find spiritual meaning and purpose of life within Nature. It is the latter quest that will be explored in this paper on the spiritual dimension of global environmental change. Thomas Berry writes of the urgent need for modern societies to find a 'new story', a new sense of the universe, to take humankind into the twenty-first century.

This universe itself, but especially the planet Earth, needs to be experienced as the primary mode of divine presence, just as it is the primary educator, primary healer, primary commercial establishment, and primary lawgiver for all that exists within this life community. The basic spirituality communicated by the natural world can also be considered as normative for the future ecological age.   (Berry, 1988: 120)

Berry is not alone in his call for fundamental and transformational changes in humankind's currently dysfunctional relationships with the natural environment at spiritual, cognitive and behavioural levels (Carroll, Brockelman, and Westfall, 1997; Hull, 1993). There are many 'old stories'—stories forgotten, distorted, or marginalized within modern Western societies—which can provide guidance during these times of change. One can also learn from many newer stories informed by an environmentalist ethic.

The primary concern of this chapter is on spiritual discourse as a means of constructing and reconstructing humankind's relationship with the natural environment. Following a brief historical review, this paper explores the spiritual and philosophical 'lessons' of ancient and modern stories concerning relationships between humankind and nature. The ways in which spiritual communities and religious organizations have worked for environmental change as well-informed contemporary eco-philosophies and environmentalist organizations is then presented. How these lessons have been accessed by individuals and collectives to effect transformational change in ecological consciousness and action will be discussed. And finally, the implications of spiritual discourse for organizations and organizing for environmental change on a global level will be addressed.

Historical Evolution of Socio-Natural Relationships

Archaeological evidence of prehistoric hunter-gatherer and agrarian societies depicts an era when humans strove to live in harmony with nature which was all-powerful (Eisler 1987). From that time to the present, nature and its forces have been personified as deities to be worshipped and revered. In the horticultural societies of south-eastern Europe in the period 7000 to 3500 BCE, female deities represented the natural fertility and generative power in nature (Gimbutus 1982). In many aboriginal and Native American societies, Mother Earth or the Great Mother was regarded as 'the beginning and end of all life on earth' (Walker 1988: 339). The reverence for nature deities was/is present in the spiritual traditions of shamanism, pantheism, paganism, and Hinduism (Wall 1994). In the ancient cradle of western civilization, the fertile Mother Goddess or Earth Goddess took the mythological forms of goddesses such as Isis (Egypt), Ishtar (Mesopotamia), Demeter and Gaia (Greece), Ceres (Roman) who were regarded as the creators and sustainers of life within the cosmos.

However, in time, these ancient urban civilizations challenged the belief that humans needed to be subservient to an all-powerful and sacred nature. In ancient Mesopotamia, humans claimed a divine right to tame the 'monstrous chaos' of nature while classical Greek humanists (Aristotle, Plato) and the early Stoics claimed that the resources of nature were there for the exclusive use of humankind (Hughes 1975; Wall 1994). The emergence of anthropocentrism (human-centredness) in spiritual, religious, and philosophical thought on humankind's relationship with nature would be central to Judaeo-Christian edicts for humans to 'be fruitful and multiply' as well as to 'have dominion over every living thing that moveth upon the earth' (White 1973). Even though the universe was still seen as organic, living and spiritual, humankind's place in that universe was regarded as separate and above that of nature and all that was nonhuman (Merchant 1980).

In western societies, the 'ascent of man' over nature was advanced by seventeenth-century Enlightenment philosophers (Bacon, Descartes, Newton, Hobbes) as essential for scientific and social progress (Ehrenfeld 1978; Merchant 1980). Mechanistic materialism, rationality and scientific reductionism became the ideological cornerstones of the Scientific and Industrial Revolutions of western societies (Bramwell 1989; W. Fox 1990). Human intellect and will would produce the science and technology to master and manage a chaotic nature. Ehrenfeld describes this ideology as the 'religion of humanism'.

The core of the religion of humanism: a supreme faith in human reason—its ability to confront and solve the many problems that humans face, its ability to rearrange both the world of Nature and the affairs of men and women so that human life will prosper. Accordingly, as humanism is committed to an unquestioning faith in the power of reason, so it rejects other assertions of power, including the power of God, the power of supernatural forces, and even the undirected power of nature in league with blind chance.   (Ehrenfeld 1978: 5)

Fundamental to the industrial–materialist–scientific world-view has been the exorcism of a nature which is organic, living, and spiritual. Instead, nature is regarded and treated as a machine in the service of humankind. In this mechanistic hierarchical world-view, both persons and non-human nature are objectified and valued only in utilitarian instrumental terms (as inputs or consumers of production) rather than for any intrinsic or spiritual value (Devall and Sessions 1985).

There is no doubt that the modern industrial age has been a period of unprecedented scientific and technological achievement. Members of western industrialized societies enjoy the highest material standard of living, economic prosperity, and physical security known to date. And yet, as we approach the twenty-first century, this same science and technology is also revealing how this course is endangering the long term survival of humans and other entities on this planet (Brown 1991; Daly and Cobb 1994). Although environmental exploitation and degradation have always been one consequence of human activity, the current nature, scale, and rate of humankind's impact on the planet is unprecedented in our history. Humankind can no longer ignore or deny its role in creating an ecological crisis which touches all aspects of the natural environment.

There are many in science and industry who are working to find scientific, technological, and industrial solutions to environmental problems (Hawken 1993; Schmidheiny 1992). There are also many in government, communities, and the environmental movement who are working to find political and institutional remedies at local, national, and international levels (Sitarz, 1993; World Commission on the Environment and Development 1987). However, there are others who speak of finding spiritual or religious ways to make peace with the planet which humankind has abused (Berry 1988; Gottlieb 1996; Hull 1993). As written by Matthew Fox (1988-9: 50), 'Mother Earth is in jeopardy, caused by the anthropocentrism of religion, education, and science during the past three centuries. A new beginning is required, centred on the *sacredness of the planet*.'

Transformational changes of the kind which many believe are required cannot happen or endure without going deep into the realm of values and beliefs—the spiritual consciousness of humanity. Developing a sustainable relationship with the environment requires a deep awareness not only of the biophysical environment within which we live but also of one's spirituality (Schwarz and Schwarz 1987). The next section of this paper presents several spiritual traditions which bring the natural environment into focus. While by no means a complete or definitive treatment of all traditions or world-views, the intent is on how nature-centred spiritual traditions, Asian religions and philosophies, and monotheist religions regard and interpret nature.

Nature-Centred Spiritual Traditions

Nature-centred spiritualities have existed since before the advent of modern human civilization. Although the early Greek and Roman deities have been relegated to the status of mythology, the reverence for nature-based entities or deities remains in many spiritual traditions. Two are shamanic spiritual traditions (specifically, in indigenous cultures), goddess spirituality and neopaganism.

For over 20,000 years, shamanic spiritual traditions have guided indigenous peoples throughout the world. In this holistic and integrative tradition, 'spirituality is not a religion with a fixed set of dogmas but rather, spirituality pervades and infuses all forms of existence—human, animate and inanimate' (Frost and Egri 1994: 7). It informs the view that all that exists in nature is living and sacred therefore deserving of respect and care (Halifax 1990).

There are three assumptions which underlie the shamanic belief system: (1) the existence of numerous coexisting and interpenetrating worlds of experience; (2) the need for holistic balance amongst these worlds; and (3) that change is a continuous transformational process (Egri and Frost 1991). In regard to human relationships with the natural environment, most important is the need for holistic balance between the ordinary world of material reality, the symbolic and social world of human societies, and the spiritual world of the universe. To ignore or deny the spiritual, cultural, emotional, and physical interconnections between humans and the rest of creation is not only disrespectful but also self-destructive.

Several different traditions talk about four or five different worlds and say that the Creator made all these worlds with one simple law: that we shall be in harmony and in balance with all things, including the sun. And time and again people have destroyed that harmony; we have destroyed that harmony. And we have done it again needlessly. Unless we bring about that balance again, this is our last chance. (Brooke Medicine Eagle, Crow Nation shaman, as cited by Halifax 1979: 91)

Shamanic spiritual traditions identify multiple sources of spiritual and practical information which can assist in healing a destructive imbalance between human societies and the natural environment (Egri and Frost 1991). However, the transformational process of healing out-of-balance relationships is not the sole responsibility of the shaman but one shared by all human beings. Native American spiritual teachers often tell of the importance of 'place' to maintain one's spiritual connection to the earth. The Native American land ethic teaches that spiritual connections to the earth are born from the heightened awareness and identification that comes from staying in one place long enough to experience, learn from and care for the spirit of the place one is in (Kelly 1993). The assumption of care and responsibility for the environment within which one lives thereby becomes natural and inevitable.

Goddess spirituality also celebrates the cycles of regeneration, diversity within unity, and humans' essential connectedness with nature (Nicholson 1989). The image of Gaia, the Greek goddess of the earth, has been adopted by those who envision the world as a living spiritual organism within which life is 'holistic, systemic, symbiotic, connective and participatory' (Spangler 1993: 93). This in turn has informed the practice of Gaian meditations and rituals to rediscover one's connections with nature (Seed, Macy, Fleming, and Naess 1988). While in one respect contemporary Goddess spirituality represents a resurgence of pantheism, neopagan spirituality (or the Old Religion) remains truer to the rituals and practices of ancient Celtic and indigenous societies (Gimbutus 1982; Merchant 1992). Pagan spirituality (or Wicca) is based on the core concepts of: *immanence* wherein everyone and everything in nature has inherent value and power; *interconnection* among the human and natural worlds; and *integrity* of thoughts, words, and practice (Starhawk, 1990).

In summary, nature-centred spiritual traditions such as shamanism, goddess spirituality, and neopaganism emphasize human beings' physical and spiritual connections with an animate and sacred nature. As an ecological belief system, they teach of the need for respect for all that exists in the natural environment as well as the need for transformational change to regain holistic balance and harmony in the cosmos.

Asian Religions and Philosophies

The ancient Asian religions and philosophies of Hinduism, Buddhism, and Taoism offer much to ponder concerning the spiritual and metaphysical connections between humans and nature. The Hindu religion teaches that earth is the Universal Mother with the rivers and earth being personified as goddesses and the winds and fire as male deities (Chapple 1993; Klostermaier 1989). Nature is the spiritual guide and teacher in a religion which has codified environmentally beneficial practices in its rituals, proverbs and stories (Gadgil and Guha 1992). For example, respect and even reverence for other species is based on Hindu beliefs that the Supreme Being is incarnated in various species and that humans themselves can be reincarnated as animals and birds. In Hindu religion, trees and plants are seen as possessing divine powers and thus are to be protected from destruction (Dwivedi 1996).

Buddhism proposes that *nirvana* is a higher ultimate spiritual reality and truth which transcends all else. The 'Middle Way' of Buddhism teaches the importance of simplicity in living, that attachment and craving for material wealth and goods stands in the way of liberation (Badiner 1990; Schumacher 1973). The Buddhist principle of the truth of personal experience emphasizes the importance of experiential learning, practising the 'art of mindfulness' to resensitize oneself to hear, see, and feel the web of life rather than limiting oneself to abstract ideas of reality (Kaza 1993; Martin 1993). The Buddhist principle of reciprocity and interdependence is based on the belief that 'all events and beings are interdependent and interrelated' in a universe which is 'a mutually causal web of relationship' as in the image of the Jewel Net of Indra (Kaza 1993: 57).

Buddhist relational ethics teach that moral actions are those which are informed, sensitive to and respectful of all beings (sentient or not) within interdependent relationships. In both Buddhism and Hinduism, violence to other beings within the biotic community is immoral and given the precept of interdependence, self-destructive. The principle of non-violence is also central to both traditions' concept of *Dharma* which has been interpreted to mean 'moral duty', 'right action' and 'the truth about right living' (Bhatt 1989). The Buddhist and Hindu doctrine of *karma* (fate or destiny) also teaches the importance of taking responsibility for moral action in all of one's relationships.

Lao Tzu, the sixth-century Chinese philosopher wrote of the *Tao* as being the creator of the universe as well as 'the way' followed by all that exists in the universe (human, animate, and inanimate). Rather than being the product of a transcendent God, the *Tao* is the infinite energy of the cosmos—a totality and unity of being and becoming which 'embraces everything, large or small, in the universe and imparts a unity of relationships in our environment' (Cheng 1986: 355). In Taoism, reality is conceived in terms of *Tao* (the way of transformation and change), *sheng-sheng* (life creativity), and *ch'i* (the vital force or energy that creates, connects, flows, and balances forms and experience). *Yin* and *yang* are the two dialectical polarities of *ch'i* which are complementary and together, represent the fundamental forces in the universe which cause the cyclic process of change (Callicott and Ames 1989; Lau 1963). Whereas *yin* is part of *K'un/The Receptive* associated with earth, death, mother, and being devoted and yielding; *yang* is part of *Ch'ien/The Creative* which is associated with heaven, life, father, and strong action in the universe (Wilhelm 1977). When there is a dynamic balance between *yin* and *yang*, harmony within and with the natural environment is attained. When there is imbalance working against the natural flow of the *Tao*, then there is disharmony and harm. As related in the *I Ching* (Book of Changes), *T'ai* or Peace is achieved when *K'un* (earth) is above *Ch'ien* (heaven) for this is 'a time in nature when heaven seems to be on earth. Heaven has placed itself beneath the earth, and so their powers unite in deep harmony. Then peace and blessing descend upon all living things . . . In the world of man, it is a time of social harmony' (Wilhelm 1977: 48). Alternatively, *P'i/Standstill* (stagnation and decline) results when *Ch'ien* is above *K'un* for during these times, 'Heaven and earth are out of communion and all things are benumbed. What is above has no relation to what is below, and on earth confusion and disorder prevail' (Wilhelm 1977: 52).

Belying its early roots in shamanism, Taoism teaches of the need for balance with nature and the spirit world (Palmer 1991) with the relationship between humans and the environment being one of holistic interdependence, interpenetration and interaction. Furthermore, interference with the delicately balanced natural order will lead to upset and disorder (Lau 1963).

> In harmony with the Tao
> the sky is clear and spacious,
> the earth is solid and full,
> all creatures flourish together,
> content with the way they are,
> endlessly repeating themselves,
> endlessly renewed.
>
> When [humanity] interferes with the Tao,
> the sky becomes filthy,
> the earth becomes depleted,
> the equilibrium crumbles,
> creatures become extinct.
>
> Lao Tzu (1988: 39)

One important lesson to be learned from the *I Ching* concerns the means by which 'peace' or 'standstill' are achieved and maintained. Peace, prosperity, and order do not happen automatically but require continuous effort and a creative attitude on the part of humans. Otherwise, peace will change and disintegrate into stagnation and decline. In contrast, times of standstill or disorder do not change of their own accord to peace and order. While not lasting forever, human effort is required to end stagnation in order to regain peace and order. Thus, purposeful action is needed to attain peace and harmony, whereas lack of action results in standstill and disorder.

Asian religions and philosophies teach that there is an intricate web of cyclic relationships within and between the spiritual and material realms, the human and the non-human environment. Asian philosophies tell us that: 'The environment is a perfect mirror of man' (Cheng, 1986: 367). If humans abuse or misuse the natural environment, then the environment responds in a harmful way. Obversely, if humans act in ways which preserve life and enhance health in the environment, then the environment responds in kind. Peace and harmony in the natural order requires active and creative effort on the part of human beings. Whether it is through disciplined meditation, personal observation and reflection or through community practice, such action needs to be informed by the principles of compassion, nonviolence and the 'virtue of non-contention' (passive resistance). The restoration of harmony and balance with nature can only be achieved through subjective and objective understanding as well as self-transformation in all aspects of human existence—spiritual, intellectual, social, and material.

Monotheist Religions

Judaic, Christian, and Islamic theologies teach that there is one omnipotent God who was the creator of all in the universe (Armstrong 1993; Rodwell 1994). Within that universe, there is a hierarchy of existences with a transcendent God, human beings, and nature. Biblical scholars have identified that this God (Yahweh, the God of Moses and of Israel) is a pure spiritual being in a realm apart from the forces of nature and matter (Armstrong 1993). Human beings are a 'microcosm of the universe' in that they have both bodies (belonging to the earth) and souls (akin to God). The human soul is the divine gift of the intellect which permits wisdom to raise humans above the flawed and mortal realm of animals and plants in nature. In turn, nature is conceived of as wilderness which man is commanded to master, subdue and transform in accordance with God's laws.

The strong anthropocentrism (or more accurately, androcentrism) of the traditional Judaeo-Christian tradition notwithstanding, there have been alternative Christian views of the relationship between humans and nature. St Francis of Assisi has been identified as one who 'tried to substitute the idea of the equality of all creatures, including man, for the idea of man's limitless rule of creation' (White 1973: 28). Early Celtic Christianity also advanced a view of the mystical intimacy of human, nature and the divine in which there was a human partnership with the natural world (Hull 1993). The Christian mystics of eleventh–thirteenth-century Rhineland Germany

(Hildegard of Bingen, Mechtild of Magdeburg, Meister Eckart, and Julian of Norwich) wrote of a creation-centred philosophy premised on a holistic and blessed cosmos in which a loving and compassionate God was both mother and father, the earth was holy and there was a unity of body and soul (M. Fox 1994; Merchant 1992). More recently, Matthew Fox has adapted this western mysticism to formulate an ecological creation spirituality while Christian theologians John Cobb and David Ray Griffin propose an eco-theology based on an ecosystems perspective (Cobb and Griffin 1976). In these ways, nature is conceived of as the sacred creation of God which ennobles the human stewardship of nature and all its creatures.

In Islam where there has been less of a separation between the sciences of nature and religion, the Islamic principle of unity (*al-tawhid*) links humans with nature (Nasr 1968). In the Qur'ān, the principles of *khalifa* (trusteeship) and *akhrah* (accountability) underlie Mohammed's edicts to humans: 'He hath appointed you his viceregents in the earth' (Sura 35); 'And commit not disorder on the earth after it hath been well ordered' (Sura 7). (Rodwell 1994) As stated by Farhadi (1989: 6–7): 'No religion on earth is so clearly vocative against destruction of domestic and wild life and against decima-tion of the God-granted natural wealth.' Thus while humankind is the master and custodian of nature, their role is to care for and protect God's creation.

Although the traditional Judeo-Christian ethic for the domination of nature has often been criticized as anti-ecological (Kinsley 1994; White 1973), some of this may be attributed to narrow interpretations of scriptural writings which deny the need for the stewardship of nature (Nash 1989). As observed by Wall (1994: 192): 'The Judaeo-Christian concept of original sin may have given rise to the doctrine that, far from being sacred and worthy of reverence, the Earth is a fallen realm that deserves little care.' The Very Reverend James Park Morton (1993: 124), dean of the Episcopal Cathedral of St John the Divine in New York City observes that, 'We forgot that *domin-ion* has its root in *dominus*—dweller in the house or caretaker, the Latin equivalent of the *oikos* in ecology.'

In response, the importance of humankind's ecological stewardship rather than domination and exploitation has led modern theologians to focus more on biblical passages such as the following.

> The earth dries up and withers,
> the world languishes and withers,
> the heavens languish together with the earth.

> The earth lies polluted under its inhabitants,
> for they have transgressed laws,

> violated the statutes,
> broken the everlasting covenant.

> (Isaiah 24: 4–5)

Recent developments within contemporary western religions demonstrate that divine concern for all of creation (and not just for humans) is not incompatible with Judaeo-Christian theology (Daly and Cobb 1994; McFague 1993). There are those who are working towards an ecological Judaism which integrates environmental principles into Judaic laws and rituals (Lerner 1994; Swartz 1996). Both Protestant and Catholic religious leaders and theologians have made the ecological crisis a central concern in their writings and meetings. Most noteworthy has been Pope John Paul II's papal addresses on ecology: 'Peace with God the creator, peace with all of creation' in December 1989 (Beyer 1992) and 'The ecological crisis: A common responsibility' message for the Celebration of the World Day of Peace on 1 January 1990 (Pope John Paul II 1990). While not totally abandoning their anthropocentric worldview, mainstream religions are endeavouring to create a theology which advances the 'integrity of creation' for both environmental and social justice (Beyer 1992; Gottlieb 1996).

Spirituality and Environmental Change

> human identity and personal fulfillment somehow depend on our relationship to nature. The human need for nature is linked not just to the material exploitation of the environment but also to the influence of the natural world on our emotional, cognitive, aesthetic, and even spiritual development.

> (Kellert 1993: 42)

As proposed by the biophilia hypothesis which seeks to explain humans' instinctual and learned responses toward the natural environment (Wilson 1984), humans' spiritual, mental, and physical well-being is innately and intimately connected to nature. The biophilia hypothesis also proposes that humankind's evolutionary experience (past, current, and future) is deeply dependent on the well-being or health of all aspects of the natural environment. However, ecopsychologists contend that before the earth can be healed, one must first heal oneself (Roszak, Gome, and Kanner 1995). Developing a sense of ecological perception or awareness is the first step towards overcoming the destructive myopia and denial which is at the foundation of the modern ecological crisis (Sewall 1995). Spiritual traditions and religions provide alternative ways of perceiving and understanding the world. To the degree that spiritual belief systems influence individual and collective values and beliefs, they create the ideational motivation to change the ecological status quo. That said, there still remains the question of whether transformational changes in the human psyche are enough to inspire changes in human action. Pessimists would highlight the numerous contradictions between espoused spiritual values and ecologically destructive behaviours of various cultures throughout history (Callicott and Ames 1989; Timm 1993). They would also point to the power of deeply rooted social and economic institutional systems to resist transformational changes of the type which are proposed (Dobson 1995).

Even so, there are many ways that nature-centred spiritual traditions, Asian religions and philosophies, and monotheist religions have informed and influenced socio-natural relationships. This section identifies and discusses the ways in which spiritual communities and religions have been forces for environmental change. First, examples of spiritual environmental activism illustrate a wide variety of change initiatives including grass-roots protest and resistance activities, the reinterpretation and rewriting of religious texts and edicts, the creation of environmentally symbolic rituals and ceremonials, the development of environmental demonstration and educational projects, and environmental advocacy for collaboration to influence government policy at national and international levels. Next, the ways that spirituality has been integrated into contemporary eco-philosophies as well as informed environmental activism is explored. And finally, the implications for organizing for environmental change are presented.

Environmental Activism of Spiritual Communities and Religions

> Earth-based spirituality provides both an imperative toward action in the world and a source of strength and renewal of the energies that often burn out in political action.
>
> (Starhawk 1989: 176)

As expressed by Starhawk, environmental activism is not inconsistent with neopagan or goddess spirituality. During the 1980s, members of Starhawk's Matrix affinity group organized political demonstrations to protest California's Lawrence Livermore Laboratory's research on nuclear weapons (Merchant 1992). They employed Wiccan rituals, chants and spells throughout this large-scale non-violent protest which resulted in numerous arrests (at one point in 1983, 1,000 persons were detained for 15 days).

In terms of the impetus and logic for political activism for environmental change, believers in neopaganism and goddess spirituality differ from those in shamanic communities. Shamanic spiritualities discourage such organized political activism. The approach of the shamanic spiritual tradition is to look into one's own culture, community, and environment for spiritual guidance and to offer only examples of how one can live according to nature-centered spiritual principles (A. Smith 1993). The uniqueness of each place's natural environment and culture requires that those who live there develop their own ways, stories and rituals (Gaard 1993). Even so, this has not precluded indigenous peoples from joining together to address common environmental problems. One example is the Indigenous Environmental Network, an alliance of fourteen North American indigenous grassroots organizations formed in 1991 to share information on environmental problems that face their communities and to work for environmental protection and sovereignty on their lands.

Kaza (1993) recounts a number of arenas of Buddhist environmental education and activism. For example, the Buddhist Peace Fellowship (founded in 1978) has worked within the peace and environmental movements to enhance environmental awareness as well as engage in non-violent anti-nuclear protests. Buddhists Concerned for Animals have worked to stop the inhumane treatment of animals in scientific research as well as in factory-farms. Buddhist values have been identified as being closest to that of an environmentally sustainable society (Badiner 1990). Schumacher (1973) adapted the Buddhist concept of 'Right Livelihood' to develop a Buddhist economics for environmental and industrial change. Specifically, he proposed an environmental ethic based on liberation through simplicity and non-violence; attaining ends with the minimum of means; and holding a reverent and non-violent attitude to all beings and entities in nature. In this way, Buddhism provides a blueprint for individual and collective efforts to effect environmental change.

Mainstream religions have also endeavoured (singly and in collaboration) to translate their theology into practice and policy for ecological change at local, national, and international levels. Christian and Jewish organizations, seminaries, and divinity schools have initiated numerous environmental projects and task forces. Among the most notable is the National Religious Partnership for the Environment which includes the US Catholic Conference, the Coalition on the Environment and Jewish Life, the National Council of Churches of Christ, and the Evangelical Environmental Network to provide educational programmes, advocate environmental legislation and policies, and organize environmental projects and action campaigns. Other noteworthy initiatives include the Friends Committee on Unity with Nature (Quakers), the Eco-Justice Project of the Center for Religion, Ethics, and

Social Policy at Cornell University, the Commission on Stewardship of the National Council of Churches of Christ, and the North American Conference on Christianity and Ecology (Washington, DC, and San Francisco). The Eco-Justice Project of the United Methodist Church has set out specific principles for Christian stewardship of the environment. Other Christian denominations which have environmental projects include the American Baptist Churches, Lutheran Church, Presbyterian, United Methodist Church, the United Church of Christ, and the Reformed Church in America. (Gottlieb 1996; Merchant 1992)

In Central and South America, liberationist Catholicism provides the impetus for aiding peasants and workers in their struggles against environmental degradation. One example is the Commisao Pastoral da Terra (CPT) created by the Organization of Brazilian Bishops. The CPT has helped local tribal communities' efforts to save the inland lakes along the Amazon River by providing ideological, technical, financial, and organizational assistance (Hadsell 1995). Another example of how organized religion can promote ecological stewardship is provided by the Association of African Earth-keeping Churches (AAEC) (Daneel 1994). Over 100 African Independent Churches (representing 2 million congregants) belong to the AAEC which serves as the thinktank and fundraiser for the Zimbabwean Institute of Religious Research and Ecological Conservation (ZIRRCON). In addition to their work on afforestation, wildlife conservation and protection of water resources projects, the AAEC has brought the environmental ethic into church teachings and liturgy through innovations such as tree-planting eucharists performed in AAEC congregations.

The Jewish ecological movement has identified several means for recovering an ecological consciousness (Lerner 1994). This includes: developing a code of eco-kosher practices relating to consumption (avoiding food produced with chemical pesticides, paper from old-growth forests, products derived from the exploitation of non-renewable resources and polluting technologies) and investment; observing *shabbat* as a seventh year of rest for the land; and celebrating *sukkot* as the Jewish thanksgiving ritual for a living planet.

At a global level there have been several interfaith initiatives focusing on ecological issues. In July 1979, the World Council of Churches addressed environmental issues at their meeting on 'Faith, science, and the future' (Brown 1981). The 300 delegates from fifty-six countries proposed that an ecological theology be developed to heal the destructive relationship between humanity and nature. They also proposed that there be an international moratorium on construction of nuclear power plants as well as remedies to resolve food shortages and hunger. Since then, environmental stewardship has been a frequent theme at gatherings of the World Council of Churches (which represents over 400 million Christians). In 1990 at Seoul the theme was 'Justice, peace, and integrity of creation' (Beyer 1992) and the 1991 General Assembly held in Canberra, Australia focused on 'Come Holy Spirit, Renew the Whole Creation' (Oelschlaeger 1994).

In June 1991, the Joint Appeal in Religion and Science (leaders of major American faith groups, scientists and US senators) convened a 'Summit on the Environment' and concluded that 'social justice and environmental integrity are inseparable' (Morton 1993: 130). And during the 1992 United Nations Conference on Environment and Development (UNCED) in Rio de Janiero, the World Council of Churches convened an interfaith gathering to draft ethical principles on the environment and development for considera-tion in the proposed UNCED Earth Charter (Hallman 1994). Although governments could not negotiate an agreement on an Earth Charter,[1] work continued on what became the *One Earth Community* document to be 'used as a guide for church programmes and for advocacy with government and industry' (Hallman 1994: 265).

In summary, these examples of spiritual environmental activism illustrate a wide variety of symbolic, behavioural, institutional, and political strategies of actions to effect environmental change. However, to what degree do these examples of spiritual environmentalism challenge the modernist status quo? Many of mainstream religions' environmental initiatives such as their reinterpretations of religious texts, creation of environmental rituals and ceremonials, and development of education programmes (cognitive and experiential) indicate an assumption of cultural continuity (Swidler 1986). Similarly, it could be argued that the political advocacy being undertaken at national and international levels represent an extension of previous social justice activities. Although the global interorganizational initiatives represent collaboration of previously separate organizations, there is less evidence that fundamental changes in internal organizational arrangements are occurring. Thus, much of mainstream religions' environmental activism (especially within the northern hemisphere) could be regarded as rites of renewal (Trice 1985) in which symbolic discourse and action serve to rejuvenate and reinforce existing systems of power and authority rather than radically transforming them.

In contrast, during periods of cultural transformation, alternative ideo-logies provide coherent belief and ritual systems which 'model new ways to organize action and to structure human communities' (Swidler 1986: 280). In this respect, the assumption that this is a period of cultural transforma-tion appears to underlie more of the environmental activism of neopagan and Buddhist spiritual organizations as well as mainstream religious organi-zations in the southern hemisphere. These organizations' grassroots protest

and resistance activities explicitly challenge existing socio-political arrangements. There also appears to be a greater unity of words and deeds in the
everyday lives of their followers. That these forms of environmental activism
are more often found in places where the evidence of ecological threat is
most visible cannot be taken as coincidental. However, the long term effectiveness of these strategies of cultural change is largely dependent on the
development of supportive structural arrangements (Swidler 1986). In this
respect, environmental activism by mainstream religions within the southern hemisphere may have the advantage whereas neopagan activism could
be regarded as too radical and Buddhist activism could be regarded as too
diffuse to be at the forefront of social transformation.

Spirituality in Eco-Philosophies and the Environmental Movement

While not all eco-philosophers are receptive to the idea of a spiritual ecology
or an ecological spirituality,[2] many have found inspiration and guidance from
various spiritual and religious traditions for developing their philosophies of
the socio-natural relationship. They recognize that human values and beliefs
concerning the natural environment do not emerge *sui generis* but rather
have a long cultural and spiritual heritage. One of the central tenets of
radical eco-philosophies is the recapturing of a pre-Enlightenment world-
view in which the universe is seen as organic, living and spiritual (Devall and
Sessions 1985; Drengson and Inoue 1995). The following explores how the
eco-philosophies of deep ecology, transpersonal ecology, and eco-feminism
propose this should be accomplished.

Deep ecology philosophers (Devall and Sessions 1985; Drengson and
Inoue 1995) have drawn from Asian and Native American spiritual traditions
in their writings on biocentrism, biospherical egalitarianism (intrinsic
value of all life forms), and the need for holistic balance with nature. Deep
ecology proposes the moral goal of *self-realization* wherein 'the interest or
interests of another being [which] are reacted to as our own interest or
interests' (Naess 1988: 261). Deep ecology's radical biocentrism advocates
the restriction of individual human freedoms (in particular, neo-Malthusian
restrictions on human reproduction) in favour of the rights of wildlife and
nature.

Transpersonal ecology extends deep ecology's focus on the alienation
caused by the mechanistic and dualistic worldview of modern industrialized
society which can only be healed by recapturing humanity's sacred connections with all aspects of creation (W. Fox 1990). Drawing from the work
of Abraham Maslow, Stanislav Grof, and Anthony Sutich, transpersonal

psychology offers proposals for personal growth or eco-actualization through a holistic identification (personal, ontological, and cosmological) with all life forms including the non-human world.

Nature-centred spiritual traditions (especially goddess spirituality) and Asian philosophies have been particularly influential in the development of ecofeminist philosophy (Adams 1993; Warren 1994). Ecofeminism posits that humankind is different from, but not equivalent to, other life forms within the ecological community. The central position of ecofeminism is that the achievement of social justice is integral to environmental justice to end all forms of hierarchical domination within patriarchal cultures. As identified by Ruether (1993), spirituality provides ecofeminists with the energy to challenge and survive (at both conceptual and behavioural levels) oppressive hierarchical systems to create new systems based on the principles of egalitarianism, inclusiveness, communitarianism, consensual decision making, mutual care and responsibility (Cheney 1987).

As the operating philosophy of radical environmental activist organizations such as Earth First!, the Sea Shepherd Society, Friends of the Earth, and Greenpeace, deep ecology provides the rationale for direct action campaigns (including ecological sabotage) and civil disobedience against those interests viewed as the enemies of nature (Manes 1990). It has been observed that radical proponents of deep ecology have quasi-religious aspirations to promote ecological consciousness as a spiritual quest (Bookchin 1994; W. Fox 1990). One could question deep ecologists' justification of the use of violent means to effect ecological balance and harmony. While professing to be guided by Taoist, Buddhist, and Native American spiritualities, deep ecologists who advocate and engage in violent acts are violating these traditions' fundamental principle of non-violent thoughts and deeds to all beings in creation. It should be noted that not all radical environmentalists who subscribe to a deep ecology perspective condone the use of violence to effect environmental change. Grassroots advocacy groups in the environmental movement have more often organized campaigns of civil disobedience and passive resistance (Merchant 1992). On several occasions, the more pacifist ecofeminist approach has been adopted by environmental activists such as the protesters who during the summer of 1993 strove to stop clear-cut logging in British Columbia's Clayoquot Sound (MacIsaac and Champagne 1994). The 'virtue of non-contention' common to both Hinduism and Buddhism was present in the passive resistance of the women's Chipko movement in northern India to prevent logging in the Himalayan foothills (Shiva 1989). Green Party candidates in Europe and North America eschew violence in favour of working within existing political systems for a peaceful transition to an ecological world (Jancar-Webster 1993; Sale 1993; Spretnak and Capra 1986). Whether informed by eco-feminist philosophy or not, the approach of the majority within the environmental movement has been one of non-violence (Day 1989; Sale 1993). While the tactics of a few 'eco-terrorists' have garnered much media attention, the majority are working in peaceful ways that involve bearing witness to environmental destruction and hazards, developing environmental educational and information programs as well as working collaboratively with legislators and industry to initiate environmental change.

Religious monastic orders have also served as models for radical environmentalist proposals for ecologically sustainable communities. In a spiritual extension of the deep ecology concept, Devall (1990) proposes that Buddhists develop ecocentric *sangha* communities within bioregions. Bahro (1994: 90) contends that 'we need a new Benedictine order' of small self-sufficient bioregional communities which will create a critical mass of spiritual consciousness to effect transformational change in society. Within the radical environmentalist literature, there are other proposals for how intentional community and communal strategies can facilitate environmental change (Dobson 1995; B. R. Taylor 1995). Ecotopian communities founded on bioregional ideals serve as exemplars from which the rest of society can learn how to live an ecologically sustainable lifestyle. However, networks of such communities can only succeed as revolutionary alternatives to the degree that they operate outside of conventional society (thereby avoiding co-optation and compromise).

Implications for Organizing for Environmental Change

> Whatever the tradition, religions are malleable. In the face of environmental deterioration, they have been mutating into forms capable of inspiring (or reinforcing) ecological activism, both by articulating ideals that participants find compelling . . . and by providing concrete institutional resources for ecological struggles.
>
> (B. R. Taylor 1995: 335–7)

This paper has presented a number of ways in which spiritually inspired ideals of environmental stewardship have motivated and guided individual and collective behaviour. Spiritual principles and teachings provide personal inspiration and guidance for those seeking ecologically sustainable lifestyles. Spiritual and religious organizations provide information and educate about the principles of environmental stewardship and respect for the natural environment. Leading by example, these organizations have translated words into action by initiating environmental projects and providing organizational support and resources for direct action campaigns to stop environmental degradation. Spiritual ideas have also inspired eco-philosophy and ecological activism in the wider environmental movement.

Spiritual traditions such as Buddhism, Taoism, and shamanism suggest that ecological transformation will be realized by letting 'a thousand flowers bloom'. That is, an accumulation of changes in individual ecological consciousness will over time, create a critical mass within groups, societies, and populations to effect a change in the collective ecological consciousness. It is a way that requires active personal commitment to work for ecological sustainability in ever-widening circles of concern (oneself, one's home, community, bioregion, nation, planet). This is a path that requires high levels of dedication, patience, and faith to achieve integrity in means and ends. What role do spiritual organizations and their leaders have to play in this process? Primarily, it is to facilitate the development of ideational motivation of individuals and collectives by offering information and guidance, by providing encouragement and support, and by providing spiritual, intellectual, and social linkages for people. To this end, modern communication and transportation technologies can accelerate the speed and broaden the scope of collaborative connections among people and organizations in disparate parts of the globe (Bilimoria *et al.* 1995).

Mainstream religions demonstrate the potential of hierarchical institutions to forge another path for change. Mainstream religions have the institutional infrastructure, knowledge, and resources to organize ecological conservation initiatives. These organizational competencies also facilitate the development and implementation of environmental initiatives with similarly organized economic, political, cultural, and religious institutions. Recent examples of interfaith dialogue and collective action illustrate the potential of adopting a global partnership approach to develop a world environmental ethic. As exemplified by the 1993 Second Parliament of the World's Religions which gathered together 8,000 individuals representing over 200 religious organizations (Tobias, Morrison, and Gray 1995) and the 1996 United Religions Initiative Summit (Khalsa and Kaczmarski 1996), disparate parties can work towards the common good despite fundamental ideological differences. In these ways religious organizations model the new forms of collaboration needed for transformational social and ecological change that transcend cultural and political factionalism (Brulle 1995).

Even so, the question remains as to the potency of such organizational initiatives to mobilize personal and institutional change. Snow and Benford (1992) argue that 'collective action frames' have greater mobilizing potential if they are more elaborated and more central to the ideology of the targets of mobilization. Thus, the reinterpretation and reintegration of the natural environment in religious teachings and edicts bode well for creating an environmental metanarrative to organize experience and guide action to challenge the status quo (Brulle 1995, Tarrow 1992). New social movement theorists (Morris and Mueller 1992) also identify that pre-existing social relationships are a critical part of the mobilization process for social change. In this regard, spiritual and religious communities also appear to be well suited as focal points for environmental activism. However, Schwartz and Paul (1992) observe that consensus social movements which have broad attitudinal support, developed social infrastructures and considerable institutional resources have lower rates of membership mobilization and greater strategic rigidity than conflict movements. As earlier identified, the magnitude and urgency of current environmental problems requires both institutional and personal changes in envisioning and enacting an ecologically sustainable world. To the degree that organized religions constitute consensus movements, change strategies which eschew conflict or confrontation may hinder their effectiveness in mobilizing their members to take personal committed action to achieve espoused environmental goals.

Spiritual Pathways for Environmental Change?

> The human community and the natural world will go into the future
> as a single sacred community or we will both perish in the desert.
>
> (Thomas Berry, as quoted by Martin 1993: 43)

In *The Dream of the Earth*, Berry (1988) writes about creating an earth community (the whole planetary ecosystem) based on a 'functional spirituality' or 'functional cosmology'. He calls for a new story, a new sense of the universe, to take humanity forward from the mechanistic orientation of the scientific world and the pathologies of modern industrial society. Interestingly, Berry (a Passionist priest) calls for a new shamanic personality, not a prophet, to help discover this story.

The shamanic type is the person that goes deep into the mystery of the universe and brings back power and direction to a society. It brings back healing, because the power is frequently healing power but supportive power. But the main thing about the shamanic personality is that it's dealing more with the powers of the natural world. We are not accustomed to dealing with the powers of the natural world. (Berry, 1990: 20)

Berry's (1993) agenda for healing the earth community is far reaching and encompasses the spiritual, technological, educational, economic, and institutional dimensions of the human community. It is also an agenda that requires changes at individual, organizational, societal, and global levels.

This chapter has presented a variety of spiritual values and beliefs concerning the relationship between humankind and the natural environment. Nature-centered and Asian spiritual traditions emphasize the need for holistic balance and harmony within the interdependent and interpenetrating webs of relationships between humans and the natural environment. They teach that thoughts and actions towards others and nature need to be respectful and informed by the principle of non-violence. Asian philosophies tell of the requirement for continuous effort and a creative attitude to achieve and maintain this peace and harmony. Both teach of the importance of experiential knowledge—that knowing one's physical place within the natural world is integral to attaining an intellectual and spiritual understanding of the universe. Monotheist religions emphasize the divine concern of God for all in creation and humankind's role as stewards of the natural world. Many environmental thinkers, writers, and activists (even the most secular) view the natural world and unity of life on the planet with awe, respect, and love. That is to say, they view life on earth as sacred and, hence, having a spiritual dimension to it even if they don't use those terms.[3]

Current global interfaith initiatives to address environmental issues demonstrate that there can be a unity in purpose (peace and justice ideals) irrespective of a diversity of spiritual and religious perspectives. This in turn can serve as an important counterbalance to the instrumental orientation (progress, efficiency, technical rationality) and individuation of functionally specialized, globally homogeneous economic and social systems (Beyer 1992). In this regard, the nature-centred and Asian concept of 'place' is a critique of the universalist meaning structures underlying modern science and technocratic societies. On the other hand, the concept of place could also serve as an exclusionary mechanism to pre-empt open debate regarding actions needed to resolve environmental problems which transcend physical and cultural boundaries. Thus, these approaches to spiritual environmentalism posit a potential dialectical tension between inclusion and exclusion which necessitates reflexive discourse.

The linkage between spirituality and environmental activism may be uncomfortable for those who believe in the importance of a strictly secular society. To be sure, history has taught us that the politicization of spirituality in the advocacy of environmental change warrants a degree of caution (Deudney 1995). However, there is little evidence that the goals of spiritual and religious leaders engaged in environmental advocacy and projects extend to a rejoining of Church and State. Instead, their agenda has been more to facilitate environmental change by re-examining their spiritual teachings, being exemplars of environmental responsibility, and working in parallel and collaboratively with existing political and economic institutions (Oelschlaeger 1994).

This passage into the twenty-first century is a social invention. It is an act of cultural imagination, and as such it provides a catalyst for other similar acts of imagination on which our collective prosperity and health—and even our survival—may rest. It is an invitation to reexamine, reevaluate, and where necessary, change attitudes and habits of culture that increasingly prove dysfunctional on the interconnected planet that we inhabit. (Spangler 1993: 70)

One recurrent theme throughout this chapter has been the role which spiritual values and beliefs can play in recapturing connections with the natural environment and guiding humankind through the modern ecological crisis. In one sense, this has been an exploration about *being* as well as *doing*. It is based on the assumption that action which is not grounded in and guided by one's values and beliefs is superficial and transitory. If, as many have observed, there need to be fundamental changes in the ecological consciousness of humankind, then one important starting point for those changes is from within. To the degree that religions and spiritual traditions influence social norms and behaviours, they provide the inspiration and personal commitment so needed for ecological self-discipline and activism (Carroll *et al.* 1997; Deudney 1995).

God has made different religions to suit different aspirations, times, and countries. All doctrines are only so many paths, but a path is by no means God Himself. Indeed, one can reach God if one follows one of the paths with whole-hearted devotion. (Ramakrishna, as cited by H. Smith 1991: 74)

The intent of this chapter has not been to propose a universal environmental belief system nor that there is one best way to relate to nature. One needs to be cognizant and respectful of the many significant and fundamental differences amongst these traditions, particularly in regards to their spiritual practices. As there is need for biodiversity on the planet, there is also a need for diversity in human expression and action which reflects the unique historical, cultural, and biophysical realities which have co-evolved throughout the world (Roberts 1990; Warren 1994). This chapter proposes that spiritual perspectives on the natural environment and ways of effecting environmental change are complementary to other necessary cognitive and behavioural initiatives which are currently envisioned and underway. While there is a richness within each spiritual tradition and religion that remains to be further explored, my intent has been to trigger our imagination and our thinking about what these spiritual traditions and religions have to offer, in terms of guiding modern secular societies during this time of ecological crisis.

PART II

Cultural Discourse in Environmental Expertise and Policy Making

4

Engineering the Environment: The Politics of 'Nature Development'

JOZEF KEULARTZ

During the past decade a new variation on 'nature conservancy' has gained acceptance in the Netherlands: 'nature development'. As the name suggests, the issue is no longer to protect and conserve existing nature, but to produce *new* nature. The fact that this variety should have arisen in the Netherlands is hardly surprising. The Netherlands is very densely populated, has an intensive agriculture and an expansive chemical sector and, as the delta of several of Europe's largest rivers such as the Rhine, the Meuse, and the Scheldt, it has become the 'cesspit' of western Europe. In response to the progressive impoverishment of nature, the country has seen the emergence of a strong nature conservation movement. The two largest nature conservation organizations, the Vereniging tot Behoud van Natuurmonumenten (Nature Monuments Association, generally called simply Nature Monuments) and the Dutch branch of the World Wide Fund for Nature (WWF), boast a membership of 800,000 and 700,000 respectively (out of a total population of some 15 million), while Greenpeace, with 585,000 members, also enjoys considerable support. This involvement by large parts of the population has certainly played an important part in the shift in official nature policies from a defensive to an offensive approach.

The idea of large-scale production of new nature can sound exciting and promising. It also appears to bear out the view that nature has now, more than ever—and in the Netherlands more than elsewhere—entered 'the age of technical reproducibility', as Gernot Böhme once said, with a nod to Walter Benjamin. Seen in this light, nature development would do justice to the progressive interweaving of town and countryside, nature and culture, and mesh with attempts in postmodern philosophy (Derrida), social constructivism (Latour) and cyberfeminism (Haraway) to escape once and for all from the binary thought regime by undermining all manner of traditional dichotomies.

But, upon closer look, things are not what they seem. The ideal behind the large-scale production of new nature is old nature. Everything revolves around the original, untrodden nature, around 'primeval nature' in which there is no place for man or his technical artefacts. The motto of the nature developers is not integration but segregation. The aim is to shield nature from human interference, so that it can once again go its own way. Yet to achieve this in the existing situation in the Netherlands requires large-scale human intervention. This attempt to drive the devil of technology out of nature with the help of Beelzebub reveals the profoundly ambivalent character of nature development. This ambivalence is already evident in the very expression 'nature development', where nature can be read as both *genitivus subjectivus* and *genitivus objectivus*. On the one hand, the phrase can refer both to a supreme, quasi-sacred subject—primeval nature—and to a profoundly manipulable object. On the other, it is precisely this ambivalence that gives nature development its strength and has allowed it to become the *cause célèbre* of a wide variety of social groups with diverging and often conflicting interests.

It can be demonstrated that nature development can be seen and described as an (implicit) form of cultural politics which manages to bind certain social groups while at the same time threatening to sideline other groups to the point where their interests and needs can no longer be voiced in politics. In doing so, I shall dwell on the cognitive roots of nature development, the main source of its social authority. I shall argue that to a large extent, these roots display that same ambiguity to which, as mentioned above, nature development owes its ideological appeal. However, the basic principles of nature development are not only ambivalent but also one-sided since nature developers systematically turn a blind eye to alternative paradigms or competing research programmes. In short, whether one looks at it from a socio-cultural or a scientific point of view, nature development in its present form is both questionable and dubious.

Power to the Primitive Imagination

An outline of the historical context in which the emergence of nature development must be seen may serve as introduction to this critique. In *Landscape and Memory* (1995) Simon Schama advanced the proposition that there have always been two kinds of Arcadia, the *pastoral* and the *primitive*. Whereas the primitive Arcadia is inhabited by people who behave like wild animals, the pastoral Arcadia is a place from which all dangerous creatures (such as the snake and the lion) have been banned and the ideal animals (such as the cow and the bee) behave like conscientious and industrious citizens. Relations between the two representations have always been tense. According to Schama, this tension also makes itself felt within the nature conservation and environmental movements, an observation that also applies to Dutch nature policy, which for decades has swung back and forth between the pastoral and the primitive representation of an ideal landscape.

The Dutch model *par excellence* of the pastoral representation is the landscape of around 1850, when society was poised on the threshold of large-scale modernization processes. Owing to the highly diversified but also highly stable forms of land use, this landscape offered a variegated panorama and a wide variety of plants and birds. It was this landscape that was embraced, most notably in circles around the Nature Monuments Association, as the model of a successful interplay between social patterns of utilization and natural development processes. In fact, it is a highly cultural–historical landscape in which the hand of man is all-pervasive. After 1850, this landscape underwent a large number of fairly dramatic changes. The sharp rise in population led to urbanization and an increase in traffic and transport. Many canals were dug and, in a relatively short period of time, a dense network of train and tram lines and motorways was constructed.

In line with the pastoral representation, the strategy of Nature Monuments has from the very outset been aimed at maintaining the status quo, the main criteria being the existing diversity of (rare) species and the cultural–historical value of the (pre-industrial) landscape. In order to maintain this landscape, human intervention is indispensable. The management of reserves by Nature Monuments therefore comes down to a continuation of traditional techniques such as hunting and fishing, reed and brushwood cultivation, tree planting and felling, mowing and turf cutting, the setting up of duck decoys and the use of water mills.

During the depression years in the 1930s, when vast areas of 'wasteland' were reclaimed in the context of unemployment relief works, conflicts arose between the nature conservationists and the farmers. This went hand in hand with the ascent of a primitive wing within the generally pastorally oriented nature conservation movement. The foremost spokesman of this wing was the biologist T. Weevers, who promoted the view that real nature cannot tolerate human intervention. Taken in a strict sense, this meant that there should be no human management of nature reserves and it presented private nature conservationists with a serious dilemma. By and large, the pursuit of 'naturalness', that is to say an undisturbed development of plant and animal communities, was irreconcilable with the demands of exploitation, the significance of cultural–historical landscape elements and the importance of the richness of varieties. This dilemma was resolved by biologist Victor Westhoff. He introduced the concept of 'half-nature' to characterize the Dutch landscape, every part of which, he believed, had been shaped by human intervention. If this landscape was to be maintained, he concluded, continued intervention was inevitable. If nature was simply left to run its course, then heaths and marshes, for instance, would degenerate irrevocably and lose their biological diversity. Westhoff's approach overtook that of the primitives around Weevers, allowing the pastoral tradition to regain its prominence in nature conservation in the first decades after World War II (Van der Windt 1995).

However, this did not put an end to the battle between the pastorals and the primitives; between 1975 and 1985 the consensus in the nature conservation movement crumbled once again. Two groups took up opposing positions. Organizations such as the Vereniging Milieudefensie (Environmental Defence, Dutch branch of Friends of the Earth) and the Landelijke Vereniging tot Behoud van de Waddenzee (National Society for the Preservation of the Wadden Sea) reproached the nature conservation movement for assuming an elitist and apolitical stance and ignoring the position of farmers. These (pastoral) organizations made a plea for the integration of nature conservation and farming and advocated environmentally friendly agriculture. Groups such as Kritisch Bosbeheer (Critical Forest Management) and Kritisch Faunabeheer (Critical Fauna Management) were opposed to such integration and instead advocated a more rigid separation of nature and agriculture. They called on the nature conservationists to stop ministering to 'degenerate' nature in the shape of production forests, grasslands, and heaths and to concentrate on 'real' nature, or 'primeval nature'. To help natural processes get back into swing, certain starting conditions had to be created, of course, but beyond that all human activity should stop.

This (primitive) approach to nature conservation, called 'nature development', gained the support of the WWF, the largest competitor of Nature Monuments, and also had a strong impact on the *Natuurbeleidsplan* (Nature Policy Plan) adopted by the Dutch parliament in 1990. This plan centres on the realization of an 'Ecologische Hoofdstructuur' (National Network of Important Ecosystems), a network of ecological core areas with a minimum area of 5 square kilometres, several smaller areas and the links between them (in the form of stepping stones and corridors). The National Network of Important Ecosystems will eventually cover quite a large area (700 sq. km.) of the Dutch territory (total surface area 3,500 sq. km.), which already includes some 450 sq. km. of designated nature areas.

The nature developers' view of the future reorganization of the Dutch landscape can be clearly seen in their 'casco' (basic or 'stripped' structure) concept, in which a distinction is made between low and high dynamism functions. Low dynamism functions mainly concern ecological processes, which require a stable environment for sustainable development, whereas high dynamism functions relate primarily to economic processes, which require a high degree of flexibility. In essence, the casco concept prescribes the spatial segregation of the two functions: the low dynamism functions are to be clustered together in a landscape framework (i.e. the 'National Network of Important Ecosystems') and the high dynamism functions in the 'utility space'. To prevent the fast-turning wheel of the economy from one day crushing the slow-turning wheel of ecology, the Dutch landscape is to be converted into a 'two-speed landscape'. In order to show how the nature developers have managed to mobilize pretty widespread social support for this view, I shall now turn my attention to the ambivalent character of the concept of nature development.

Subject of Adoration and Object of Manipulation

The nature developers reject taking the landscape of 1850 as an objective reference point for nature policy, basing themselves instead on the 'Ecological Reference', which indicates what nature would be like in the Netherlands today if it had never been ravaged by human beings. Their particular point of reference is the situation as it is assumed to have existed in the last interglacial era, partly because from a climatological point of view this era is closest to our own times, but more especially because at that time man did not yet possess long-range weapons (such as the javelin or bow and arrow) and was therefore not yet able to eliminate his natural enemies. The reconstruction of this 'primeval' nature relies on geological, physical–geographical, and biological–archaeological research. In addition, research is being carried out into surviving ecological communities which are very similar in terms of species composition to the ecological communities in Europe during the last interglacial era. Such ecological communities are still to be found in the national parks of India and Sri Lanka and in a clutch of African nature reserves.

   Human beings have only a very modest role to play in this primeval nature, namely 'as a hunter, gatherer or scavenger', as the main background document to the *Nature Policy Plan* puts it, without the slightest trace of irony. 'Even though, ecologically speaking, man is an omnivore, his choice of prey nevertheless puts him in the category of the large predators.' (*Natuurontwikkeling* 1989: 40) Nature has been going rapidly downhill ever since humankind progressed beyond the primitive stage of hunter, gatherer, and scavenger.

Whereas the nature aspired to by traditional conservationists depends on the application of old agricultural crafts, the nature championed by nature developers is reconcilable with only the most primitive techniques. However—and this constitutes the main paradox of nature development—this alleged primeval nature has been absent from the Netherlands since 1871 when Beekberger Woud, the last remaining patch of primeval forest, was cut down in a matter of days, and can therefore only be reproduced by technological means. In other words, the romantic ideal of primeval nature rests on a hidden rational practice which might best be described as 'ecotechnology'.

From an ecological point of view the Netherlands is nothing less than a disaster area, according to nature developers. Land reclamation, cultivation, dike-building, and canalization have curbed or completely eliminated various natural processes, such as the flooding and drying up of river forelands. But living nature has also been completely disrupted, say the nature developers: on the one hand, certain species are no longer present in our landscape because of human intervention; on the other hand, our nature is ridden with 'exotics', plants and animals which 'by nature' do not really belong here. The only genuinely autochthonous or indigenous organisms, they claim, are those that arrived in the delta region entirely of their own accord after the last Ice Age. Sheep, for instance, are not among them and neither are pheasants, grouse, house sparrows, or house-martins. Their presence is regarded as 'fauna fraud'. Even our sparse woods turn out to consist mainly of exotics like the Canadian Douglas fir and the Japanese larch. This 'genetic pollution' by exogenous material is alleged to have had a highly detrimental effect on the vitality of the Dutch forests.

So, not even the vestiges of primeval nature remain in the Netherlands. In order to bring it back, all sorts of dynamic processes will have to be reactivated. One example of this is 're-meandering', a process whereby bulldozers are used to make twists and bends in streams and rivers that were once neatly canalized. To give free reign to the dynamics of wind and water, dozens of summer dikes are breached, layers of clay are cut, parallel ditches are dug and high grounds are raised. Living nature requires a lot of work as well. Nature developers wish to remove exotic creatures and (re)introduce vanished species. Unfortunately, a number of species said to have settled here after the last Ice Age have since died out. This is true of the Irish deer and also of the mammoth, who would presumably have migrated to the lowlands in severe winters. However, good replacements can be found for some species that have become extinct. Thus the Heck ox can serve as a surrogate for the aurochs (†1627) and the konik can do the honours for the tarpan (†1887), the European wild horse. Because the Heck ox is unsuitable for areas where recreational activities are allowed, a human-friendly version is currently being bred: the 'Ecolander'.

Nature development is a purely technological enterprise, as is obvious in the rhetoric accompanying the (retro)breeding and (re)introduction programmes. (Re)introduced animals are being presented primarily as the instruments of a modern style of nature management that is supposedly cheaper and more efficient than traditional nature management. By redeploying large herbivores, grazers (such as cattle), pruners (deer and elk), and 'intermediate feeders' (red deer and European bisons) the forests can be prevented from overgrowing, allowing the landscape to develop into a mosaic of open and densely wooded patches with a rich vegetable and animal population. Provided, that is, the reintroduction of large predators such as wolves and lynxes is pursued with equal energy. If this is not done, the herbivores will not disperse sufficiently and the forests will not get a chance to regenerate properly.

Just how strongly nature developers cherish an entirely instrumental view of these animals is revealed in the mechanistic metaphors they deploy. Frequent use is made of terms such as 'tuning the grazing pressure' exerted by herbivores, or the 'number regulation' of these cheap 'mowing and pruning machines' by their natural enemies and so forth. Another example of the engineering mentality of nature developers is the way they portray nature as the 'main contractor' of nature management. This frequently used phrase betrays just how much this spontaneous, self-regulating, self-ordering nature that is nominally the highest good, is in fact an out-and-out technological product.

The New Coalition

But it is precisely this ambivalent combination of a romantic image of nature and a rational planning practice to which nature development owes its ideological appeal. Nature development nurtures the hope that action can be taken to stop the deterioration of nature, that it is even possible to make some big gains, while at the same time allaying the fear and loathing many conservationists feel towards technology which is, after all, blamed for the impoverishment of our natural environment. It is this ambiguous, two-sided appeal that has enabled nature development to become a strong binding force for widely divergent social groups.

The new approach, worked out by a group of young ecologists at the Ministry of Agriculture, Nature Management, and Fisheries, was soon adopted enthusiastically by the planners and civil engineers of the Rijksplanologische Dienst (National Land Use Planning Agency) and Rijkswaterstaat (Directorate General for Public Works and Water Management). The latter department, in particular, had run out of work after the completion of the Delta Works and in 1994 it published the report *Natuur aan het werk* (Nature at Work) in which it was proposed that the nature areas be considerably extended (beyond what had been foreseen in the Nature Policy Plan). Ironically, this proposal centred largely on the cutting of dikes and inundation of polders, some of which had previously been designed and constructed by that very same Department. It goes without saying that the proposal was very well received by the dredging and brickmaking industries. The strength of the alliance between government and industry is evident in the energy they have put into the Grensmaasproject (Border Meuse Project), one of the most ambitious nature development projects of the moment. This project is being sold to the general public under the catchy slogan of 'Green for Gravel', thereby inadvertently revealing the thoroughly technological character of nature development. The project involves a new technique of shallow rather than deep quarrying, a method that has yet to be developed and tested.

In addition to certain government sectors, the new approach was eagerly welcomed by the WWF, which in 1996 launched a major campaign under the motto of 'The Netherlands twice as beautiful' aimed at doubling the area 'under nature' in the Netherlands, from 5 to 10 per cent. It is believed that the land required to achieve this aim can be withdrawn from agriculture, a solution that appeals greatly to a number of leading agriculturalists given the need for drastic reorganization in a sector that has long been in a state of severe crisis. While the aforementioned government agencies see nature development primarily in relation to practical activities such as planning, dredging, digging, heightening, and deepening, the WWF aims to enable the Dutch to undergo 'wilderness experiences' in their own country. By emphasizing this aspect, the WWF has succeeded in winning the support not only of Dutch Rail but also of the largest tourist association, the very association that happens to represent the interests of the car-borne day tripper. In addition, the WWF plays on public concerns, arguing that new nature creates a favourable business environment and, consequently, employment opportunities. Finally, the WWF has even managed to win over the Nature Monuments Association, previously fiercely opposed to the whole idea, with the argument that nature development is cheaper and more efficient than traditional methods (aimed at maintaining the agricultural landscape) of nature management.

Nature development, however, is not only a binding factor in nature policy: it has also been a cause of discord and resistance because its adoption leads to certain groups being excluded from nature policy. But before going into such political effects I would like first to focus on the scientific basis of the idea of nature development. The ambivalence to which it owes its practical power to bind together disparate groups, can be traced back to its foundations in theory. Nature development is always of two minds about nature. On the one hand, it rests on a cybernetic conception of nature as developed in systems ecology; on the other hand it appears to cling—implicitly rather than explicitly—to a metaphysical holism which, although characteristic of the pre-war forerunner of systems ecology, has now been replaced in ecology by a purely methodological holism.

Clockwork Nature

Scientifically speaking, nature development can be traced back to cybernetics, which flourished in the United States in the early post-World War II years, in a climate of technocratic optimism. The politicians, having proved unable to cope with the problems of a complex industrial society, were urged to make way for social engineers who would then manage society as a self-regulating machine. One of these technocrats, Evelyn Hutchinson, was to leave an indelible mark on post-war ecology (P. J. Taylor 1988).

In a pioneering paper published in 1946, 'Circular Causal Systems in Ecology', Hutchinson distinguished between two closely related approaches, the 'biogeochemical' and the 'biodemographic' approach. Seen from a biogeochemical perspective, the entire biosphere appears as a giant cyclical system of energy, matter, and information which is able to maintain a dynamic equilibrium thanks to the presence of a series of feedback mechanisms. This perspective was elaborated in particular by Hutchinson's student Howard Odum and his brother Eugene Odum. They repeatedly compared the biosphere, inclusive of mankind and society, with a complex clockwork. This comparison reappears in the main background study of the Dutch Nature Policy Plan. 'In complete ecosystems all the wheels in the machinery are in place and everything runs on solar energy without any additional external input' (*Natuurontwikkeling* 1989: 39).

The biodemographic approach deals with groups or communities of organisms, the so-called 'populations'. In conformity with the cybernetic principle shared by the two approaches, these populations are also perceived as systems attempting to maintain their stability under ever-changing conditions by means of feedback mechanisms. This approach was further elaborated by another of Hutchinson's students, Robert MacArthur. In the 1960s, in collaboration with Edward Wilson, he developed a theory on the biogeography of islands, the 'island theory'. Using the size of the island and the distance to the mainland as its main parameters, the theory predicts the number of species on a given island. MacArthur and Wilson, too, assumed a dynamic equilibrium: although the taxonomic composition on the island is subject to continuous change, the number of species (which is determined by the rates of extinction and colonization) remains constant.

Since its introduction in the early 1980s, the island theory has had a lightning career in Dutch nature policy. Together with the ecosystems theory, it was used to underpin the National Network of Important Ecosystems, in the sense that nature areas are perceived as 'islands in a sea of cultivated land'. The theory serves as a basis for the attempt to maximize the size of contiguous nature areas and the number of links between them.

All attempts to test the island theory empirically have so far failed to come up with any conclusive evidence and the theory is still fiercely contested nowadays. This holds true with even greater force for the application of the theory to cultural landscapes, where the boundaries between the isolated nature areas and the surrounding environment are of course far less well defined than in the original situation. Three discussions currently in progress touch on the essential aspects of the island theory (Shrader-Frechette and McCoy 1993). Firstly there is the question of which is better: a large area or a multitude of smaller areas. The acronym SLOSS (Single-Large-Or-Several-Small) is sometimes used to refer to this discussion. Secondly, there is the question of whether the spatial distribution of the nature areas makes any significant difference. This discussion is also referred to by an acronym: CONC (Circular-Or-Not-Circular). And thirdly there is the question of whether the advantages of wildlife corridors outweigh the disadvantages (Mann and Plummer 1995). Corridors are intended to increase the survival chances of populations by creating links that facilitate a two-way exchange of individuals. However, corridors also allow greater freedom of movement for undesirable organisms such as exotic species, predators, viruses, and parasites. What is more, a free exchange of genetic material can pose a threat to genetic diversity.

Ambivalent Holism

But there is another reason to be sceptical. There is something half-hearted about the way the nature developers exploit the legacy of Hutchinson.

Although his ecology can undoubtedly be characterized as 'holistic', this holism no longer bears the stamp of metaphysics, as did much of pre-war ecology, but is purely methodological. The nature developers are clearly ambivalent on this issue, seeming always to hesitate between metaphysical and methodological holism.

Metaphysical holism emerged in the second half of the 1920s in opposition to the materialistic and mechanistic cosmology devised in the seventeenth century by Galileo, Descartes, and Newton, the inherent reductionism and epistemic dualism of which were held responsible for the decline in community spirit and the alienation from nature. During the inter-war years, metaphysical holism was popular not only among philosophers of repute (such as Alfred North Whitehead and Adolf Meyer-Abich) but also among prominent ecologists (such as Warder Allee and Karl Friedrichs). One of the most influential exponents of metaphysical holism within ecology was American botanist Frederic Clements. He referred to plant communities literally as super-organisms subject to a process of succession, in the course of which plant species succeed each other in a well-ordered fashion for as long as it takes to reach a stable final situation, the so-called 'climax'. This theory was linked by his South African disciple John Phillips to the views expounded by Jan Christiaan Smuts, whose 1927 book *Holism and Evolution* had drawn worldwide attention among the general public.

The political message of metaphysical holism is that a community's chances of survival are totally dependent on the unselfish and unconditional subservience of its members to the greater whole, of their readiness to exercise self-discipline, self-denial and self-sacrifice. This message rings loud and clear in a famous passage from *Science and the Modern World* (1925), where Whitehead cites the Brazilian forest—a 'triumph of the organization of mutually dependent species'—as an example for society, a triumph that can only be achieved if we are prepared to put up with the loss of individual opportunities for growth (244). Smuts is even more unequivocal on this issue. 'Throughout the entire range of organic nature one is impressed with the essential selflessness, the disregard of self, and the transcendence of self in the reproductive process, which harnesses the individual to the needs of the race, exhausts its reserves of strength, and often costs it its life. On that process is stamped, as on the very heart of Nature, the principle of sacrifice, of the subordination of the part to the whole, of the individual to the race or type' (Smuts 1927: 83). This message, a repudiation of liberal individualism, instantly lost any appeal it possessed following the rise of Stalinism and Fascism and the outbreak of World War II.

Post-war systems ecology is often referred to as 'neo-Clementian'; it, too, proceeds on holistic premises, but this holism is of a methodological rather than a metaphysical nature. The 'whole' that is more than the sum of its parts is no longer interpreted realistically but serves exclusively as a scientific working hypothesis, as a construct. In effect, this radical shift does not cause systems ecology to proceed in a less reductionist fashion than the classic natural sciences, but its reductionism is of a totally different order. Reductionism in the classic natural sciences refers to a reduction to elements, such as atoms or molecules, that are identical in a *material* sense. Systems ecology, on the other hand, is concerned with components that are identical in a *functional* sense because they perform the same function within the ecosystem, for example that of producers (green plants), consumers (herbivores, carnivores, and omnivores), or decomposers (bacteria and fungi). Such reductionism allows for a trade-off, as it were, between organisms with a similar function with the aim of optimizing the biomass yield (Trepl 1983: 9).

In view of the purely methodological character of its holistic principles, systems ecology quite naturally discards as unscientific the question of which *specific* species actually belong to a certain ecosystem. The same holds true for the related island theory which takes no interest in the identity of the species but only in their number. Yet it is this very question that is constantly exercising the nature developers' minds. Did the European bison or the lynx live here in the past or did they not? If not, would these species have settled here if mankind had not prevented them from doing so? One detects an allergy to exotics and an obsession with the truly autochthonous and authentic. Primeval nature is the be-all and end-all. In order to regain this lost primeval nature, expensive research is conducted into ecosystems from far-off times, or in far-off regions where shreds of wilderness are thought to have survived. This restless quest for the untrodden and original shows how the nature developers are forever swinging back and forth between a metaphysical and a methodological holism, between a romantic image of nature (where there is room for only the most primitive forms of technology) and a rational planning practice (using the most advanced forms of ecotechnology).

The Democratic Deficit

The quest for an all-encompassing world view on a holistic basis is not only obsolete in a scientific sense, it is an anachronism in a social sense as well. It can be seen as a nostalgic reaction to the disintegration of the quasi-organic unity that characterized the societies of the *ancien régime*. Under democratic conditions, state and society become separated; politics, econo-my, justice, science, and art fall apart and each of these discourses, more-over, is subject to a tremendous proliferation of competing paradigms. As a result of this decomposition of the societal body, the future becomes highly unpredictable and unmanageable for there is no central position or point of view from which the truth about society can be established once and for all (Lefort 1983).

In reaction to this, there have been repeated attempts since the early nineteenth century to restore the lost unity by bringing new 'Grand Narra-tives' into circulation. Contemporary philosophy has sealed the fate of such Grand Narratives by pointing out the totalitarian consequences which they entail. It follows that the call of the radical ecologists for a new world-view is a plea best left ignored, rejected in the name of a democracy that thrives on differences that can be bridged only temporarily by debate and deliberation.

As is well known, it was Jean-François Lyotard in particular who force-fully advanced the proposition that we should make a clean and total break with all grand narratives and get used to the idea that there exist a multi-tude of language games or 'genres', such as science, law, economics, ethics, and aesthetics. These genres are heterogenous since they are governed by different rule systems. In Lyotard's view there simply are no 'meta rules' which apply to all genres. Pursuing this thought he distinguishes between two forms of struggle. When a conflict arises between parties who partici-pate in the same genre, one can speak of litigation ('litige'). Such a conflict can be brought before a judge who can pass judgement according to the pre-vailing rules which apply. However, when a conflict arises between parties who adhere to different genres, the absence of meta-rules renders it impos-sible to issue a legal verdict. In such a case Lyotard speaks of a 'differend' (dispute). In practice, says Lyotard, a dispute is often accompanied by injus-tice. This is the case when a particular genre has gained supremacy and has made it impossible for the complainants from other genres to get a hearing. Unable to bring their complaints before the seat of justice of the dominant genre they are quite literally 'struck dumb'. As such, the dispute is 'smoth-ered' in argumentation or, as Lyotard puts it, "litigation".

These two forms of struggle serve to throw my criticism of the nature development discourse into sharper relief. In both environmental philoso-phy and nature policy, a social dispute is constantly in danger of being smoth-ered by scientific argumentation, with the result that all positions and considerations not based on ecology are systematically brushed aside. But argumentation is repressed as well, since the nature developers base them-selves one-sidedly on the image of nature emanating from systems ecology.

In particular, they totally disregard the perspective of evolutionary ecology, which since World War II has emerged as a formidable rival to systems ecology. The fact that nature developers have succeeded in presenting their image of nature as the only objective and scientifically legitimate representation is the very reason why they have been able to monopolize the social debate on nature and landscape.

The Smothered Dispute

The nature developers blame all the trouble and strife that surrounds nature conservation on the existence of different images of nature . ('My definition of nature is not your definition. The one is just as good as the other. Where will it end? Anything is nature, so nature conservation is always OK. Soon even the farmers will be able to produce nature! Hail to postmodern nature.') A cheap swindle, the advocates of prehistoric nature will say: 'We don't have five definitions of a clean environment either, or ten definitions of iron, do we?' (Vera 1994).

Although nature developers present their Ecological Reference as the only objective standard, their standard does not succeed in putting an end to all discussion. For instance, as Vera (1992: 22) explains, the disagreement about 'whether a species such as the European bison was naturally indigenous to the Netherlands, but that is a discussion that can be fought out with scientific arguments—it is not a matter of taste, as in the case of cultural landscapes'. It is the very fact that traditional nature conservation took the agrarian, man-made landscape of 1850 as its point of reference that makes it unacceptable to the nature developers. 'By using the term "nature" as a synonym for situations created by various forms of agriculture, the concept has been given all kinds of subjective and contradictory meanings' (ibid. 19).

These quotations demonstrate that the nature developers' strategy amounts to an attempt to smother the social differend about where we as a society want to go with nature in scientific litigation. It is a strategy that threatens to put the lid on language games or genres other than those based on ecology. Claiming to be the only ones who can recreate 'real' nature, the nature developers exclude other interested parties from nature policy-making. Prominent among those stricken by this fate are all individuals and parties who advocate or have an interest in functional integration rather than segregation. A group of painters and writers, for instance, have expressed the fear that implementation of existing plans to cut the dikes and allow the old polders to be flooded will spell the end for the river landscape as a cultural historical monument.

But, more than the historical landscape, it is the modern agrarian cultural landscape that the nature developers really abhor. Their plans present a grave threat, for instance, to farmers who wish to combine their business with nature management. Such 'farmers' nature' fills the nature developers with nothing but loathing. 'Farmers' nature is the same as razing the whole Amazon area to the ground and calling the result nature,' says nature developer Frans Vera (1994). And Ed Nijpels, the chairman of the WWF, says farmers' nature is equal 'by definition to sickly nature, in need of constant care'. Instead, the WWF opts for nature that can stand on its own feet . 'A project like the Border Meuse, where the forelands of the Meuse are dug out, now *that* is nature' (Nijpels 1995). Ecological and bio-dynamic agriculture, the production of foodstuffs without resorting to chemicals and in harmony with nature, is not to be encouraged therefore. Nature development benefits from intensive agriculture with a high yield per hectare. For only this will free sufficient acreage to be used for new nature. A number of nature conservation organizations, such as the Wadden Sea Society, Environment Defence and the Nature and Environment Foundation, are opposed to further intensification of agriculture and make a plea for equal treatment of nature and cultural landscapes.

It goes without saying that as well as farmers' nature, village and town nature are likewise in danger of falling victim to the nature development ideology. The extent to which this ideology has already begun to permeate the policies with regard to 'public greenery' is evident in the complaint uttered by Rob Leopold, one of the most prominent spokesmen of a new generation of Dutch garden artists.

Nowadays, if you just say that it's ecological green management, which comes down to letting things run wild a bit, putting up with a few more dandelions and nettles, you're sitting pretty because it is not only nice and cheap but also natural. Ecologists often still nurture a prejudice against horticulture, hence gardening art, because it is species management and therefore culture. Plus, ecology is a science. A science is not supposed to have any aesthetic ambitions, for then it becomes recreational and recreation has nothing to do with nature.

The marginality of aesthetic considerations in current nature policy is also evident in the *Landscape Report* of 1992 which, together with the *Nature Policy Plan* of 1990, constitutes the basis for specific regional policies in the National Network of Important Ecosystems. This remark may seem at odds with the fact that landscape planning is repeatedly presented as resting on the so-called 'Three Es': (A)esthetic, Ecological, and Economic quality. On closer inspection, however, it turns out that these three Es are not treated equally. This is because the Landscape Report gives pride of place to the 'casco' (or 'stripped') concept introduced by the nature developers. As we saw earlier, this concept is exclusively concerned with ecology and economics, while aesthetics play no role whatsoever. Or, in the euphemistic wording of the main background study for the *Landscape Report*: 'The aesthetic component is not specifically indicated by this concept' (Sijmons 1992: 30). According to the author, this component cannot be given any substance except in practice, on the drawing board of the landscape architect whose job it is to link a specific programme to a certain landscape. He compares the relationship between a planning concept and an architectural concept with that between a story and the storyteller. 'Without a story the storyteller is speechless and without the storyteller the story remains a dead letter' (ibid. 54). In short: aesthetics has no story of its own and does not deserve to be heard at the highest level of planning. Its help is only called in at the moment when the 'two-speed landscape' is to be given concrete form.

Ethical considerations tend to be as much ignored as aesthetic considerations in nature development projects. The nature developers, so runs the chief complaint of the Dutch Society for the Prevention of Cruelty to Animals, sacrifice the health and welfare of individual animals to their crusade to restore primeval nature. The herds of reintroduced cattle and horses have to undergo a process of 'de-domestication'. Complementary feeding and veterinary care are withdrawn, exposing them directly to starvation and dehydration, to parasites and predators, all for the sake of regenerating natural selection processes. Under the pressure of these processes they have to learn once again to procreate on their own strength and according to a seasonal cycle, to organize themselves into harems and acquire all the skills needed for survival. That a serious ethical problem is at issue here becomes clear when one realizes that on average only some 10 per cent of all reintroduction programmes are successful. The stress and, hence, the mortality among animals subjected to de-domestication, are staggering. (B. Beck 1995: 155)

The average holidaymaker and the ordinary nature lover, finally, are also left out in the cold by this policy. Their experience of nature is somewhat scornfully dismissed as irrelevant, as the following quotation demonstrates: 'In the Netherlands we call the South Limburg hills nature. They look pretty, they are fun to take your children out for a walk without being bothered by all kinds of wild animals, but they have little to do with full-blown nature. Most of our so-called nature areas are disused cultural landscapes. Although the landscape may look quite attractive here and there, Dutch nature is in fact dismantled nature. From an ecological point of view, the Netherlands is a disaster area' (Baerselman and Vera 1990). But the professional opinions of the nature developers have little in common with the preferences of the public at large, as has been confirmed by empirical research into people's perception and appreciation of landscapes. Apart from the nature landscapes that are the be-all and end-all of the nature developers, people distinguish agricultural landscapes, village landscapes, urban landscapes, and industrial landscapes. Another interesting finding is the fact that people tend to ex- perience as natural anything that appears to have grown spontaneously and harmoniously. Thus, old farms, overgrown dikes, and even old city centres create an impression of naturalness.

Beyond Suppressed Deliberation: Evolutionary Ecology

As we have seen, there is a clear tendency in the practice of nature devel- opment to smother the social dispute about what kind of nature and what kind of landscape we want, in scientific argumentation. But there is clear evidence of injustice in the scientific argumentation itself, too. The nature developers are guilty, in other words, of double one-sidedness: not only do they turn a deaf ear to all arguments not based on ecology, they also make a highly selective use of ecological findings.

What the two approaches that determine current nature policy—systems ecology and the islands theory—have in common is the underlying image of nature as a self-regulating system. Both cherish the image of an orderly, balanced nature which in principle is fully knowable and manageable. Time and coincidence, irreversible and unpredictable events have no place in either of these theories. It is no accident that Sharon Kingsland concludes her book on the history of population ecology, *Modelling Nature* (1985), with a chapter centring on the island theory entitled 'The Eclipse of History'. The basic principle of nature development is 'actualism' which 'implies that natural processes are timeless and will always reappear once the necessary condi- tions are in place. When this is the case, nature will resume working in its own way' (Vera 1992: 23).

This static view of nature is relegated to the realm of fantasy by an increasing number of ecologists. Their view is most eloquently expressed in a book published in 1990 by Daniel Botkin under the telling title *Discordant Harmonies*. Wherever we look for stability, Botkin notes, we find change. Undisturbed nature is not constant, neither at the level of populations nor at the level of ecosystems, whichever time interval or spatial scale we choose.

We must abandon the old image of a static landscape continuing into eternity like a single musical chord. 'The true idea of nature is by its very essence discordant, created from the simultaneous movement of many tones, the combination of many processes flowing at the same time along various scales, leading not to a simple melody but to a symphony at some times harsh and at some times pleasing' (Botkin 1990: 25).

The idea that change is more 'natural' than stability is widely accepted among evolutionary ecologists, who have traded in the holistic concept of community for an individualistic concept that goes back to Clement's opponent Henry Allan Gleason. Their image of nature is not so much deterministic as stochastic. According to the evolutionary ecologists, nature is less predictable and consequently also less manageable and controllable than the systems ecologists would have us believe. The evolutionary ecologists have abandoned the idea of a neatly defined, stable, self-regulating system; they call attention to situations that have grown wildly 'off-balance' and demand recognition for the role of unique events and historical occurrences.

A recent evaluation of the oldest nature development project in the Netherlands, the Duurse Waarden, appears to bear out the evolutionary point of view. Five years after the start of this project, nature was found to behave far more capriciously in the wild than on the drawing board. One of the most explicit aims had been the preservation of the rare corncrake, but this very bird was the first to go. The attempt to reintroduce the sand-martin also failed; the bird refused to make its abode in the steep wall specially constructed for it. Moreover, less grass and marshland and more woodland developed than had been expected. To top it all off, the Scottish highlanders and Iceland ponies proved useless because of their unpredictable grazing behaviour and are now being replaced by galloways in the hope that these will function better. The fact that the natural mowing and pruning machines do not behave in accordance with policy ecologists' expectations had already become apparent earlier in the Biesbosch marshland. The beavers set out here were supposed to set to work on the willows and so create room for rare species of trees. However, the beavers refused to do the job they were hired for—thinning out the thick willow brushwood—and instead feasted on the very species they had been intended to clear the way for.

Evolutionary ecology not only employs a different image of nature than systems ecology, it also holds out the promise of a less rigid, more flexible nature policy. This is because evolutionary ecology does more justice to the ever-increasing complexity of the interaction between nature and society than systems ecology. While systems ecology views functional disentanglement as an essential pre-condition for a healthy nature, evolutionary ecology sees nature as open to human design, with all the opportunities but also, of course, all the dangers this entails.

Evolutionary ecology also compares favourably with systems ecology in that it is prepared to acknowledge that science is not in a position unilaterally to lay down the criteria for nature policy (such as the Ecological Reference of the nature developers). Because of its principled openness to other genres and vocabularies, evolutionary ecology is more in tune with a democratic culture than systems ecology, which is impelled by its holistic nature to issue compulsory directions as to how we should interact with nature.

Finally, the very awareness that there are diverse visions of nature at work within ecology itself—and that references to 'the' ecology are therefore highly deceptive and misleading—can give a new impetus to the social debate about nature. The idea is not to gag the ecologists, but to give the final word back to society. It is not the ecological but the democratic landscape that should be the ideal of nature policy.

Concluding Remarks

This appeal to democratic deliberation appears to have recently gained some ground. The resistance put up by farmers and inhabitants of prospective nature development areas has sparked off debates here and there as to the whys and hows of nature development. The most important debate to date was organized by the Rathenau Institute, whose mission it is to stimulate public debates on the social and ethical aspects of technological developments. The debate on nature development, which took four months and was organized in a fashion similar to that of the American *citizens' juries*, was conducted by a 32-member panel. In the course of its work the panel, composed of laymen and experts, also visited four nature development areas and had in-depth discussions with inhabitants and users. The concluding debate was held on 1 July 1996, the very day on which the World Nature Fund and its allies staged the final manifestation of their 'The Netherlands twice as beautiful' promotion campaign.

In its concluding statement, the panel stated that the debate on nature policy is unjustifiably dominated by biologists and ecologists and that nature development plans are too often implemented in a top-down manner by government. The panel demanded that in future greater weight be given to social priorities and local potential and argued the case for an open planning procedure which expressly permits discussion of different solutions and scenarios. The panel also came out strongly against an overly narrow view of nature in which all the emphasis is on 'spontaneous nature', advocating instead a broader perspective which leaves room for urban nature and (traditional as well as modern) farmers' nature. If this message, which has also been heard in other recent debates, were finally to reach the policy makers, then nature development could become an exciting and adventurous project—a (democratic) experiment in the true sense of the word.

5

Eco-Managerialism: Environmental Studies as a Power/Knowledge Formation

TIMOTHY W. LUKE

Before scientific disciplines or industrial technologies turn its matter and energy into products, nature already is being transformed by discursive work-ups into 'natural resources'. Once nature is rendered intelligible through these interpretative processes, it can be used to legitimize many political projects. One vital site for generating, accumulating, and then circulating such discursive knowledge about nature, as well as determining which particular human beings will be empowered to interpret nature to society, is the modern research university. As the primary structure for accrediting individual learners and legitimating collective teachings, graduate programmes at such universities do much to construct our understanding of the natural world (Gibbons *et al.* 1994). Over the past generation, graduate study in environmental science on many American university campuses has become a key source of new representations for 'the environment' as well as the home base for those scientific disciplines that generate analyses of nature's many meanings. Indeed, a new environmental episteme has evolved over the past three decades, allowing new schools of environmental studies either to be established *de novo* or to be reorganized out of existing bits and pieces of agriculture, forestry, science, or policy studies programmes.

These educational operations now routinely produce eco-managerialists, or professional-technical workers with the specific knowledge—as it has been scientifically validated—and the operational power—as it is institutionally constructed—to cope with 'the environmental crisis' on what are believed to be sound scientific and technical grounds. Increasingly, graduate teaching in such schools of the environment has very little room for any other social objectives beyond the rationalizing performativity norms resting at the core of the current economic regime. To understand the norms of this regime, as Lyotard asserts, 'the State and/or company must abandon the idealist and humanist narratives of legitimation in order to justify the new goals: in the discourse of today's financial backers of research, the only credible goal is power. Scientists, technicians, and instruments are purchased not to find truth, but to augment power' (Lyotard 1984: 46).

This chapter asks how specialized discourses about nature, or 'the environment,' are constructed by American university programmes in graduate-level teaching and research to train eco-managerialist workers. Professional–technical experts working on and off campus create disciplinary articulations of 'ecoknowledge' to generate performative disciplinary systems of 'geo-power' over, but also within and through, what is worked-up as nature in the managerial structures of modern economies and societies. These institutionalized attempts to capture and contain the forces of nature by deploying advanced technologies, and thereby linking many of nature's apparently intrinsic structures and processes to strategies of highly rationalized environmental management as geo-power, develops out of university-level 'environmental studies'. It is a strategic supplement to various modes of bio-power defined by existing academic 'human studies' in promoting the growth of modern urban–industrial populations (Foucault 1980a: 140–1). Moreover, rules of economic performativity now count far more in these interventions than do those of ecological preservation, because they provide managerial solutions that blur the central role of capitalist economic growth in causing the environmental crisis (Fischer 1990).

The first efforts to realize these goals in the United States began with the Second Industrial Revolution and the conservation movement over a century ago as progressively-minded managers founded Schools of Forestry, Management, Agriculture, Mining, and Engineering on many university campuses to master nature and transform its material stuff into 'goods' and 'services' (Hays 1959). In the ecological upheavals of the 1960s and 1970s, however, schools of the environment or colleges of natural resources went beyond the conservationist project when they began training new even more specialized experts in environmental science—ranging from ecotoxiology to national park administration—needed to define, develop, and deploy new varieties of geo-power more broadly in all dimensions of everyday work and play. The mission of redefining and then administering the earth as 'natural resources,' as it is articulated, for example, by Yale's School of Forestry and Environmental Studies, powerfully expresses these managerial goals:

The mission of the School of Forestry and Environmental Studies is to provide leadership, through education and research, in the management of natural resource

systems and in the solution of environmental problems. Through its focused educational programs, the School develops leaders for major institutions concerned
with the earth's environment. Through its research activities, the School fosters
study in selected areas of particular importance for resource and environmental
management.   (Yale School of Forestry 1996: 10)

The entire planet can be reduced by environmental studies at research universities to a complex system of interrelated 'natural resource systems',
whose ecological processes are left for humanity to operate—efficiently or
inefficiently—as the geo-powers of one vast terrestrial infrastructure.
Directed at generating geo-power from the more rational insertion of
natural and artificial bodies into the machinery of global production, the discourses of eco-managerialism produced by graduate programmes in environment studies define physical and social ecologies where environmental
professionals operate in diffuse projects of 'ecological modernization' (Hajer
1996: 246–68).

There are scores of academic programmes across the United States that
now offer this kind of comprehensive scientific instruction in environmental studies. This brief analysis cannot survey all of them to determine
what the general foci of their curricula are or how each specific programme
varies in its substantive concerns. Instead it selects four well-known and
highly regarded programmes—two at elite private universities, two at
respectable public institutions—from around the nation—one in the Pacific
region at the University of California-Berkeley, one in the Mountain States
at Colorado State University, one in the North-East at Yale University, and
one in the South at Duke University. Such programmes provide suggestive
examples of how contemporary university training re-imagines nature as
'the environment' in graduate courses of study and professional codes of
self-interpretation. While other American universities might yield additional
insights, these institutions represent the most crucial disciplinary tendencies
in mainstream academic environmental discourses today.

These university training discourses comprehensively reframe 'the environment' as a highly complex domain far beyond the full comprehension of
ordinary citizens or traditional naturalists. Because it sustains economic
growth, ecology becomes something to be managed by expert eco-
managerialists armed with coherent clusters of technical acumen and
administrative practice (Perkin 1996). Reading through the self-representa-
tion of environmental studies at these colleges of natural resources or
schools of the environment in the United States, one sees this ideology at
work as deans, directors, and department heads promise to prepare prospective students for the ins-and-outs of resource managerialism, risk assessment,

and/or recreationist management. Resources, risks, and recreationists become 'the three Rs' of education in contemporary environmental studies, giving students and faculty specific new foci for their specialized knowledge and managerial power in technocratic work settings.

Environments and Geo-Power

Surveying the rhetorical representations of 'the environment' or 'natural resources' at American universities with a distinguished 'school of the environment' or an outstanding 'college of natural resources' is very instructive. Because so many environmental professionals and natural resource workers from all over the world are being trained in these academic settings, one gains an important sense of how their professional practices both are shaped by, and, in turn, shape academic environmental discourse. Investigating the language used to enlist students for graduate study in their ecological curricula at such schools of the environment also permits us to reappraise what 'the environment' means at these schools and which 'natural resources' are valorized at such colleges.

As actions on the behalf of nature have shifted from the avocational register of literary naturalist writings into the professional–technical knowledge codes of environmental science, larger public discourses about ecological degradation, resource waste, or environmental remediation also have changed significantly. On the one hand, many see this shift as positive: scientific personnel with positivistic technical knowledges allegedly now can identify ecological problems objectively as well as design efficient solutions for the most pressing ones. On the other hand, this change is regarded by others with suspicion: a spirit of 'shallowness' occludes the enchantments of Nature in the dark shadows of anthropocentrism, capitalism, and statism as 'the environment' often is treated as being little more than terrestrial infrastructure for global capital. Techno-scientific knowledge about the environment, however, is, and always has been, evolving in response to changing interpretative fashions, shifting political agendas, developing scientific advances, and meandering occupational trends. Such variations designate 'a will to knowledge that is anonymous, polymorphous, susceptible to regular transformations, and determined by the play of identifiable dependencies' (Foucault 1977: 200–1).

This polymorphous combination of anonymous scientific environmental knowledge and organized market and/or state power is disclosed most baldly by the stated purposes of Berkeley's Environmental Science, Policy, and Management faculty in the Division of Resource Institutions, Policy, and Management. That is, schools of the environment or colleges of natural resources are engaged quite concretely in 'how current and historical configurations of social, economic, and political institutions, as well as cultural values lead to different environmental outcomes and consequences for the composition, level, and distribution of social well-being' inasmuch as their students, teachers and administrators 'study and contribute to the formation of natural resource policy, the administration and management of natural resources institutions, and issues of territory, property, and sovereignty at different temporal, spatial, and institutional scales' (Department of Environmental Science 1996: 2–3).

As Berkeley's mission statement indicates, the channels of authority flowing within transnational corporate enterprise and modern nation-states have not carried many ideas, for example, from biocentric deep ecology into more widespread practice in either official American environmental policies or established academic teachings. Notions associated with anthropocentric shallow ecologies, however, have fused more coherently and cohesively in the power effects of such social formations. Their power, as Foucault indicates, 'traverses and produces things. . . . It needs to be considered as a productive network which runs through the whole social body, much more than a negative instance whose function is repression' (Foucault 1980a: 119). Schools of environmental studies and colleges of natural resources now provide vital networks in which the relations of this productive power shape the categories of knowledge and limits of professional practice through the training of eco-managerialism. In accord with the prevailing regimes of truth in instrumentalist technoscience, academic centres of environmental studies reproduce those bodies of practice and types of discourse, which the top executive personnel now managing most of the contemporary American state and social institutions regard as 'objective', 'valid', or 'useful' to facilitate economic growth. From their discourses, one can define, as Foucault suggests, 'the way in which individuals or groups represent words to themselves, utilize their forms and meanings, compose real discourse, reveal and conceal in it what they are thinking or saying, perhaps unknown to themselves, more or less than they wish, but in any case leave a mass of verbal traces of those thoughts, which must be deciphered and restored as far as possible to their representative vivacity' (Foucault 1994: 353).

Where life, labour, and language conjoin in discourses of environmental studies, one finds an analytic of power/knowledge 'which shows how man, in his being, can be concerned with the things he knows, and know the things that, in positivity, determine his mode of being' (Foucault 1994: 354) in highly focalized academic constructions of 'the environment'. The environment, if one follows Foucault's lines of reasoning, must not be understood either as the naturally given sphere of all ecological processes that human power keeps under control or as a mysterious domain of obscure terrestrial events which human knowledge works to explain. Instead, it emerges as a very historical artifact of expert management that is largely constructed by techno-scientific interventions, because it cannot remain an occluded reality that is difficult to comprehend for a modern economy. In this network of interventions, the simulation of spaces, the intensification of resources, the incitement of discoveries, the formation of special knowledges, the strengthening of controls, and the provocation of resistances all can be linked to one another as 'the empiricities' of Nature for academic environmental studies (Foucault 1994: 362–3).

The Three 'Rs' of Eco-Managerialism

The scripts of eco-managerialism embedded in environmental studies are rarely rendered totally articulate by scientific and technical discourses. The advocates of more radical ecological movements, like deep ecology, eco-feminism, or social ecology, dimly perceive the destructive biases in these scripts in their frustrations with 'reform environmentalism', which weaves logics of geo-power in and out of the technocratic eco-managerialism that has defined the mainstream of environmental science and traditional natural resource policy-making (Luke 1997). Three foci of eco-managerialist interventions coalign in schools of the environment as the theories and practices of resource, risk, and recreationist managerialism.

The mission statements and core curricula of such educational operations identify and initiate the discursive practices which encircle 'the environment' or 'the resources' their training gives students knowledge of and power over as expert professionals. The association of resource managerialism, risk assessment, and recreationist administration in range management at Berkeley, environmental toxicology at Duke, or tourist management strategies at Colorado State with 'the environment' as a terrestrial infrastructure gives professional workers the discursive practices they need for 'the delimitation of a field of objects, the definition of a legitimate perspective for the agent of knowledge, and the fixing of norms for the elaboration of concepts and theories' (Foucault 1977: 199).

Resource Managerialism

Resource managerialism can be read as a geo-power/eco-knowledge of modernizing economies. While voices in favour of conservation can be found in Europe early in the nineteenth century, the real establishment of this stance comes in the United States with the Second Industrial Revolution from the 1880s through the 1920s and the closing of the western frontier in the 1890s. Whether one looks at John Muir's preservationist programmes or Gifford Pinchot's conservationist codes, an awareness of modern industry's power to deplete natural resources, and hence the need for systems of conserving their exploitation, is well established by the early 1900s. Over the past nine decades, the fundamental premises of resource managerialism have not changed significantly. At best, this code of eco-knowledge only has become more formalized in bureaucratic applications and legal interpretations.

Evolving from the managerial logic of the Second Industrial Revolution, which empowered technical experts (engineers and scientists) on the shop floor and professional managers (corporate executives and financial officers) in the main office, resource managerialism imposes corporate administrative frameworks upon nature in order to supply the economy and provision society through centralized state guidance. These frameworks assume that the national economy, like the interacting capitalist firm and household, must avoid both overproduction (excessive resource use coupled with inadequate demand) and underproduction (inefficient resource use coming with excessive demand) on the supply side as well as overconsumption (excessive resource exploitation coming with excessive demand) and underconsumption (inefficient resource exploitation coupled with inadequate demand) on the demand side.

Even to construct the managerial problem in this fashion is to reduce nature—through the encirclement of space and matter by national as well as global economies—to a system of geo-power systems that can be dismantled, redesigned, and assembled anew on demand to produce 'resources' efficiently when and where needed in the modern marketplace. As a cybernetic system of biophysical systems, nature's energies, materials, and sites are redefined by the eco-knowledges of resource managerialism as manageable resources for human beings to realize great material 'goods' for sizeable numbers of some people, even though greater material and immaterial 'bads' also might be inflicted upon even larger numbers of other people, who do not reside in or benefit from the advanced national economies that basically monopolize the use of world resources at a comparative handful of highly developed regional and municipal sites. Echoing California-Berkeley's declaration that environmental studies boil down to mobilizing the biological, physical, and social sciences to address the major social and political effects of current and future anthropogenic environmental problems, Yale's Dean Cohon tells would-be environmental studies students that their professional power/knowledge will be crucially significant in the coming years: 'Your role in helping to protect and manage the integrity and survival of natural systems and human health globally could not be more important. Since so much is now in human hands, people are needed, more than ever, who are focused, informed, and dedicated to learning' (Yale School of Forestry 1996: 9).

Such environmental beliefs, as they are embraced by eco-managerialists, infrastructuralize the earth's ecologies. The earth becomes, if only in terms of techno-science's operational assumptions, an immense terrestrial infrastructure. As the human race's 'ecological life-support system,' it has 'with only occasional localized failures' provided 'services upon which human society depends consistently and without charge' (Cairns 1995: 3). As the environmentalized infrastructure of techno-scientific production, the earth generates 'ecosystem services,' or those derivative products and functions of natural systems that human societies perceive as valuable (Westmen 1978: 960–4). This complex system of systems is what must survive; human life will continue only if such survival-sustaining services continue. And, as Colorado State's, Yale's, Berkeley's, or Duke's various graduate programmes all record, these infrastructural outputs include: the generation of soils, the regeneration of plant nutrients, capture of solar energy, conversion of solar energy into biomass, accumulation/purification/distribution of water, control of pests, provision of a genetic library, maintenance of breathable air, control of micro- and macro-climates, pollination of plants, diversification of animal species, development of buffering mechanisms in catastrophes, and aesthetic enrichment. Because it is the terrestrial infrastructure of transnational enterprise, the planet's ecology requires highly disciplined re-engineering to guide its sustainable use in the most performative fashion. In turn, academic practices must monitor, massage, and manage those systems which produce all of these robust services. Just as the sustained use of any technology 'requires that it be maintained, updated and changed periodically,' so too does the 'sustainable use of the planet require that we not destroy our ecological capital, such as old-growth forests, streams and rivers (with their associated biota), and other natural amenities' (Cairns 1995: 6).

This infrastructuralization of the environment can be illustrated in Colorado State's Forest Science recruitment brochure, which casts its knowledge as being dedicated to 'Valuing our Forests and Natural Resources' both inside the classroom and outside in the mountains. To imagine what forests are and do, the Department of Forest Science asks:

Have you ever stopped to think how the health of our forests affects your own life? Without forests, there would be no wood for homes or fiber for countless paper products we use every day. Forests also help maintain watersheds and keep our air free of harmful pollutants. And, for centuries, forests have been a very special place where people go to see and enjoy nature. Whether you live in a city or small town, forests impact your life in many ways.   (Department of Forest Science 1996: 2)

Forests here become open infrastructural networks, or quasi-subjective agencies whose health, growth, and location are quasi-objective structures needed by human beings as building materials, watershed maintenance mechanisms, air cleaners, or human enjoyment zones.

The environmental infrastructure of our forests 'need people who can understand and manage them' but, as Colorado State claims, 'only with well-educated professionals can we ensure that our resources will be available for the benefit of present and future generations' (Department of Forest Science 1996: 2). To rightly manage this vital green infrastructure, it provides four concentrations of discursive understanding and applied practice—forest biology, forest fire science, forest management, and forest business—to prepare environmental professionals. Learning about forests 'from actual experience, not just from textbooks', Forest science pledges comprehensive training as forest biology focuses 'on the biology of trees and the ecology of forest'; forest fire science examines 'fire as a forest management tool' as students 'learn how prescribed fire can be used to enhance wildlife habitat, prepare seedbeds, control forest insects and disease, and reduce fuel hazards'; forest management concentrates on how state and commercial agencies exploit 'forest productivity, economics, and conservation, along with the latest in computer-based management tools'; and, forest business teaches business applications 'if you seek employment with a private timber company, or you wish to develop your own forest business' (Department of Forest Science 1996: 3–4).

Colorado State's Forest Science Programme promises to open doors to jobs that oversee the techno-scientific nexus of discipline / sovereignty / terri-toriality in managing forest resources as students either are able 'to qualify as a professional forester and work with traditional national and interna-tional resource organizations' or find avenues that 'pursue employment in fields such as land use planning, youth agency administration, natural resource communications, mining reclamation, business, law enforcement, or conservation biology' (Department of Forest Science 1996: 4). Forest

science here produces the discursive truths which environmental professionals need 'to manage forests for maximum growth; to protect forests
from fires and disease; and to conserve forest, soil, and water resources,'
because such mediations of power do provide 'a truly unique and reward-
ing opportunity' (Department of Forest Science 1996: 2) to exercise their
professional–technical power/knowledge ecologically.

Risk Managerialism

As Beck (1992) suggests, risk managerialism is now an integral part of the
self-critical production and reproduction of globally thinking, but locally
acting, capitalism. Schools of environmental studies train students to conceptually contain, actuarially assess, and cautiously calculate the many
dimensions of ecological risk in their ecotoxicology, environmental assessment, or eco-remediation courses. Yet, the assumptions of such modelling
techniques constitute only a scientized first take for the sweep of reflexivity.
They do not, and indeed cannot, capture the depth, scope, duration,
or intensity of the damage they pretend to measure. Colorado State's
Department of Fishery and Wildlife Biology, for example, casts itself as an
international leader in the areas of risk assessment and analysis. Combining
practical laboratory experiences and field studies, it suggests that areas of
growing emphasis are risk-analysis centred concerns, like integrated
resource management, conservation biology, and environmental risk analysis (Department of Fishery 1996: 3). This focus upon quantitative surveillance and evaluation in risk analysis also can be found in the other graduate
programmes' curricula.

  Yale's graduate course, Ecological Resource Risk Assessment and
Management, for example, hints that related course work in statistics, ecotoxicology, and environmental chemistry will help its students to understand
the impact of pollution, disease, and ecological management practices on
the health of ecosystems. However, 'assessment of risk of an adverse impact
on an ecological resource caused by one or more chemical, biological, or
physical stressors, and monitoring the status and trends of an ecological
resource are priority needs of contemporary environmental management'
(Yale School of Forestry 1996: 31). Likewise, Duke's highly economistic
reading of environmental studies stresses the benefits and costs of policies
relating to sustaining resource productivity and maintaining environmental
quality in its risk analyses. Its graduate course, Survey of Environmental
Health and Safety, directs the attention of students toward 'environmental
risks from the perspective of global ecology, biology, chemistry, and radia-
tion' such that 'the nature and scope of environmental hazards' might be

addressed by its understanding of 'risk assessment and management strategies' (Duke Nicholas School 1996a: 101), the economics and ecologies of risk, then, create tremendous new opportunities for cadres of educated professionals to work productively as better resource managers.

Risk management at colleges of natural resources presumes its calculations 'are based on a (spatially, temporally, and socially circumscribed) accident definition' or that its analyses truly do 'estimate and legitimate the potential for catastrophe of modern large-scale technologies and industries' (U. Beck 1996: 32). Superfund site after supertanker spill after superstack bubble, however, indicate that this degree of managerial knowledge is precisely what risk management sciences at schools of environmental studies fail to produce, 'and so they are falsifications, and can be criticized and reformed in accordance with their own claims to rationality' (U. Beck 1996: 33). This trend towards developing a fully self-conscious risk managerialism grounded in economistic trade-offs also surfaces fully in the curriculum of the Yale School of Forestry and Environmental Studies, whose recent strategic restructuring commits it fully to risk assessment methods because these techniques are 'redefining forestry to encompass all of the social and political factors which we know from experience to be fundamental to good forest management' (Yale School of Forestry 1996: 2).

These visions of environmental science recapitulate the logics of capitalist technics as they work in the world's states and markets. Rather than the environment surrounding humanity, the friction-free global marketplace of transnational capital is what now envelopes nature. Out of its metabolisms are produced ecotoxins, biohazards, hydrocontaminants, aeroparticulates, and enviropoisons whose individual impacts generate inexorable collective risks. These policy problematics unfold now on the global scale, because fast capitalism has colonized so many more sites on the planet as part and parcel of its own unique regime for sustainable development. As Yale's Dean Cohon asserts:

The challenge we all face now, as you know, is not limited to one resource in one nation, but extends to the protection of the environment worldwide. The fabric of natural and human communities is currently torn or tattered in many places. There is hardly a place on earth where human activity does not influence the environment's current condition or its prospects for the future.   (Yale School of Forestry 1996: 2)

Well-trained environmental professionals must measure, monitor, or manage these risks, leaving the rational operations of global fast capitalism wholly intact as 'risks won' for their owners and beneficiaries, while risk

analyses performed by each environmental school's practitioners and programmes deal with the victims of 'risks lost'.

Recreationist Managerialism

Schools of environmental studies must also prepare their students for more
tertiary uses of Nature as recreational resources. As the Forest Service and
Bureau of Land Management say about their managed public lands, the
natural environment is 'a land of many uses', and mass tourism, commercial recreation, or park administration all require special knowledges and
powers to be conducted successfully. Instead of appraising nature's resources
as industrial production resource reserves, recreationist managerialism
frames them as resource preserves for recurring consumption as positional
goods, scenic assets, or leisure sites. The entire idea behind national parks
or protected areas is to park certain unique sites or particular undeveloped
domains beyond the continuous turnover of industrial exploitation for
primary products or agricultural produce. The recreational pursuits of
getting to, using, and appreciating such ecological assets then are mass produced through highly organized sets of uniform practices. Consequently,
recreationist managerialism 'develops expertise in managing public lands
and waters and in providing quality outdoor recreation experiences to their
visitors' (Department of Natural Resource 1996: 2).

As Colorado State University's Department of Natural Resource
Recreation and Tourism puts it, 'there is an exciting trend to establish park
and outdoor recreation programs worldwide' (1996: 1). This graduate programme moves beyond undergraduate studies of 'recreationists and tourists'
to examine other publics, like 'concessionaires, private land owners, policy-
makers, agency personnel, communities, and special interest groups', which
need to be managed as part of providing 'quality outdoor recreation experiences' to visitors of parks and protected areas (Department of Natural
Resource 1996: 1). Focusing upon 'the human dimensions of natural
resources' in recreationist management, in turn, permits this disciplinary
unit to tout its Human Resources Survey Research Lab to prospective
students, assuring them that this 'state of the art telephone survey lab helps
to develop skills in measuring preferences, perceptions, and behaviors
among outdoor recreationists' (Department of Natural Resource 1996: 1).

Armed with this knowledge about recreationist management, graduates
are assured secure professional placement because the programme 'is
oriented to employment with federal and state agencies, counties, and
municipalities' (Department of Natural Resource 1996: 1). Beyond the
recreationist management functions of governmental resource management

agencies, this graduate programme also underscores a US Department of Commerce study that forecasts tourism will be the world's largest industry by the year 2000. Prospective students are assured how easily recreationist managerial knowledge can be pitched to 'that sector of the tourism industry that is dependent on natural resources: park and recreation concessionaires, adventure and tour guide companies, private campgrounds and hunting/fishing preserves, destination resorts, ecotourism establishments, and tourism development boards and advertising companies' (Department of Natural Resource 1996: 1) to embed eco-managerialism in private sector pursuits.

The obligation to supervise human recreationists rightly in 'the conduct of their conduct' within the natural environments is summarized by Yale's Dean Cohon, who characterizes environmental studies as almost another mode of police work, or 'helping to protect and manage the integrity and survival of natural systems and human health globally', because recreationist management, like all environmental studies, needs skilled people 'who are focused, informed, and dedicated to leading' (Yale School of Forestry 1998: 9). Discourses of eco-managerialism give dedicated students the correct disciplinary paths for leading others to the right kind of information produced by professional schools of the environment. Their power/knowledge foci, in turn, authorize and legitimate the acts taken by 'a corps of professionals' whose policing of anthropogenic environmental crises will bring about more positive recreational experiences.

The discursive reconstruction of the environment around these 'three Rs' as an ensemble of technocratic sites for managerialist intervention is quite significant, because, as Yale's Dean of Forestry and Environmental Studies suggests, their faculties have a long history of socializing 'generations of leaders of government agencies, university faculties, and private forest products companies' (Yale School of Forestry 1996: 1). Moreover, such training purports to engage 'the broad range of issues of environmental conservation and protection' through 'the inclusion of biological, physical, and social science perspectives to provide basis for realistic, effective approaches to what are often subtle and complex issues' (Yale School of Forestry 1996: 1).

Those who imagine that all environmentalists are some sort of countercultural resistance fighters only need to consult the Nicholas School of the Environment at Duke to get a sense of where academic environmental studies actually lead. While some of its graduates—only 16 per cent—end up working for advocacy non-profit organizations, like the Rain Forest Alliance, World Wildlife Fund, or Chesapeake Bay Foundation, many also find positions with staid groups like Worldwatch, the Nature Conservancy, or the National Geographic Society. Another 32 per cent work for federal and state governments, and 42 per cent work for private consulting and industrial firms, like ABT Association, ERM, Inc., ICF Kaiser International, General Motors, Texaco, or Westvaco Corporation (Duke Nicholas School 1996b: 1). The key validation of academic environmental studies at Duke is wholly careerist: good placement and respectable salaries for newly graduated natural resource professionals. Marketability of their labour equals effectiveness for their education. The performative truths such schools impart must be valid; otherwise, big business, federal agencies, and global NGOs would not be dropping by to recruit their graduates. Their training in Ecotoxicology and Risk Assessment, Resource Economics, or Forest Resource Management does not stress post-anthropocentric deep ecology; likewise, the Nicholas School will not count holistic New Age Deep Ecology Studies among its in-house graduate programmes. Techno-scientific truths here are those of eco-managerialism, which is, in turn, tied to reproducing environmental studies as the coda of careerist knowledge and professional power.

In these curricula and their professional tracking, the discourses of resource managerialism/risk assessment/recreationist administration become, as Foucault argues, 'embodied in technical processes, in institutions, in patterns for general behavior, in forms of transmission and diffusion, and in pedagogical forms which, at once, impose and maintain them' (Foucault 1977: 200). Environmental studies graduates find in their professional labour the callings of eco-managerialism—mediated through their formal knowledges of environmental study and implemented through their institutionalized powers over natural resources. Under this managerial regimen, power/knowledge systems bring 'life and its mechanisms into the realm of explicit calculations', making the disciplines of environmental knowledge and discourses of managerial power into many concrete networks devoted to the 'transformation of human life' (Foucault 1980a: 143).

Eco-Managerialism as Heterogeneous Engineering

The 'three Rs' of environmental studies now implicitly acknowledge how thoroughly most human ecologies on Earth are 'a socio-technical order'. As Law suggests, the networks of humans and machines, animals and plants, economies and ecologies, which now constitute our environment, are mixed media of power and knowledge: 'what appears to be social is partly technical. What we usually call technical is partly social. In practice nothing is purely technical. Neither is anything purely social' (Law 1991: 10). Approaching the environment as terrestrial infrastructure, at the same time, admits that the professional–technical graduates of environmental studies programmes are in many ways trained to operate as 'heterogeneous engineers.' That is, the eco-managerialist must work 'not only on inanimate physical materials, but on and through people, texts, devices, city councils, architectures, economics, and all the rest,' such that if his/her designs are to work as a system, then he/she always must travel effectively 'between these different domains, weaving an emergent web which constituted and reconstituted bits and pieces that it brought together' (Law 1991: 9).

Few articulations of environmental studies acknowledge these basic operational conditions, but they form the socio-technical terrains upon which eco-managerialists must negotiate their professional work lives in order to heterogeneously engineer Earth's ecologies as the infrastructures of anthropogenic environments. Transforming the raw stuff of nature into natural resources, while minimizing the associated risks of such processing and maximizing the aggregate access of recreationists to yet-to-be or never-to-be transformed nature, is a constant challenge for heterogeneous engineers from the environmental science disciplines. Likewise, the green fixation of so many environmental activists makes it difficult, if not impossible, for environmental studies to recognize all of the natural/artificial networks that environmental experts must oversee in their projects of heterogeneous engineering. Owning up to these immense tasks, however, leads those who would be the tenders of nature to the project of 'terraforming', or reshaping the earth so completely that it becomes an essentially planetary order of complex socio-technical systems.

The earth no longer is allowed to exist or evolve as such; instead it has been consigned to terraforming professionals with graduate training in the environmental sciences. Duke University asserts 'the mission of the School of the Environment is education, research and service to understand basic environmental processes and to protect and enhance the environment and its natural resources for future generations' (Duke Nicholas School 1996a: 9). This engagement at 'protecting' and 'enhancing' the environment to transmit its natural resources to future generations is seconded by California-Berkeley, whose Ecosystem Sciences mission statement virtually writes the job description of terraforming technicians: 'Ecosystem Sciences are concerned with quantitative understanding of ecosystem properties and processes, and the controls on these features. Central to this mission is a full partnership between physical and biological scientists, leading to an integrated understanding of ecosystem structure and function, and the extension of these findings in modeling and implementation activities'

(Department of Environmental Science 1996: 2). The labour of eco-managerialist professionals must be dedicated to protecting *and* enhancing the performativity of our environments.

Whatever surrounds our performative global economy must also be made operationally adaptable, flexible, and productive through the operations of, as Colorado State labels them, problem-solving knowledges for riparian management, land rehabilitation, habitat evaluation, range economics, biotelemetric surveillance, wood engineering, resource interpretation, or visitor strategies. While students may enter schools of environmental studies and colleges of natural resources in search of wisdom from Aldo Leopold or John Muir, they mostly leave as eco-managerialists, or adept practitioners of ecosystem management/analysis, ecological risk analysis, and recreation resource administration. Forests, range lands, waters, game animals, and soils all are integral components in terrestrial infrastructures for the vast machineries of commodity production, circulation, consumption, and accumulation, which are, in turn, terraforming the unruly ecologies of earth to suit their mainly commercial requirements. Because, as the Dean of Yale's School argues, 'there is hardly a place on Earth where human activity does not influence the environment's current condition or its prospects for the future', environmental studies and colleges of natural resources produce techno-scientific experts, or those new 'cadres of educated professionals', or who truly believe 'that the best hope for developing sound knowledge and workable management solution for environmental problems is to bring science and policy together' (Yale School of Forestry 1996: 9).

Truths about ecology are not objective timeless verities, but rather are the operationalized findings of continuously evolving practices for those forms of heterogeneous engineering that have been constructed by major research universities. These institutions are sites where 'truth', or 'a system of order procedures for the production, regulation, distribution, circulation, and operation of statements' (Foucault 1980*b*: 133), arises from knowledge formations, like the disciplines of environmental science, to help steer power formations, like the decision-making bureaux of liberal democratic states and capitalist firms. As Foucault asserts, 'there are manifold relations of power which permeate, characterize and constitute the social body, and these relations of power cannot themselves be established, consolidated nor implemented without the production, accumulation, circulation and functioning of a discourse. There can be no possible exercise of power without a certain economy of discourses of truth which operates through and on the basis of this association' (Foucault 1980*b*: 95). Environmental science reveals multiple traces of this vital cycle of cogeneration by which power charges truthful knowledges even as truthful knowledges mediate power in the scope and substance of its discursive construction at schools of environmental studies and colleges of natural resources.

Conclusion

This approach to some environmental discourses circulating through modern research universities may offend many in the academy because it asks how involved, and in what ways have academicians become implicated, in causing the current ecological crisis, even though they might believe themselves to be ameliorating it. This is where the heterogeneous engineering cultures of mainstream environmentalists—or conventional understandings manifest in the acts and artefacts of these social groups—are both produced and reproduced. Here one can discover how and why environmental studies are shaped by its disciplinary discourse as every environmental professional gets his or her education to protect and manage the earth (Trzyna 1995). A few may be engaged, on the one hand, by dreams of preservationist restoration ecology, but most are devoted, on the other hand, to vast projects of conservationist eco-rationalization in which Nature's forests, lands, and waters are to be re-engineered as terrestrial infrastructures for resource/risk/recreationist managers to administer. For the emerging sciences of industrial ecology, this infrastructuralization of Earth is carried to its logical conclusion. As Frosch asks, 'let us consider, industry, indeed, the whole of humanity and nature, as a system of temporary stocks and flows of material and energy' (Frosch 1996: 201). If industrial ecology comes to dominate environmental studies, then all ecological questions may become tied to 'a framework for thinking about materials and their flows in the context of industrial waste, about the balancing of costs and environmental impacts in possible future states of industry, and about a method of policy examination' (Frosch 1996: 211).

There are limitations to the present analysis. On one level, it cannot delve beneath the manifest intentions of such schools and colleges as they portray themselves in their own literature. One must assume that they are what they profess to be, and actually do what their documents promise. On a second level, it cannot catch any resistances or all deviations from the official institutional line, which clearly are always afoot in any academic institution. Many courses carry bland descriptions of totally conformist approaches, but their instructors and students may very well follow none of them when their classes actually convene. And, on a third level, it does not consider how state or corporate power centres, in the last analysis, often will ignore or belittle academic knowledge, because its guidance contradicts what their organizational powers can, or will, in fact, do against all informed advice to act otherwise. Well-trained professionals, even when armed with sound science, can be used to serve the far more expedient goals of naked power agendas. Nonetheless, this very tentative survey of the professional–technical practices fostered at schools of environmental studies discloses a great deal about how their techno-scientific discourses frame regimes of eco-managerial performance in the everyday workings of economic production.

The heterogeneous engineers behind global capitalism's ever moderniz-ing economies must articulate eco-knowledges for economic growth to acti-vate their command over the earth's geo-power as well as operationalize a measure of managerial discipline over environmental resources, risks, and recreationists in their reconstruction of contemporary governmentality as eco-managerialism. Like governmentality, the disciplinary articulations of eco-managerialism now centre upon establishing and enforcing 'the right disposition of things' by policing humanity's 'conduct of conduct' in nature and society (Foucault 1991: 98). Nature loses transcendent qualities. Its locales, resources, and systems are pre-processed in the academy and become mere 'environments' full of exploitable (but also protectable) 'natural resources', which university faculty and graduate students manipu-late to rationalize how particular research-oriented and management-oriented applied sciences will get down to the business of administering them as terrestrial fast capitalism's 'natural resource systems'.

6

Mapping Complex Social-Natural Relationships: Cases from Mexico and Africa

PETER J. TAYLOR

> In this actual world there is . . . not much point in counterposing or restating the great abstractions of Man and Nature. We have mixed our labour with the earth, our forces with its forces too deeply to be able to draw back and separate either out. Except that if we mentally draw back . . . we are spared the effort of looking, in any active way, at the whole complex of social and natural relationships which is at once our product and our activity.
>
> (Williams 1980: 83)

Social interactions and negotiations are always implicated in environmental change. They also shape how society, nature, and society–environment relations come to be known or represented. Such intersections between social and natural processes generate considerable complexity, evident in the social and environmental situations that researchers study, as well as in the social situations that enable different researchers to do their research. And such complexity only increases when researchers promote change in either or both of these situations. The goal of this essay is to chart ways that might help researchers address, without suppressing, the complexity of intersecting social–natural processes. Or, in the words of the English/Welsh cultural analyst, Raymond Williams, I hope to stimulate researchers to examine from new angles 'the whole complex of social and natural relationships which is at once our product and our activity'.

I introduce and link three projects—political ecology, heterogeneous constructionism, and mapping workshops—that are concerned with, respectively, the complexity of the situation studied, the complexity of the researcher's situation, and researchers self-consciously employing their understanding of the latter to change the ways they deal with the former.

Each additional strand of complexity increases the range of relevant social agents, the diversity of resources they mobilize, and the possible points of engagement for the different agents. In short, complexity becomes ever more *distributed*, which leads me in the final section to reflect on open questions concerning what I call the '*logic* of complexification' and the *pragmatics* of drawing readers into the projects I describe.

Complexity of the Environmental Situation: Political Ecology and Intersecting Processes

The words *political ecology* have often been applied in recent years to research that analyses the complexity of social, and environmental change as something produced by intersecting and conflicting economic, social, and ecological processes operating at different scales. These processes range from the local institutions of production and their associated agro-ecologies, the social differentiation in a given community and its social psychology of norms and reciprocal expectations, through to national and international political economic changes. The rich descriptions produced by this kind of political ecology tend to exhibit a number of features. They connect local struggles and changes related to land, labour, and other resources to disputes over roles and responsibilities, draw upon the historical background of the current processes, highlight the dynamics related to inequality, and attend to critical developments in the larger political economies (Blaikie 1985; Peet and Watts 1996a; Hall and Taylor 1998).

To make these features concrete and to develop some of their implications, I present a synopsis from some political ecological research undertaken in the mid-1980s by my Mexican collaborator, resource economist Raúl García-Barrios, and his ecologist brother, Luis. These two researchers traced severe soil erosion in a mountainous agricultural region of Oaxaca, Mexico to the undermining of traditional political authority after the Mexican revolution (García-Barrios and García-Barrios 1990).

The soil erosion of the twentieth century is not the first time this has occurred in Oaxaca. After the Spanish conquest, when the indigenous population collapsed from disease, the communities moved down from the highlands, abandoning terraced lands, which then eroded. The Indians adopted labour-saving practices from the Spanish, such as cultivating wheat and using ploughs. As the population recovered during the eighteenth and nineteenth centuries, collective institutions evolved that re-established and maintained terraces and stabilized the soil dynamics. Erosion was reduced and soil accumulation was perhaps stimulated. This type of landscape transformation also needed continuous and proper maintenance, since it introduced the potential for severe slope instability. The collective institutions revolved around first the Church and then, after independence from Spain, the rich Indians, *caciques*, mobilizing peasant labour for key activities. These activities, in addition to maintaining terraces, included sowing corn in work teams, and maintaining a diversity of maize varieties and cultivation techniques. The caciques benefited from what was produced, but were expected to look after the peasants in hard times—a form of moral economy (Scott 1976). Given that the peasants felt security in proportion to the wealth and prestige of their cacique and given the prestige attached directly to each person's role in the collective labour, the labour tended to be very efficient. In addition, peasants were kept indebted to caciques, and could not readily break their unequal relationship. The caciques, moreover, insulated this relationship from change by resisting potential labour-saving technologies and ties to outside markets.

The Mexican revolution, however, ruptured the moral economy and exploitative relationships by taking away the power of the caciques. Many peasants migrated to industrial areas, returning periodically with cash or sending it back, so that rural transactions and prestige became monetarized. With the monetarization and loss of labour, the collective institutions collapsed and terraces began to erode. National food pricing policies favoured urban consumers, which meant that in Oaxaca corn was grown only for subsistence needs. New labour-saving activities, such as goat herding, which contributes in its own way to erosion, were taken up without new local institutions to regulate them.

Although brief, this synopsis of the García-Barrioses' account allows me to draw out several implications of political ecology.

1. *Differentiation among Unequal Agents*: Sustainable maize production depended on a moral economy of cacique and peasants, and the inequality among these agents resulted from a long process of social and economic differentiation. Similarly, the demise of this agro-ecology involved the unequal power of the state over local caciques, of urban industrialists over rural interests, and of workers who remitted cash to their communities over those who continued agricultural labour.

2. *Heterogeneity of Elements*: The situation has involved processes operating at different spatial and temporal scales, involving elements as diverse as the local climate and geo-morphology, social norms, work relations, and national political economic policy.[1]

3. *Historical Contingency of Processes*: The role of the Mexican Revolution in the collapse of nineteenth-century agro-ecology reveals the contingency

that is characteristic of history. The significance of such contingency rests not on the event of the revolution itself, but on the different processes, each having a history, with which the revolution intersected.

4. *Inseparability*: Processes of different kinds and scales, involving heterogeneous elements, are interlinked in the production of any outcome and in their own ongoing transformation. Each is implicated in the others, even by exclusion (C. A. Smith 1984), such as when caciques kept maize production during the nineteenth century insulated from external markets. I use the expression *intersecting processes* to convey this inseparability or mutual implication (P. J. Taylor and García-Barrios 1995).[2] It means that no one kind of thing, no single strand on its own, could be sufficient to explain the currently eroded hillsides. In this sense, political ecology contrasts with competing explanations that centre on a single dynamic or process, e.g. climate change in erosive landscapes; population growth (or, during the twentieth century, population decline) as the motor of social, technical, or environmental change; increasing capitalist exploitation of natural resources; modernization of production methods; or peasant marginalization in a dual economy (Peet and Watts 1996b).[3]

5. *Structuredness*: Although there is no reduction to macro- or structural determination in the above account, the focus is not on local, individual–individual transactions. Regularities, e.g. the terraces and the moral economy, persist long enough for agents to recognize or abide by them. That is, structuredness is discernable in the intersecting processes.

6. *Distributed Social Agency*: The social agency implied in the account of the García-Barrioses was distributed, not centred in one class or place. In the nineteenth-century moral economy caciques exploited peasants, but in a relationship of reciprocal norms and obligations. Moreover, the local moral economy was not autonomous; the national political economy was implicated, by its exclusion, in the actions of the caciques that maintained labour-intensive and self-sufficient production. Although the Mexican revolution initiated the breakdown in the moral economy, the ensuing process involved not just political and economic change from above, but also from below and between—semi-proletarian peasants brought their money back to the rural community and reshaped its transactions, institutions, and social psychology.

7. *Intermediate Complexity*: The García-Barrioses include heterogeneous elements in their account, but, as my synopsis indicates, different strands can be teased out. The strands, however, are cross-linked; they are not torn apart. In this sense, the account has an intermediate complexity—neither highly reduced, nor overwhelmingly detailed. By acknowledging complexity, the account steps away from debates centred around simple oppositions, e.g.

ecology-geomorphology vs. economy-society, or ecological rationality vs. economic rationality. Similarly, by placing explanatory focus on the ongoing processes involved in the historically contingent intersections, the account discounts the grand discontinuities and transitions that are often invoked, e.g. peasant to capitalist agriculture, or feudalism to industrialism to Fordism to flexible specialization.[4]

8. *Multiple, Smaller Engagements*: Distributed social agency, intermediate complexity, and the other features of intersecting processes have implications, not only for how environmental degradation is conceptualized, but also for how one responds to it in practice. Accounts of intersecting processes do not support government or social movement policies based on simple themes, such as economic modernization by market liberalization, sustainable development through promotion of traditional agricultural practices, or mass mobilization to overthrow capitalism. They privilege multiple, smaller engagements *linked together* within the intersecting processes.

This shift in how the problem is conceived requires a corresponding shift in scholarly practice. On the level of research organization, accounts of intersecting processes highlight the need for transdisciplinary work grounded in particular sites. Such a perspective does not underwrite the customary, so-called interdisciplinary projects directed by natural scientists, nor the economic analyses based on the kinds of statistical data available in published censuses. Rather, representing is inseparably bound up with the task of intervening in a way that further extends the ideas of distributed complexity and social agency (P. J. Taylor 1995).

Complexity of the Researcher's Situation: 'Heterogeneous' Construction of Science-in-the-Making

It is rare for accounts of environmental change to embrace more than a few of the complexities that political ecology highlights. In order to make sense of the ways that social–natural processes are simplified, the social influences on the making of scientific knowledge need to be examined. My approach to this task seeks to expose diverse practical considerations implicated in the social situation of the scientists. An emphasis on what it means *practically* for *agents* to *modify* science makes it appropriate to use the term *construction*. I use the adjective *heterogeneous*, however, to establish some distance from standard views about social construction, which tend to imply that scientists' accounts *reflect* or are *determined by* their social views (P. J. Taylor 1995).[5] I

aim to evoke the connotations construction has of a process of agents building by combining a diversity or heterogeneity of components or resources,
as in people building a house or a nation rebuilding its economy after a war.[6]
To illustrate the significance of the heterogeneous construction of science,
I present excerpts from a case study involving computer modelling of
nomadic pastoralism (P. J. Taylor 1992).

Nomadic pastoralists are people who spend part of the year moving
their herds in search of pasture, which varies from year to year in quality
and location according to the patchy and variable rainfall. The 1968–74
drought in sub-Saharan Africa resulted in decimation of the pastoralists'
herds and famine. Western attention was drawn to the region, not only for
relief efforts, but in subsequent studies of the ecological and social arrangements of pastoralists. One such study formed part of a $1 million project at
the Massachusetts Institute of Technology (MIT) funded by the United
States Agency for International Development (USAID) during 1973–5 to
examine the long-term future of the sub-Saharan region.

After a three-week visit to the region a graduate student at MIT, Anthony
Picardi, with a background in systems analyses of population and ecological issues, constructed and reported on a sequence of three system dynamics models 'for understanding the ecological and social dynamics of the
pastoral system' (Picardi 1974: abstract, p. i). Picardi's system dynamics
models of pastoralists included many factors and mathematical relationships, and allowed many scenarios to be investigated. Picardi saw a common
pattern, which he summarized in terms of the 'tragedy of the commons',
in which overstocking and overgrazing are held to be the inevitable outcome
of resources being held in common (Hardin 1968).[7]

Many social worlds intersected in Picardi's making of science—those of
different researchers at MIT, both in the USAID project and in the modelling and management fields more generally, in addition to the worlds of
USAID, the US Congress, Africanists at the United Nations, and Africans,
including the pastoralists themselves. Choosing Picardi's modelling work as
my entry point into these social worlds, I reviewed applications and critiques
of system dynamics, attended classes and conducted interviews with the
System Dynamics Group at MIT, manipulated Picardi's model on a computer, and reviewed subsequent analyses of nomadic pastoralists in sub-
Saharan Africa. From these different sources I distilled nine consistent
aspects of system dynamics modelling, which can be summarized in the following terms: fixed rules and system structure; history as a source of long-
term values; generic systems; uniform individuals, which can be simply
aggregated; constant parameters; temporal and spatial variability leave
system structure unchanged; systems decomposable into subsystems; exter-

nal forces simply mediated; responses to crises require overall policy changes. (Illustrations of two of these are given below. See P. J. Taylor 1992 for the full analysis.)

I then characterized *alternatives* for each aspect, illustrating them using examples abbreviated from the literature on African pastoralism. The contrasts were not meant to be read as indicating technical limitations of Picardi's models *per se*. Instead, I asked what it would have meant *practically* to pursue the alternatives, given the many social worlds intersecting in Picardi's making of system dynamics models? By exploring the implications of pursuing these *counterfactuals*, I aimed to expose the ways Picardi's work was facilitated by his staying with the conventional aspects of system dynamics. That is, my goal was to expose the *resources* with which he made his science. Let me illustrate this counterfactual method by teasing out two of the contrasts.

Rules and System Structure: Fixed vs. Changing

Picardi designed his models as an effort to understand 'the ecological and social dynamics of the pastoral system' (abstract, p. i).[8] For Picardi, as for other system dynamicists, it was unquestioned that the world—at whatever level of resolution examined—is composed of systems. In system dynamics a system connotes more than the orderly collection of interacting components subject to scientific management. A system in system dynamics is a bounded integrated entity, the behaviour of which is primarily determined by internal interactions or rules (Picardi 1974: 4, 7, 19 ff.; Forrester 1969: 17 ff.). External factors are simply mediated, like energy into an ecosystem or people migrating out of a pastoralist society (Picardi 1974: 7, 15).

In contrast to analysing complex interactions as self-determining and enduring, one might analyse the changes in the structure of those interactions and rules governing them. Let me give an example:

During the mid-19th century, Fulbe peoples codified conventions for land use and access in the floodplain of the inland Niger delta of what is now Mali. This code or Dina divided the floodplain into clan lands. A jooro or tax collector/pasture manager for each clan controlled access for livestock from other clans, in particular the timing of access. Under the colonial and post-colonial governments the jooro have less power to enforce their control over land use and access. Rice cultivators, for example, have encroached on lands traditionally grazed by the pastoralists' livestock. At the same time more jooro have begun to extract monetarized taxes for their personal benefit, further reducing their authority to regulate land use.   (Turner 1993)[9]

In principle, it is possible for modellers to incorporate changing rules in their models. To do so they need to anticipate the restructuring that may result from crises, such as loss of livestock during the 1968–74 drought, or from external interventions, such as the administrative actions that are progressively undermining the *Dina*. The modeller then incorporates the range of system structures into the model from the outset and specifies transitions or switches among those structures. In practice, however, such prior specification is difficult. It is no trivial issue for pastoralists themselves to anticipate the new arrangements they will make when, say, they rebuild their herds after a drought or they react to encroachment. An outsider wanting to anticipate structural change might get drawn into detailed comparative study to see how other pastoralists had responded to similar situations. Or, the outsider might live with pastoralists long enough to observe how they respond to change. Given the short study time dictated by USAID, Picardi did not follow either of these courses. He considered only a small number of switches within the model system, corresponding predominantly to policy changes such as initiation of taxation to enforce destocking (323 ff.). Moreover, these changes were to be imposed from the outside, not generated by the pastoralists.

Although USAID's short study time constrained Picardi's modelling, this also facilitated his work. The time limit relieved him of any expectation of undertaking more detailed study or developing a sustained engagement with pastoralists. Furthermore, USAID had requested an evaluation of long-term strategies for the region, intending to use the results to advise the US Congress and the United Nations in assisting the region. Specific strategies for international intervention were called for. Picardi was well aware of the need to communicate his results to clients (4, 6, 19, 216–17). Moreover, if Picardi's evaluation of nomadic pastoralism had been replete with pathways branching according to possible restructuring of arrangements, then significant translation would have been expected of Picardi by the project's sponsors, USAID (or of USAID by their sponsors)—especially if the possible restructuring depended on future initiatives of the pastoralists themselves, and not the external interventions.

Of course, Picardi's actions were not determined by this one relationship with USAID. Other elements of the intersecting social worlds were implicated in his emphasizing system-ness and de-emphasizing restructuring. Each element reinforced each other, rendering them harder to modify in practice. This cross-reinforcement will be evident if I consider another of the contrasts and examine the practical consequences.

Uniform Units vs. Strata of Differentiating Individuals

In Picardi's models all individual households, livestock, and plants behaved identically. In contrast, a modeller could consider the effects of differences, say, in the wealth and power of households. More detailed data would, of course, be needed. In addition, an alternative to system dynamics (or patience in its use) would be required because system dynamics computer implementation was not designed for multiple variants (arrays) of each basic variable. The speed of computer operations and the clarity of diagrams used to illustrate the system drops rapidly as variables proliferate. Modelling the process of differentiation of strata would, however, have been more difficult. The characteristics of the strata change as they accumulate or become impoverished. In fact, the very structure of the system may change, e.g. herders become agriculturalists and wage labourers. As in the case of modelling a changing system structure, the modeller would have to anticipate these changes.

To model differentiation Picardi would also have had to work without exemplars to follow because in 1974 there were no system dynamics models of differentiation. Nor were data pertaining to differentiation in West Africa available. The uniform model of pastoralists Picardi used obviated data on strata or differentiation, thus facilitating his work in similar ways to his fixed rules and system structure. Stratification was, in any case, less apparent in the locality Picardi chose as the basis of his model. In that locality, Tuareg pastoralists had not become sedentary nor were they deeply implicated in the agricultural economy. They were thus closer to the systems analyst's desired pure or generic system.[10]

Uniformity of model individuals facilitated Picardi's modelling in an additional way. When system dynamicists seek to establish the realism of their models, their prime means of persuasion is not to demonstrate close correspondence of model predictions with actual observations. Instead they render their models plausible by directing their presentations at non-specialists in the area in question, and drawing the listener or reader into the logic of the model. The rationality of modelled individuals is validated by the listener's personal experience—would you decide any differently in the same circumstances? (Picardi 1974: 199) The system dynamicist then uses system dynamics to demonstrate that locally rational decisions, when worked through feedbacks in the models, generate unanticipated and counterproductive outcomes. The scenario of Hardin's 'tragedy of the commons' which Picardi's models represented for the first time using system dynamics (abstract, p. i), has achieved widespread recognition by the same means.

If, however, a system dynamics model specified a heterogeneity of individuals, its realism would be harder to establish by personal validation and weight of logic. The outcomes would no longer be simple and inexorable—with which of the strata would the listener identify? With all pastoralists alike, persuasion by logic was possible. Direct empirical evidence of selfish individual exploitation of the common range was not needed (162 ff.). Some specialists have proposed contrary or more complex possibilities,[11] but these could remain out of Picardi's picture. USAID, in turn, was spared the difficult, politically charged task of considering explicitly how their programmes of assistance and support for state policies would differentially affect pastoralists who had unequal access to resources, in particular, to the 'common' rangeland.

Situatedness and Change: Mapping Heterogeneous Resources

Social agency is distributed in my analysis of Picardi's science. Notwithstanding the focus on his modelling, the analysis moved readily out into the intersecting social worlds around that modelling. His modelling work could have been modified, but this would not have followed from a mere change of world-view on his part, but would have involved many practical considerations and social negotiations.[12] The question then arises, how can this heterogeneous constructionist insight be employed to change the ways that society and nature are scientifically represented? One possible means is through *mapping workshops*, which encourage participants to be more explicit and strategic about modifying their social context of research and their research together (P. J. Taylor and Haila 1989; P. J. Taylor 1990).

Mapping workshops begin by asking researchers to focus on a key issue— a question, dispute, or action in which the researcher is strongly motivated to know more or act more effectively. They then identify *connections*, things that motivate, facilitate, or constrain their inquiry and action. The ultimate goal is to analyse the diverse resources mobilized or mobilizable by the researcher. However, in the interest of exploring the range of potential resources, participants are not expected to evaluate carefully the significance of every connection before including it in their initial maps. Things connected to the key issue might include theoretical themes, empirical regularities, methodological tactics, organisms, events, localities, agents, institutional facilities, disputes, debates, and so on.

Each researcher then draws a *map*, a pictorial depiction employing conventions of size, spatial arrangement, and perhaps colour that allows many connections to be viewed simultaneously. The metaphor of a map is not intended to connote a scaled-down representation of reality, but instead a map serves as a guide for further enquiry or action—to show the possible pathways. Finally, mapping is undertaken in a workshop setting so that each participant's thinking is exposed to questioning by other participants. The workshop interaction is intended to lead to participants clarifying and filtering the connections and, eventually, reorganizing their maps so as to indicate which connections were actually significant resources.[13]

To illustrate this work let me use one map drawn by a Finnish ecologist studying carabid beetles in the leaf litter under trees (Figure 1). I should note that this has been streamlined and redrawn on a computer for publication and cannot do justice to the real-time experience of an actual workshop. The central issue on this ecologist's map is very broad, namely, to understand the ecology of carabids in urban environments. Below this issue the map includes many theoretical and methodological sub-problems, reflecting the conventional emphasis in science of refining one's issue

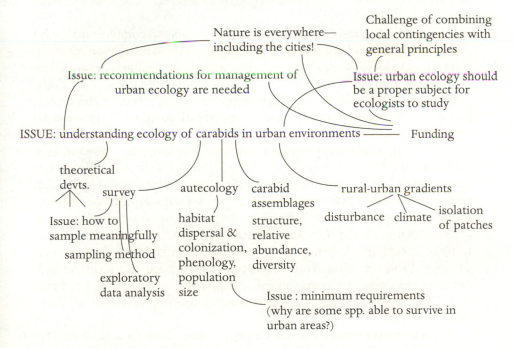

FIG. 1.   Understanding the ecology of carabids in urban environments.

into specialized questions amenable to investigation. Above the central issue are various background considerations, larger and less specific issues, situations, and assumptions that either motivate work on the central issue or are related to securing support for the research. The ecologist's research alone would not transform the urban public into recognizing that 'nature is everywhere—including in the cities', but by combining the upward and downward connections, he reminded himself that work on the background issues, not just refining a working hypothesis, would be necessary to keep being able to do his research (Fujimura 1987).

In narrating his map, the ecologist mentioned some additional history. Many of the ecologists with whom he collaborated had been studying a forest area, but the group lost their funding when the Forestry Department asserted that forest ecology was their own domain. It did not matter that animals are barely mentioned in the ecology of forestry scientists. The ecologists self-consciously, but of necessity, turned their attention to the interconnected patches of forest that extend almost to the centre of Helsinki, and explored novel sources of funding and publicity, including a TV documentary. The upward connections were thus a recurrent, if not persistent, influence on the ecologist as he defined his specific research questions.

As it turned out, the Finnish ecologist was not able to complete his study of urban carabid ecology. Indeed, reflecting upon the construction of one's research provides no guarantee of being able to change the available resources to one's advantage. Further experience with mapping workshops is needed in order to illuminate when, in practice, such reflection can stimulate scientists to modify and reconstruct the situations in which they undertake research.

The initial, exploratory work on mapping workshops raised many methodological and theoretical issues, one of which I want to mention here: maps tend to be *idiosyncratic*.[14] Although leaders of future workshops could urge a standard format for maps, idiosyncrasy ought not be dismissed lightly. It may be an inevitable outcome of leading scientists to reflect on and to consider changes in the situation in which they do their research. In contrast to political ecology's intermediate complexity, maps highlight the potential for what I call the *unruliness* of complexity. To explain this term, let me outline a number of issues that mapping raises, issues that would, I believe, be relevant to other attempts to promote researchers' reflection on their work situations.

The *boundaries* of maps call out for negotiation—how far away from the individual researcher should the 'horizon' of the map be drawn? Should the researcher's issue remain at the centre? Instead of a web of resources supporting a scientific claim, why not a web supporting scientific activity? In this sense, the rise and fall of autonomous peasants' movements in Mexico probably contributed to the generation of the scientific activity of the García-Barrioses as international concern for pastoralists in West Africa definitely did for Picardi's research.

Once such shifts in focus are entertained, the appropriate *categories* for interpreting and intervening in science hardly remain obvious. The traditional focus of scientists and philosophers on scientific claims can be stabilized only by separating research questions from research work and social support. These *levels*, however, are routinely traversed by scientists' actions, even though they often talk in terms of 'science *versus* society'. If one acknowledges the existence of resources for scientists in the work situation or in the wider social context, and one recognizes regularities or structure in those resources, should one attempt to *generalize* about the situations in which research is done? Yet, if generalizations discount or filter-out the contingency and idiosyncrasy of scientists' actions, is a degree of determinism injected which is not apparent in the individual situations? Finally, we might ask, as answers are decided to these questions of representing the situation of scientists, what *social actions* are privileged and facilitated?

Open Questions: The Logic and Pragmatics of Complexity

Questions about boundaries, categories, levels, generalization, and social actions facilitated by representations add complexity not only to the practice of mapping workshops, but also to heterogeneous constructionist and political ecological analyses. These questions can be asked, moreover, of anyone who foregrounds research into some situation while backgrounding inquiry into the situation of the researcher. Or of anyone who foregrounds research into either of these situations while backgrounding efforts that change them. There is nothing natural about these separations, nothing that ought to be taken for granted, once we acknowledge that, in all these endeavours, researchers mobilize multiple, diverse resources in establishing what counts as knowledge and in pursuing their work more generally.

Clearly, the main vector of the chapter lies in the direction of additional complexity. Yet, because of my emphasis on what it means practically for agents to modify their work, I can expect few readers to be moved by the *logic* of complexification or by written work more generally. Over and above representations of, and arguments for, complexity then, what resources might I provide for drawing readers into the projects I have been describing? I could imagine, for example, that researchers in mapping workshops might be better able to revise their maps in response to interaction with other participants if I developed suitable computer software to draw and redraw maps. I also think that, at a more fundamental level, I need more institutional resources, status, skills, and spare time in order to attract advanced researchers into mapping workshops and to sustain their interaction long enough for new complexity-addressing collaborations to emerge.

The recurrent theme in this chapter of distributing the complexity of the different projects lessens the pressure on any one person to convey the full complexity or to deliver the resources needed for others to do likewise. At the same time, with practical facilitation of researchers' work in mind, I have to recognize that simpler themes are easier to communicate to a general audience than particular reconstructions of the complexity in environmental situations and in the social context of researchers. Themes such as 'population growth will lead to environmental degradation', and 'Picardi's modelling reflects the technocratic managerial setting in which he worked at M.I.T.' appear to provide the bases for effective social mobilization—whether at the level of global environmental politics or, more modestly, at the level of teaching and influencing colleagues.

Yet, the logic of this chapter's progressive addition of complexity implies that simpler, more adaptable, accounts are only *apparently* simple. Their impact and importance depends on how they are linked to other resources by scientists and other agents negotiating their contributions to the complex, intersecting processes of knowledge-, society-, and nature-building (P. J. Taylor 1997). In this light, the challenge that has emerged in this essay is for political ecologists, heterogeneous constructionists, and self-reflexive researchers generally to discipline unruly complexity without suppressing its ever-presence. The resulting accounts would always point to the unruly complexity that is temporarily backgrounded when attempting to communicate to others. They should also, by extension, point to the complexity of social–natural processes that have to be addressed, in practice, when particular users build on the accounts in their own settings.[15] Clearly further work—intellectual, practical, and political—is needed to be able to deal productively and creatively with links between the complex situations that researchers study and the complex situations that enable researchers to do their research.

7

Security and Solidarity: An Anti-Reductionist Analysis of Environmental Policy

MICHAEL THOMPSON

Preamble

The idea that it is environmental degradation, brought on by rapid increases in population, that is inflaming the wars of the world is now much bruited about (e.g. Renner 1996, Kaplan 1994, and Homer-Dixon *et al.* 1993). Security experts, however, are not well versed in the intricacies of ecological theory, soil erosion, population dynamics, hydrological regimes, and natural resource management; their eyes have been focused elsewhere: on evil empires, rogue states, international terrorists, arms build-ups, fundamentalist movements, resurgent nationalisms, etc. Their attention has also been directed towards the large-scale actors: nation-states, in particular. Certainly they have not been peering down into the grassroots, but that of course is where they should be looking if it is environmental degradation that is the cause of all the trouble in the world. So the whole notion of *environmental security* is novel and challenging:

stabilising population, reducing social inequalities, conserving soil and water and slowing global warming are now more important for preserving international security than conventional military forces.   (Bellamy 1996)

Security, we begin to see, is not just something that states provide for their citizens. Individuals—farmers on the mountain slopes of Nepal, for instance—can become insecure if their fields are being eroded, their forests are being used faster than they can regenerate themselves, their climate is becoming drier because of global warming, and their animal's manure is all needed for cooking and no longer available to fertilize the rice-fields. As their resource-base disappears (quite literally) from beneath them, these farmers and their families, no longer able to support themselves, become *environmental refugees*, fleeing in disarray to somewhere—anywhere—where they can find enough to eat. Add all these tiny individual losses of security together and you have a major national, or regional, or even global security problem.

Security, in other words, is something that can be created and destroyed at every scale level—from the household all the way up through firms (large and small, all of whom are concerned about things like contract security), to nation-states and, ultimately, through regional (and other) groupings of states (NATOs, OPECs, G7s, G77s, ECs, SEATOs, SAARCs, and so on) to the sorts of international regimes (as they are called) that are increasingly required for the management of things like ozone layers, climates, and whale populations.

At the large-scale end of things, security experts have long known what they need to do—assess the threats and, as the song has it, reckon up their battleships—but what on earth would be the equivalent responses at the level of a single Himalayan farmer? That is the question the idea of environmental security requires us to ask. The answer, perhaps surprisingly, is that it is not just a matter of finding some way of turning down the heat—the root causes of population increase and soil loss—beneath the social pressure-cooker. Rather, it has to do with *solidarities*: the ways in which those inside the pressure-cooker bind themselves to one another and, in the process, determine their interactions with their physical surroundings.

If our Himalayan farmers are flying apart from one another in a 'beggar thy neighbour', Hobbesian war of all-against-all then all the awful consequences predicted by the pressure-cooker model will indeed come to pass. The fields will erode, their productivity will decline, the forests will be chopped down, the pastures will be grazed away to bare earth, and not one farmer will dare venture away in search of a little bit of 'off-farm employment' for fear of the predations he will suffer in his absence. But if our farmers are all pulling together, in any of a small number of possible ways, then the outcome is likely to be quite different. The fields will be skilfully maintained, so that they receive more deposited silt (from their irrigation) than they lose by erosion; their productivity will increase, thanks to the manure that is deposited (all in one place by the now largely stall-fed animals) and then laboriously carried up to the fields by their owners; the forest will be in better shape, thanks to the mutual respect between the villagers and the forest guardians they have themselves appointed; the pastures will be in good heart, thanks to the responsible behaviour of their users (and to their having switched towards the stall-feeding of their animals); and many farmers will take off from time to time on trading expeditions, or portering for tourist treks, secure in the knowledge that their neighbours will keep an eye on things and, if need be, lend a hand in their absence.

If the solidarities are arranged in this virtuous way then there need be no end to the good news: eventually, undreamed of billions of us will be living the life of Reilly in space colonies and on 'terra-formed' celestial bodies, and the pressure-cooker model will be totally invalid. Environmental security, therefore, is all about solidarities. If the appropriate solidarities are not there, and if they are not interacting with one another in the appropriate ways, then the pressure-cooker model will be valid. It is as simple (or perhaps I should say as complex) as that!

The idea of environmental security does encourage us to see that changes in security at any scale level—household to international regime—can cause changes at any of the other levels. Too much of a focus on *national* security has tended to obscure this global-to-grassroots complexity. It has prevented us from seeing that the loss of security, far from being a flame that breaks out at just one place—the interface between nation-states—is like St Elmo's Fire, running up and down the rigging, unpredictably it would seem, all the way from lofty mast-head to lowly decking.

The primary concern here is with the responsiveness of micro-level actors—mountain farmers, in particular. The argument is that responsiveness is shaped by the various forms of social solidarity that those micro-level actors are the components of. Since forms of solidarity are plural—fourfold it is argued—policy approaches that are based on the idea that people are unresponsive (just sitting there having their lives made safer, cleaner, richer, healthier, or whatever), or on the idea that they are all responsive in the same way (changing their behaviour in line with a single rationality when confronted with sticks and carrots), or even on the idea that they are responsive in two ways (the familiar markets and hierarchies) are not going to be effective. Fourfold responsiveness requires a very different approach to the interplay between micro and macro: an approach which seeks to harness the plurality, not reduce it.

This is not an easily accepted message for those who analyse, formulate, and implement policy, because they are at present strongly committed to the commonsense idea that you will get nowhere until you have a single agreed definition of what the problem *is*. Only then, they reason, can you come up with single metrics—cost/benefit analyses, probabilistic risk assessments, quality adjusted life years, and so on—and you have to have those if you are to have a rational basis for deciding between policy options. But this—reducing the plurality from four to one—is precisely what you must not do. At any rate, it is precisely what you must not do if you want to nurture trust and consent, and if you want to avoid all sorts of unwelcome surprises. Recognizing the different problem definitions (and solution definitions) at every scale level (household to international regime) and then encouraging institutional arrangements for negotiating between them, is what an anti-reductionist approach requires us to do, and that is the approach for which this chapter is endeavouring to lay the foundations.

There are two main thrusts to this anti-reductionist approach. The first is to serve notice on 'realism': the long-dominant insistence that international relations generally, and security in particular, be analysed in terms of unitary actors—nation-states—each of which interacts with the others (like economic agents in a neoclassical marketplace) with a view to protecting and advancing its interests. The second thrust is more positive: to open up a prospect in which all forms of security (social security, job security, energy security, international security, contract security, food security, supply security . . . on and on) can be seen as facets of a process in which the different forms of solidarity are interacting with one another on every scale level and between every scale level. Nor, of course, are all these institutions (which is what solidarities *are*, once they are acting at a scale level) only impinging on one another. They also impinge on the one earth they all inhabit and on which they rely for so much of the security they are all the time trying to gather together. So there is a third thrust that is entailed in the first two: to treat the environment as part-and-parcel of security, not as a rather late in the day add-on.

Us and It: An Interacting and not Easily Grasped Whole

Much policy analysis rests on the assumption that people are no different from cattle: they have certain specifiable basic needs (food, water, shelter, and so on) which have to be met. If they are not too numerous the range will support them, but if their numbers exceed the range's carrying capacity then they, and their supporting environment, will be in trouble. On this reductionist view, people and population are synonymous, and an increase in population inevitably translates into an environmental stress.[1] For instance, the I-PAT equation (environmental Impact equals some multiplication of Population, Affluence, and Technology; see also the contribution by Haila, this volume) incorporates this assumption, whilst also allowing for two multiplier effects: basic needs being compounded by proliferating derived needs, and advances in technology making it easier and cheaper for us to get all these ever increasing things that we want (Ehrlich and Holdren 1974). Cattle, of course, have not got any derived needs (the cud, not caviar, is their unchanging preference) nor are they renowned for their technological know-how. So there is something missing from the I-PAT equation: people.[2]

People, unlike populations, have some distinctly human characteristics. People have social solidarities; they have institutions, they have ways of knowing, they justify to themselves and others the various actions they take. People can learn; they can innovate, they can adapt, they can engage in discourse. People, in other words, are not cattle. So what happens to policy analysis when we put that which is ignored by the people-and-population-are-synonymous approach—the solidarities—at its very centre?

The short answer is that our attention becomes focused on the interaction of human and natural systems. This is an answer which, on the face of it, is unlikely to appeal to those who espouse ecocentrism. Humans, they will insist, are part of nature and cannot therefore be separated from it. Indeed, this false separation—anthropocentrism—is, they hold, at the root of our present ills.[3] At the very least, they will argue, if you do make this separation you should be quite clear that your singling out of the human species is entirely arbitrary, and that it would be just as valid to speak of the relationship between, say, bovine and natural systems. But human and bovine systems are *not* interchangeable in this way; humans have all the human characteristics I have just listed. In other words, they have *culture*: all the things that, as the flippant definition puts it, we have that monkeys do not. To deny this uniqueness is to fall back, I-PATwise, into the reductionism that requires us to ignore the very things—the social solidarities—that should be at the centre of our attention.

So humans are both a part of nature and apart from nature; human and bovine systems are not equivalent.[4] We cognize (see *and* know); they do not. More important still, the different forms of social solidarity of which we are the vital parts result in our knowing in several different ways, and it is this plurality of knowledges—often contradictory knowledges—that has to be addressed if we are to have effective policies: policies that enhance security, especially environmental security.

Why 'especially'? Environmental security becomes privileged (in the sense that environmental risks 'trump' all other risks) once it encompasses things like ozone holes and greenhouse effects, because it is then concerned with 'whole system' threats: the possibility that, in one way or another, we may be sawing off the branch on which we are all sitting. Other forms of security—social security, for instance, or job security or national security—do not have this 'whole system' quality (though a diminution of any one of them may, of course, contribute to a loss of environmental security).

The Anti-reductionist Approach

There are two words that should be consigned to oblivion: 'sustainable' and 'development'. Usually, when I say this, I meet with the enraged response: 'You *can't* be serious!' If the whole world has now decided that sustainable development is what we need, the argument runs, what point is there in suggesting that it is unattainable? A powerful argument, I concede, but one that, if accepted, would have some serious consequences for the pursuit of knowledge. Indeed, once accepted, we would become more bovine by the minute!

The Trouble With 'Development'

Development has now become an Orwellian word: one that, if used, is best enclosed in inverted commas. The British commentator Bernard Levin used to argue that any country with the word 'democratic' in its title isn't, and much the same seems true of 'development'. Any project or institution with the word 'development' in its title, it is pretty safe to assume, is propelling things in the reverse direction. Witness that famous conference 'Can Nepal Afford International Aid?' and the new and growing field of study that goes by the acronym DIDI: Development Induced DIsplacement. Didis (if I may call them that) are people who have been made *into* refugees *by* development projects, and there are now a lot of them. In India, for instance, hydro projects alone have displaced almost 20 million people in the fifty years since independence, few of whom have been effectively compensated (Maloney 1990). And in neighbouring Nepal, even in the case of the comparatively small number of families (222) displaced by the World Bank-funded Marsyangdi Project, the explicit World Bank guidelines on compensation (Cernea 1988) were not implemented. 'Even today', Dixit (1994: 80) writes, 'the affected people have neither been provided with employment support nor have there been any efforts to facilitate them in increasing income . . . The members of the affected families make a living as daily-wage workers.'

Of course it will be objected that you cannot make an omelette without breaking eggs, but what is by no means clear here is that there *is* an omelette. That there are broken eggs—the Didis—is not in doubt, but can we point to some among the Non-Didis who have obtained an increase in security sufficient for them to be able to compensate the Didis and still be more secure than they were before? If we can, then, according to the Pareto Principle, we can be confident that there has been development. Rawls, contra

Pareto, would insist that the compensation actually happens: that no one ends up less secure than they were before, which, of course, is not the case here.[5] So development, once we expose the different ideas of fairness that are at work within it, becomes something of a conjuring trick: 'Now you sees it; now you don't!' Framing things in terms of security allows us to get behind the conjurer. Are there institutional reforms that might enable the Nepalese state to become a provider of security to its poorest citizens? Alternatively, are there other institutional actors (in the informal sector, for instance) who, if some subsidiarity principle was invoked, could do what the state cannot? These are the questions to ask, but 'development' does not ask them.

This growing disenchantment with 'development' has been elegantly articulated by Goldman (1998) in his framing of the Trans National Institute's recent project: Re-Inventing The Commons. He begins by boldly capturing the past twenty or so years of work on the commons into a dialectic between those who accept the 'tragedy of the commons' and those who reject it. The tragedy, according to its most famous proponent Garrett Hardin (1968), is that no single user of the commons will be prepared to do what he would do—moderate his use—if only everyone else was prepared to do the same. The overuse and collapse of the commons, therefore, is inevitable, human nature being what Hardin tells us it is. 'Not so!', cry those who are ranked against him, 'The tragedy is not inherent to the commons.'

Those who accept the tragic explanation move, without further ado, to one or other of the solutions this explanation allows: either to privatize the commons (a solution that is favoured by many economists and much touted by libertarian think-tanks) or to change human nature[6] (a solution that is built into Aldo Leopold's (1970) 'earth ethic'[7] and into the deep ecologists' insistence that we develop 'a whole new relationship with nature', before it is too late). Those who reject the tragic explanation also reject this stark policy choice, turning instead to the painstaking elucidation of the conditions (such as those that, as we will see in a moment, have prevailed in the Swiss village of Davos for the last seven centuries) under which the tragedy does not occur.

But Goldman discerns that something else is now beginning to happen. This dialectic, for all the disagreement that it contains, is ultimately contained within a wider area of agreement—that development is inevitable and desirable—that is now becoming the thesis in a new dialectic: a new dialectic in which the two original camps (the Hardinites and the Painstaking Elucidators), joined together by their shared and unquestioned assumptions, are pitted against an antithesis that explicitly questions these assumptions. My distaste for 'development' (and for 'sustainable') locates me firmly in this new anti-thesis. It is from this position that I am arguing in this paper.

The Trouble with 'Sustainable'

The idea that we are operating unsustainably, or are in imminent danger of doing so, really cannot be detached from the 'carrying capacity' way of seeing things: the notion that there are some limits out there on the range, that if we are on the wrong side of them we are in trouble, and that if we can somehow get ourselves on the right side of them everything will be just fine. Implicit in this reductionist framing is the assumption that human and natural systems can be brought into some harmonious and stable relationship with one another. The assumption is that we can get it right (and keep it right) but this would be true only if both human and natural systems were *simple* (that is, linear, predictable, deterministic, equilibrium-seeking, insensitive to initial conditions, and so on). Certainly, there are plenty of theories in both natural and social science that assume this— thereby encouraging us to believe that if we can put a man on the moon (the earth and the moon *are* a simple system) we can make ourselves sustainable—but the evidence increasingly points to these systems being *complex* (that is, non-linear, unpredictable, indeterministic, disequilibrating, and highly sensitive to initial conditions).[8]

The Trouble with 'Sustainable Development'

If development projects deliver a net loss of security as often (more often, perhaps) than they deliver a net gain, then 'development' becomes indistinguishable from whatever the word is that is its opposite (and it's not 'stagnation').[9] Put it together with the word 'sustainable', and apply the combination to a system that does not provide us with any lasting limits that we can discover and get ourselves on the right side of, and you really will have committed yourself to an unwise course of action.

Of course, Goldman's 'dialectic piled upon dialectic' and my suggestion that both natural and social systems are not simple but complex each require volumes of explication and substantiation (cf. Taylor, Ch. 6, this volume), but at least we can see that a reasoned case can be made (indeed, has been made) for ditching the whole idea of sustainable development. Let me therefore move on to the constructive part of my argument: what to put in the place of sustainable development. My candidate, as I have already indicated is *security enhancement*: a goal that avoids both the unidirectional assumptions that are built into the word 'development' and the stable and harmonious Never Never Land that is promised by the word 'sustainable'.

Framing Things in Terms of Security and Solidarity

In mountain villages you will often find that the houses and the agricultural land are privately owned whilst the grazing land, and sometimes the forest, are communally owned.[10] Management of the privately owned resources is taken care of by the judgements of the individual farmers, and by their inter-actions with one another and with the wider world beyond the confines of their village. The communally owned resources, however, require some sort of *commons managing institution*, and often you find that the villagers appoint 'guardians' whose task it is to assess the ecological status of the pastures or forest, year-by-year or season-by-season, and then to decree how much overall use will be permitted. Usually there are some time-honoured proce-dures for sharing this permitted use among the commoners, and there are usually some time-honoured sanctions (small fines, for instance) for those who do not fully respect these stipulations.[11]

So here are two forms of social solidarity—*individualism* and *hierarchy*, both niched at a rather micro social scale (the village) and each generating its distinctive management style: its distinctive form of interaction between the human and natural systems. And these forms of interaction, in their different ways, deliver a wide range of securities to the villagers. But some-times we find the commons being managed, not in this hierarchical, expert, top-down way, but by a much more egalitarian, bottom-up, all-in-the-same-boat sort of commitment among the commoners. The famous tree-huggers of the Indian Himalaya, for instance, turn out *en masse* to prevent their communally owned village forests from being appropriated by the rapacious logging contractors, and Swiss villagers all lend their hands to the repair and maintenance of the structures that protect their privately owned houses from avalanches. So this is a third form of social solidarity—*egalitarianism*— and, as with the others, it generates its own distinctive management style; its distinctive form of human/natural interaction. It also, of course, deliv-ers securities that are not delivered by the other two solidarities. Nor is that the end of the stylistic plurality. Sometimes none of these three things get done, either because people are convinced that nothing they can do will make any difference, or because they are all pulling in different ways, with the result that they might just as well have not pulled at all! A shared experience of that sort of thing, too, is a form of social solidarity—*fatalism*—and it too gives rise to a distinctive (and sometimes rather destructive) form of interaction between the human and the natural systems. It also, we should note, delivers securities that are not delivered by the other three. To know that nothing can be (or could have been) done is often a great comfort. It also avoids the wastage of time and money that is entailed in believing otherwise.

This little account of the mountain village can be read in two ways: as an accurate description of the stylistic plurality by which these seemingly simple folk have kept themselves and their environment in place (though not unchanged) over the centuries, or as a parable about all the things that are going on (and going wrong) in the wider world. The Soviet collectivization of agriculture, for instance, can be likened to a bunch of over-zealous pasture guardians extending their hierarchical management style to the privately owned fields and houses. And George Soros's (1997) recent pronouncement—that democracy's greatest enemy now is not communism but capitalism—carries considerable conviction, once we relate it to a mountain village which, having found that its pasture guardians have not been doing a very good job, hits on the spiffing idea of privatizing the whole caboodle: the pastures, the forests, and even the avalanche defences. Indeed, I am sure we are all familiar with colleagues whose eyes are aglint with one or other of these monomaniacal solutions: everything controlled by the hierarchy, everything tipped into the marketplace, everything decided by the voluntary agreement of everyone!

Clearly, there is something profound and important in this everyday story of village folk, and the essence of that something is that they have somehow managed to resist the urgings of the monomaniacs. So let us take a closer look at what they are doing.

Solidarities In Action and Interaction

Over the centuries that the Davos valley, in the Swiss Alps, has been settled both the fields (in the valley bottom) and the grazing land (high above) have expanded at the expense of the forest that is sandwiched between them. But on all the steeper slopes the trees have stayed in place, acting both as a source of timber and as a barrier against avalanches. However, it is difficult (impossible, perhaps) to achieve both these functions simultaneously and, in managing the forest for timber production, the Davosers have often set in train changes in their forest's age structure which, decades later, have resulted in exceptional avalanches reaching the valley floor and threatening the destruction of the entire community.

Every time this unpleasant surprise has befallen them the Davosers have responded by switching their forest management to the all-in-the-same-boat, egalitarian style. Later, it has sometimes shifted to the hierarchist style, often to the individualist style (with farmers owning long thin strips of forest running all the way from valley floor to alpine pasture) and sometimes to the fatalist style (as happened, for instance, when the avalanche danger was clearly perceived yet timber extraction continued in response to the demands of various mining booms and, in more recent years, the demand for ski-runs).

Surely, you might think, they would have got it right by now. But to think that is to assume that there *is* one right way, and that is not the case. There is no way of ever getting it right, because managing one way inevitably changes the forest, eventually to the point where that way of managing is no longer appropriate. This would happen even if there were no exogenous changes (like the mining and tourist booms) which, of course, there always are. Security, therefore, can only be achieved by 'covering all the bases': by the villagers ensuring that they have the full fourfold repertoire of management styles, and by their being prepared to try a different one whenever the one they have been relying on for one part of their security shows signs of no longer being appropriate. 'Always learning; never getting it right!' that is the message we need to hear, and that is the message that is all the time being blocked by the idea of sustainable development.

Getting the Message

That the stylistic plurality of the village level provides such an apt parable for goings-on at much higher levels—the national and international, for instance—helps open the way for a counter-intuitive but wonderfully helpful proposition: that cultural dynamics[12] (the interplay of the four solidarities) are independent of social scale. Where conventional social science (Keohane and Ostrom 1995, for instance) sees hierarchy as something that emanates from the nation-state, and the commons as cosy communitarian set-ups that can exist only in those places—remote mountain villages and tenuous international regimes—to which the nation-state's writ does not effectively run, the *proposition of independence* allows us to entertain the idea that all four cultural styles (all four solidarities) are to be found at every scale level: all the way from households to Global Environmental Facilities.

The trick is to parcel out your transactions to the appropriate styles *and* to the appropriate scales. In the mountain village example we were looking at this trick in just two dimensions—the village level—but we began to get a feel for the third dimension once we got into the parables. Now we can see that they are not really parables at all; they are simply some of the other components in the big picture. The big picture is organized by some surprisingly simple principles.

- The first is that, at every scale level, the solidarities self-organize by defining themselves against one another. Discourse is one of the means by which they do this, with each solidarity generating its distinctive definition of both solution and problem and pitting them against those that are generated by the other solidarities.
- The scale levels' organization hardly needs to be explained. It is the inevitable concomitant of social life, and the physical transactions that sustain it, being spread out in time and space. Individuals fit inside households, households fit inside villages, villages fit inside cantons, and so on up to, at present, the international regimes that encompass the whole of the earth's surface (and up to any astronauts who happen, for the moment, to be absent from that surface).
- Securities wax and wane in a way that is reminiscent of Tolstoy's happy and unhappy families. There is only one way in which they can be enhanced: by lodging transactions at their appropriate styles and at their appropriate scales. But there are three ways in which they can be diminished: appropriate style/inappropriate scale, appropriate scale/inappropriate style, and inappropriate style/inappropriate scale.
- Appropriate today, however, as the Davosers' experiences make clear, is no guarantee of appropriateness tomorrow. In other words, without continuous plurality-based learning, security, rather like negentropy, will always tend to zero.

All in all, it warms the cockles of those economists who go by the label 'Austrian' (Schumpeter, for instance, and Hayek) and who refuse to countenance the equilibration that other economists find so comforting. But there is one big difference: the four solidarities, only one of which—individualism—is consonant with the 'Austrian' view of human responsiveness.

Why the solidarities exist, and the difference their presence makes, clearly, are large and important questions that require empirical research. One way to get a feel for the answers, however, is to focus more precisely on this multidimensional picture through a few examples of the interrelationships between cultural styles and social scales.

The Snakes and Ladders of Security

People, in their daily lives, face all sorts of risks: unemployment, natural disasters, ill health, external aggression, traffic accidents, stock market crashes, and the consequences of anthropogenic climate change, to mention but a few. And they feel themselves to be secure, not when all these risks have been eliminated (for that is impossible), but when they perceive them to be satisfactorily coped with.

Few, if any, of these risks are coped with through the unaided efforts of the person concerned; they are coped with through institutional arrangements: family ties, insurance companies, national defence forces, state-funded pensions, environmental legislation, international agreements on carbon emissions, and so on. In other words, it is to solidarities—the familiar markets and hierarchies and the less familiar egalitarian and fatalistic arrangements—that people look for their security, and they obtain different kinds of security from different kinds of solidarity. These different kinds of solidarity, as we have seen, can then be lodged at different points on the micro/macro social scale: anywhere from the household to the supranational 'regimes' that are becoming so prominent a feature of what is sometimes called 'ecological modernization'.[13] Since modernization used not to be prefixed by the word 'ecological', we can perhaps use this terminological adjustment to locate ourselves on a transition from a situation where all forms of solidarity were more or less equivalent to one in which environmental security, by virtue of what are now perceived by many to be 'whole system' threats, is privileged.

The challenge, therefore, is to conceive of risk 'in the round', applying the insights of those who have been working on environmental and technological risks, for instance, to the problems that are being grappled with by those charged with the reform of social security systems, and (despite the plausible priority of the former) *vice versa*. A tall order, I agree, but a necessary one, given that so many of these risks (those associated with capital markets, for instance) are now global in their scale or consequences. Security in one part of the world is now likely to be undermined by its absence somewhere else. A loss of environmental security in the South, for instance, may result in a loss of economic (or even national) security in the North, as those who have been displaced by the rising sea-levels that are predicted in some scenarios become a flood of migrants that threatens to overwhelm those Northerners who have been fortunate enough to have avoided that environmental risk.

Interdependence, however, does not lead to uniformity. The mix of risks that has to be coped with if a Nepalese peasant is to perceive himself as secure is not the same as that which, uncoped with, would render a Norwegian shipyard-worker insecure. Nor, when we take one of the risks that *is* present in both mixes, do we find the Nepalese peasant and the Norwegian shipyard-worker looking to the same solidarity, or to the same scale level, for their security. The Norwegian shipyard-worker will look to the state (and perhaps to the insurance market) for his social security; the Nepalese peasant will look to his family and to his personal network within the informal economy. If we colour-in these two characters on the three-dimensional picture we can see just how different they are. The Norwegian shipyard-worker's sources of security are on fairly high scale levels (the national for his pension, and the national and global if he has a private pension); the Nepalese peasant's sources are much more micro (the household and, in the case of his informal sector network, probably no more than the canton). There are stylistic differences too. The Norwegian shipyard-worker's pension comes from the hierarchical solidarity and, if he has a private pension, from the individualist (market) solidarity. The Nepalese peasant's household and family (like households and families everywhere) may be quite plural culturally (Hindu households tending towards hierarchy, Buddhist ones towards individualism) but the 'friend in need, friend indeed' response is strongly tinged with egalitarianism. Out on the personal network, however, it is individualism all the way.

Try swapping these two characters around and all sorts of inappropriatenesses avoided, and appropriatenesses overlooked, are revealed. The Nepalese peasant, for instance, is not missing out on anything by not looking to a state that cannot even compensate the 222 families that have been displaced by one of its aid-sponsored hydro projects. Yet the Norwegian shipyard-worker, especially at a time when state pensions are becoming rather insecure, might well profit by looking where his Nepalese counterpart looks: to his family and his personal network. Indeed, he quite likely *is* looking in those places; it is just that, being in Norway's informal sector (which is minute in comparison to Nepal's), these sources of security are none too visible to an outside observer!

Nepalese forests, to take another example, have suffered badly in recent decades. Indeed, they have provided those who promote the 'tragedy of the commons' explanation with some of their best ammunition. The trouble with this tragic explanation, however, is that the village forests have been commons for centuries whilst their decline only set in in the late 1950s. The tragedy-rejectors have an explanation for this: an institutional explanation. The forests started to decline, they argue, because they were nationalized, following the overthrow of the Rana regime in the 1950s, and control vested in a national forestry service. The villagers' commons managing institutions were destroyed and the new arrangements, for a variety of fairly obvious reasons, did not work. For instance, a villager might have to walk for several days to get permission to cut a tree to replace a beam in his house (where before he had only to pop round to a neighbour's) and the district forestry officer, for his part, could not see what was actually going on in all the forests he was responsible for (there being some rather large mountains in the way). Meticulous research on the age-structure of village forests, together with ethno-ecological studies that have thrown light on the villagers' various land-use strategies, and on the way a lapse into fatalism can trigger the 'nibble effect' (which can quickly remove an entire forest by over-extraction at its accessible edge and under-extraction from its more remote parts), have now lent strong support to the tragedy-rejecting hypothesis.[14] The Nepalese forestry service, for its part, is now devoting itself to a task that is the exact opposite of that with which it was originally charged; it is handing the forests back to the villagers[15] and helping them get them into the sort of shape that is best suited to their farming systems (which, of course, vary considerably from village to village).

If we refer this silvan saga to the three-dimensional picture we can see that both the village-level commons managing institutions and the national forestry service share the same cultural style—the hierarchical; it was the change in social scale—a change that has now been reversed—that was inappropriate. So there are now two managing institutions—one lodged at the village level, the other at the national and district levels—both of which are hierarchical in style. But, rather than clashing head-on, a long and seemingly messy process of negotiation between levels and styles (village forests have to mesh constructively with privately owned fields and so on) has ensured that both, for the moment, are sources of security. The present outcome, we should note, is light-years away from either of the solutions that the tragedy-mongers allow (privatize the commons or change human nature) yet it seems to be working quite well, thanks to the subsidiarity principle that is now built into the forest service/village forest relationship. The forest service only does those things (researching and developing the techniques for regenerating seriously denuded slopes, for instance) that cannot, at present, be done at the village level.

In conclusion, North and South, rich and poor, donors and recipients, are all bound up together in a cat's cradle of solidarities: a cat's cradle in which things can go seriously into reverse if an inappropriate solidarity is relied upon, or if that support is provided at an inappropriate scale level, or both. Understanding more about that cat's cradle, and teasing out ways of increasing the appropriateness of the solidarities and scale levels that comprise it, is the task we begin to discern once we have placed ourselves in the latest anti-thesis of Goldman's 'double dialectic'. That is how we shift ourselves away from sustainable development and onto security enhancement.

PART III

Environmental Politics and Cultural Difference

8

The Environment of Justice

DAVID HARVEY

> The bourgeoisie has only one solution to its pollution problems: it moves them around.
>
> (Adapted from Frederick Engels)

The Movement for Environmental Justice

The Economist (8 September 1992) reported on a leaked World Bank internal memorandum (dated 12 December 1991) from the pen of Lawrence Summers, then a Harvard economist of considerable reputation (nephew of Paul Samuelson and son-in-law of Kenneth Arrow, both Nobel prize-winners in economics). Summers, then chief economist of the World Bank and subsequently Undersecretary of State for Trade in the Clinton administration wrote:

Just between you and me, shouldn't the World Bank be encouraging more migration of the dirty industries to the LDC's [less-developed countries]? I can think of three reasons:

1. The measurement of the costs of health-impairing pollution depends on the foregone earnings from increased morbidity and mortality. From this point of view a given amount of health-impairing pollution should be done in the country with the lowest cost, which will be the country with the lowest wages. I think the economic logic behind dumping a load of toxic waste in the lowest-wage country is impeccable and we should face up to that.

2. The costs of pollution are likely to be non-linear as the initial increments of pollution probably have very low cost. I've always thought that under-populated countries in Africa are vastly under-polluted; their [air pollution] is probably vastly inefficiently low compared to Los Angeles or Mexico City. Only the lamentable facts that so much pollution is generated by non-tradable industries (transport, electrical generation) and that the unit transport costs of solid waste are so high prevent world welfare-enhancing trade in air pollution and waste.

3. The demand for a clean environment for aesthetic and health reasons is likely to have a very high income elasticity. The concern over an agent that causes one in a million change in the odds of prostate cancer is obviously going to be much higher in a country where people survive to get prostate cancer than in a country where under-5 mortality is 200 per thousand. Also, much of the concern over industrial atmosphere discharge is about visibility of particulates. These discharges may have little direct health impact. Clearly trade in goods that embody aesthetic pollution concerns could be welfare enhancing. While production is mobile the consumption of pretty air is a non-tradable.

The Washington office of Greenpeace faxed copies of the memo around the world. Environmental groups had, and continue to have (see, for example, Bullard 1993; Pepper 1993) a field day. The World Bank, already a strong focus for criticism for its lack of environmental concerns, was put very much on the defensive at the very moment it was seeking to influence the Rio Summit on the Environment through publication of its 1992 report on 'Development and the Environment'. Brazil's Secretary of the Environment described Summers's reasoning as 'perfectly logical but totally insane'. Summers was featured in *People Magazine* in its special 'Earth Day' issue as one of the top eight 'enemies of the earth' and even the *Financial Times* thought it time to save planet earth from economists (Rich 1993: 246–50). *The Economist*, however, editorialized that his economic logic was indeed 'impeccable'.

The Summers memo appears to endorse 'toxic colonialism' or 'toxic imperialism'. The final paragraph of the memo points out, however, that the problem with all of these arguments is that they 'could be turned around and used more or less effectively against every Bank proposal'. This suggests that Summers was not himself endorsing such ideas but trying to point out to his colleagues, steeped in neoclassical economic theory, the logical consequences of their own mode of thought. While this may exculpate Summers somewhat, it broadens the questions the memo raises to a whole mode of discourse about environmental and economic issues.

So what objections can be raised? To begin with, the class situatedness of the argument is transparent. Affluent groups, including most professional economists (median weekly earnings of $889 in the United States in 1994, according to Uchitelle (1995)) do not have to accept toxic wastes on their own doorstep to survive whereas child-care workers ($158 per week), janitors, and cleaners ($293 per week), and sewing machine operators ($316 per week) do not have the same range of choice. The logic also pays scant attention to questions of distributive justice, except in the narrowest sense that trade in toxins is meant to be 'welfare-enhancing' for all. This presumes that one way to raise incomes of the poor is to pay them to absorb toxins (largely generated on behalf of the rich). Any negative health impacts, it should be noted, will then be visited on those least able to deal with them. Since most of the poor and the disempowered are people of colour the impact is racially discriminatory. And if we care to think about it at all, there is a symbolic dimension, a kind of 'cultural imperialism' embedded in the whole proposal: are we not presuming that only trashy people can stomach trash? The question of stigmatization of 'the other' through, in this instance, association of racially marked others with pollution, defilement, impurity, and degradation becomes a part of the political equation. If, as Douglas (1984: 3) claims, 'some pollutions are used as analogies for expressing a general view of the social order', and if 'pollution beliefs can be used in a dialogue of claims and counter-claims to status', then claims about pollution as 'matter out of place' cannot be separated from claims about the impurities and dangers of 'people out of place'.

Questions of how and why 'wastes' in general and hazardous wastes in particular are produced in the first place are, of course, never even mentioned in discussions of the Summers' sort. Yet, as Commoner (1990) has, among others, again and again emphasized, the question of prevention surely should take precedence over disposal and cure of any side effects. But posing that question requires a discursive shift to the far more politically charged terrain of critique of the general characteristics of the mode of production and consumption in which we live.

Though the 'impeccable economic logic' advanced by Summers is not hard to deconstruct as the characteristic discourse of a particular kind of political–economic power and its discriminatory practices, it unfortunately approximates as a description of what usually happens. The market mechanism 'naturally' works that way. Property values are lower close to noxious facilities and that is where the poor and the disadvantaged are by and large forced by their impoverished circumstances to live. The insertion of a noxious facility causes fewer disturbances to property values in low-income areas so that an 'optimal' lowest cost location strategy for any noxious facility points to where the poor live. Furthermore, a small transfer payment to cover negative effects may be very significant to and therefore more easily accepted by the poor, but largely irrelevant to the rich, leading to what I long ago referred to (Harvey 1973: 81) as the 'intriguing paradox' in which 'the rich are unlikely to give up an amenity "at any price" whereas the poor who are least able to sustain the loss are likely to sacrifice it for a trifling sum'. If, as is usually the case, areas where low-income, disempowered, and marginalized 'others' live are also zones of more political organization, and weak political resistance, then the symbolic, political, and economic logic for the location of noxious facilities works in exactly the way that the Summers's memo envisages.

As a consequence, one of the best predictors of the location of toxic waste dumps in the United States is a geographical concentration of people of low income and of colour. The dumping of toxic wastes on indigenous Indian reservations or in communities of colour (African-American or Hispanic) across much of the south and west of the United States is now well documented (Bryant and Mohai 1992; Bullard 1990, 1993, 1994; Hoffrichter 1993). Even more remarkable, are the bidding wars between, for example, different native-American groups or less-developed countries to accommodate the waste in return for money incomes. While that practice might be better understood in the case of dictators or military regimes who receive all the benefits while visiting the costs on their own populations, it is not unknown for reasonably democratic debate to generate a political consensus in favour of accepting toxic waste facilities on the grounds that this generates otherwise unavailable income and employment. In Alabama's 'Blackbelt', for example, the question of hazardous landfills in Sumter County is politically contested: those who have most to lose from denying the facility, in terms of jobs and incomes (the poor and people of colour), are in this instance at odds with the middle-class and often white environmentalists who seek to close such facilities down (see Bailey *et al.* 1993). The same conflict holds in Mississippi (Schneider 1993). The political economy of waste creation and circulation under capitalism incorporates Summers's logic, including some of its inherent social contradictions.

The practice of that logic has, however, sparked militant resistance. In the United States, the movement for environmental justice and against environmental racism has become a significant political force. It is a political movement that has been long in gestation, owing its most recent reincarnation to two particular incidents. First, the celebrated case of Love Canal in 1977, when houses built on top of an infilled-canal in Buffalo, New York, found their basements fall of noxious liquids with serious health effects on resident children (Gibbs 1982; Levine 1982; Szasz 1994). This led to the formation of a Citizens Clearing House for Hazardous Waste which, according to D. Taylor (1993) now works with over 7,000 community and grass-roots groups nation-wide. The second arose out of the 1982 protests in Warren County, North Carolina, when a mostly African-American community was selected as the site for burial of soil contaminated with PCBs. The vigour of the protests (multiple arrests of well-known civil rights figures) and the involvement of a wide range of organizations focused attention on what soon came to be known as 'environmental racism'. In 1991, a very dispersed and highly localized movement came together around the

First National People of Colour Environmental Leadership Summit held in Washington, DC. There it adopted a manifesto defining environmental justice in no less than 17 different clauses (see Grossman 1994). I select just a few:

Environmental justice

affirms the sacredness of Mother Earth, ecological unity and the interdependence of all species, and the right to be free from ecological destruction

mandates the right to ethical, balanced and responsible uses of land and renewable resources in the interest of a sustainable planet for human and other living things

demands the cessation of the production of all toxins, hazardous wastes, and radioactive materials, and that all past and current producers be held strictly accountable to the people for detoxification and the containment at the point of production

affirms the need for urban and rural ecological policies to clean up and rebuild our cities and rural areas in balance with nature, honouring the cultural integrity of all our communities, and providing fair access for all to the full range of resources

opposes the destructive operations of multi-national corporations . . . military occupation, repression and exploitation of lands, peoples and cultures, and other life forms

requires that we, as individuals, make personal and consumer choices to consume as little of Mother Earth's resources and to produce as little waste as possible; and make the conscious decision to challenge and reprioritize our lifestyles to insure the health of the natural world for present and future generations.

I shall return to these principles later, though it is not hard to see how many professionals might regard them as just as 'insane' as Summers's memo, while lacking the virtue of elementary let alone 'impeccable' logic. The militant local struggles for environmental justice that coalesced to advance these theses created sufficient national political ferment, however, to force the EPA, even in its most recalcitrant Reagan–Bush years, to take up the issues of environmental equity. The EPA's 1992 report on that issue conceded that there were problems of unequal exposure of minority and low-income populations to environmental risks, but asserts that there was not enough hard information to substantiate effective discrimination (except in the case of lead poisoning). In February 1994, however, the Clinton administration— responding to its constituencies of environmentalists, minorities, and the poor—issued an executive order to all federal agencies to ensure that programmes would not unfairly inflict environmental harm on the poor and minorities. This means that the environmental needs of low-income and minority communities must be fairly addressed and that environmental issues can be adjudicated in terms of civil rights.

That move did not pacify many in the environmental justice movement in part because they recognized that co-optation into such a legal–political quagmire would be the kiss of death. The reason that hardly any new hazardous waste sites have been opened these last ten years has to do precisely with the fact that movements against such sites have been organized outside of 'channels'. For this reason too, the environmental justice movement has frequently been at odds with the main environmental groups (such as Friends of the Earth, The Sierra Club, the Environmental Defense Fund, etc.—usually referred to as 'the Big Ten'). The division here reflects class, race, and gender. It also reflects an intense politics of place (cf. Chapter 9) versus the more abstract politics of the mainstream environmental movement. 'People of Colour' and working-class women have been most active in the grass-roots movement in particular places where the Big Ten are dominated, in membership but more particularly in organization, by white, middle-class professional men, largely concentrated in the centres of political power (such as Washington, DC). Lois Gibbs, organizer of the original Love Canal protest, recalls her attempt to bring these groups together:

It was hilarious. . . . People from the grassroots were at one end of the room, drinking Budweiser and smoking, while the environmentalists were at the other end of the room eating yoghurt. We wanted to talk about victim compensation. They wanted to talk about ten parts per billion benzene and scientific uncertainty. A couple of times it was almost war. We were hoping that, by seeing these local folks, the people from the Big Ten would be more apt to support the grassroots position, but it didn't work out that way. They went right on with the status quo position. The Big Ten approach is to ask: What can we support to achieve a legislative victory? Our approach is to ask: What is morally correct? We can't support something in order to win if we think it is morally wrong.   (Cited in Greider 1992: 214)

This sort of distinction in allegiance and membership has been playfully characterized as follows:

Citizen's Clearinghouse—'typical member: quit the church choir to organize toxic dump protest', Natural Resources Defense Council—'typical member: Andover'63, Yale'67, Harvard Law'70, Pentagon anti-war marches'68,'69,'70', Environmental Defense Fund—'typical member: lawyer with a green conscience and a red Miata. . . .'   (Greider 1993: 214)

This does not imply that all forms of cooperation are ruled out: Greenpeace, for example, helped the Concerned Citizens of South Central Los Angeles (organized primarily by women) to fight off the LANCER mass-burn incinerator (designed to serve 1.4 million people throughout the city) that was to be located in a poor and heavily minority community (Blumberg and

Gottlieb 1989: ch. 6). Nevertheless, the environmental justice movement preserves its fiercely independent 'militant particularism'. It rejects government and broadly 'bourgeois' attempts at co-optation and absorption into a middle-class and professional-based resistance to that impeccable economic logic of environmental hazards that the circulation of capital defines.

Discourses of Complicity and Dissent

In recent years the 'environmental issue' has generated a vast diversity of antagonistic and mutually exclusive discourses. There are, to be sure, some common underpinnings. Most—apart, of course, from those who enter only to scoff at the whole idea—accept that there exists a class of problems which might reasonably be dubbed 'environmental' and many use a language of actual or potential crisis. Most also argue that the difficulties arise out of the particular way we relate to something external to us called 'nature' and that some ameliorative or in some instances revolutionary measures must be taken to put us on some more 'sustainable' or 'harmonious' trajectory of development. Beyond that, the multiplicity of discourses becomes confusing. I now want to take a closer look at how and why this might be the case, focusing particularly upon the political and environmental vision incorporated in discourses about environmental justice. Elsewhere I argued that discourses do not exist in isolation from beliefs, social relations, institutional structures, material practices, or power relations (1996: ch. 4). Discourses internalize effects from all of these domains while reciprocally entering in, though never as pure mirror images, to all of the other moments of the social process.

The advantage of construing things thus is that it allows me to look on a discourse about environmental justice not simply as a philosophical and ethical debate, but rather in terms of the 'environmental' conditions (beliefs, institutions, social material practices and relations, forms of political–economic power) that give rise to such a discourse and become internalized within it. It also permits a closer analysis of how a discourse about environmental justice might 'do work' within other moments of the social process (affecting beliefs, imaginations, institutions, practices, power relations, and the like).

All environmental–ecological arguments are arguments about society and, therefore, complex refractions of all sorts of struggles being waged in other realms. Aldo Leopold's land ethic, for example, arose out of a fusion of a discourse on national identity (the role of the frontier and encounter with wilderness in shaping US national identity), religion (the epiphany of looking into the eyes of a mountain lion dying from the hunt), and Darwinian science. Garrett Hardin's 'tragedy of the commons' is relentlessly built up through fusion of contemporary Darwinian thinking, the mathematical logic of diminishing returns, and a political economy of an individualized, utility-maximizing, property-owning democracy. Animal rights theorists accept the liberal rhetoric about individual rights and seek to extend it to sentient beings or, as Regan prefers to call them 'subjects of a life'. Ecological modernization theory (see below) forges a unity between doctrines of efficiency in production and the efficient as well as equitable workings of ecological aggregates. Ecofeminism builds a powerful link between traditional liberal humanism and a vision of women's role as close to nature through nurturing and caring. Each one of these composite discourses shapes a unique blend of complicity and dissent with respect to existing beliefs, institutions, material social practices, social relations, and dominant systems of organizing political–economic power. This is their specific virtue: they pose problems of defining relations across different moments in the social process and reveal much about the pattern of social conflict in all realms of social action.

Consider, for example, the general content in which Summers's version of what to do with toxic wastes becomes possible. It is not sufficient here to argue that it is a typical manifestation of neoclassical economic logic—itself an engaging set of particular metaphors—in which welfare-enhancing trade in waste can be envisaged under conditions of resource-scarcity. For there is a prior question to be answered: why is it that neoclassical economics is such a well-accepted discourse in relation to the dominant forms of political–economic power in capitalist society? And what effects does the privileging of neoclassical economic discourse have on beliefs, the functioning of institutions, social relations, material practices, and the like? I shall not attempt to answer these questions directly here, though I believe a strong case could be made for the deep penetration of neoclassical ways of economic thought into all of these realms. Instead, I shall look more closely at some dominant forms of environmental–ecological discourse in an attempt to gain some insights as to why they hold the particular positions they do and how, given their character and their extensive grip upon the public imagination and public institutions, they have created a set of environmental conditions in which the movement for environmental justice has been forced to articulate its oppositional arguments (and to some degree shape its practices) in very particular ways. With this in mind, let me begin by outlining what seem to be the dominant forms of discourse about the environment in the late twentieth century.

The 'Standard View' of Environmental Management

Capitalism has frequently encountered environmental problems. Over the last two centuries or so institutions, scientific understandings, public policies, and regulatory practices have been evolved to deal with them. These practices have converged over time into something that I will call 'the standard view' of environmental management in advanced capitalist societies.

In the standard view, the general approach to environmental problems is to intervene only 'after the event'. This strategy in part stems from the belief that no general environmental concerns should stand in the way of 'progress' (more precisely, capital accumulation) and that any 'after the event' environmental difficulties can be effectively cleaned up if need be. This implies no irreversibility problems of the sort that arise with species extinction or habitat destruction and that a 'remedial science' exists to cope with any difficulties that do arise. This 'after-the-event' emphasis means that environmental issues are essentially regarded as 'incidents'—the result of 'errors' and 'mistakes' (often based on ignorance)—that should be dealt with on a case-by-case (and often place-by-place) basis. The preference is, furthermore, for environmental clean-ups of particular sites and 'end-of-pipe' solutions (e.g. soil remediation, the installation of scrubbers on smokestacks, catalytic converters in cars, etc.) rather than for pre-emptive or proactive interventions.

The only general problem sometimes admitted under the standard view is so-called 'market failure' which occurs because firms (or other economic entities such as governments and households) can 'externalize' costs by free use of the environment for procuring resources or for waste disposal. The theory of the firm developed in neoclassical economics effectively describes why it might be economically rational for individual firms to plunder common resources like fisheries (the famous 'tragedy of the commons' argument advanced by Hardin), to pollute, to expose workers to toxic hazards and consumers to environmental degradation under conditions of market failure. It then becomes the task of the state to evolve a regulatory framework that either forces firms to internalize the external costs (generate a more perfect market that factors in all real costs including those attributable to environmental degradation) or to mandate standards that firms (or other entities) must meet with respect to resource management, occupational safety and health, environmental impacts, and the like. It also becomes the task of the state to provide those public goods and public infrastructures conducive to environmentally sound conditions of public health and sanitation. Periodically, as was the case in the progressive era (see Hays

1959) and in the early stages of the New Deal, this leads to the idea of considerable state intervention to ensure the proper conservation and efficient management of national resources, thus challenging the rights of private property in the interest of a state-managed class strategy for capital accumulation. Against this, neoclassical economics has also evolved a defence of private property solutions under the aegis of the so-called Coase (1960) theorem which holds that both the polluter and any injured party can equally be regarded as wrongdoers since the presence of the latter limits the property rights of the former to emit pollutants.

All state interventions, the logical tool of environmental management, are typically limited under the standard view by two important considerations. First, intervention should occur only when there is clear evidence of serious damage through market failure and preferably when that damage can be quantified (e.g. in money terms). This requires strong scientific evidence of connections between, for example, exposure to asbestos in the workplace and cancers developing later or power plant emissions and acidification of lakes hundreds of miles away. And it also requires careful measurement of costs of pollution and resource depletion because the second constraint is that there is thought to be a zero-sum trade-off between economic growth (capital accumulation) and environmental quality. To be overly solicitous with respect to the latter is to forgo unnecessarily the benefits of the former. This is the domain of monetized cost-benefit analysis which now plays such an important role in shaping environmental politics under the standard view.

Getting to the heart of what the trade-offs might be (theoretically and empirically) requires a particular combination of engineering and economic expertise coupled with scientific understandings of ecological processes. The translation of the environmental problem into the domain of expert discourses permits the internalization of environmental politics and regulatory activity largely within the embrace of the state apparatus or, more loosely, under the influence of corporate and state finance of research and development. This entails an application of bureaucratic–technocratic rationality under the dual influence of the state and corporations. The rough and tumble of democratic politics is generally viewed as getting in the way of proper, rational, and sensible regulatory activities. The preferred strategy, except in those periods of euphoric state strategizing, is to negotiate out solutions between the state and the private sector often on an ad hoc and case-by-case basis.

Under the standard view, the basic rights of private property and of profit maximization are not fundamentally challenged. Concerns for environmental justice (if they exist at all) are kept strictly subservient to concerns for economic efficiency, continuous growth, and capital accumulation. The view that capital accumulation (economic growth) is fundamental to human development is never challenged. The right of humanity to engage in extensive environmental modifications is tacitly accepted as sacrosanct (turning the standard view into a doctrine complicit with the hubristic version of the domination of nature thesis). The only serious question is how best to manage the environment for capital accumulation, economic efficiency, and growth. From this standpoint, negative externality effects (including those on health and welfare) deserve to be countered (provided no serious barriers are created to further accumulation) and serious attention should be given to proper conservation and wise use of resources. Given the framework, ecological issues within the standard view are generally viewed as a concern of the nation-state, in some instances devolving powers to lower levels of government. National politics and cultural traditions (for example, with respect to the importance of wilderness or the forest) then typically play an important role in affecting the way in which the standard view gets worked out and presented in different nation-states and even in different localities. Put in the prevailing terms of economics, socially based and often locally specific preferences for environmental qualities can be factored into the argument as a particular manifestation of consumer preference.

A powerful and persuasive array of discourses are embedded (sometimes without even knowing it) within this standard view and its associated practices, institutions, beliefs, and powers. Environmental economics, environmental engineering, environmental law, planning and policy analysis, as well as a wide range of scientific endeavours are ranged broadly in support of it. Such discourses are perfectly acceptable to the dominant forms of political–economic power precisely because there is no challenge implied within them to the hegemony of capital accumulation. Financial and logistical support therefore flows from the state and corporations to those promoting such environmental discourses, making them distinctive discourses of power.

This is not to say that there is no contestation within the standard view. There is abundant room for dispute over the scientific evidence of connection between environmental change and social effects, the extent and measure of damage, the designation of liability, where the trade-offs between economic growth and environmental quality (or equity) should lie, how divergent consumer preferences for environmental qualities might be measured and expressed, how far into the long run environmental concerns should be projected (the literature on discount rates and time-preferences is extensive), and how comprehensive state regulation should be. The intensity of debate within this overall discursive frame often precludes general discussion of broader let alone radically different alternatives. But, the debates have sometimes generated contradictions that do prepare the way for discursive shifts into radically different ways of thinking. While, for example, the apparent intent of Summers's memo was to wake up some of his colleagues to a stronger sense of how to negotiate issues of environmental equity and market forces within the standard view, it subsequently became an icon whose shock value could be used to press for an alternative discourse of environmental justice.

The standard view has a considerable history. Beginning with the extensive public health measures in nineteenth-century urban settings and following through to present-day efforts to improve air and water quality in many areas of the advanced capitalist world, the working out of the standard view has not been without a substantial record of successes to its credit. Were this not the case, it would long ago have been abandoned. At its best, even some of its seemingly negative features have a virtuous side; for example, the ad hoc and fragmented approach has sometimes permitted a degree of local and particularist sensitivity to consumer preferences and considerable flexibility in environmental interventions. But there are, plainly, serious limitations to the effectiveness of the standard approach and in recent years some of its more glaring internal contradictions have spawned the search for some alternative way to look at environmental issues.

Ecological Modernization

The thesis of 'ecological modernization' (see Hajer 1995) has periodically emerged as one way to structure thinking about the dialectics of social and ecological change. In the United States it became popular during the progressive era (when the name of Pinchot dominated discussions) and remerged during the 1930s in the soil conservation movement and within institutions like the National Resources Planning Board (Hays 1987). In recent years there are signs of its adoption/co-optation by both environmental pressure groups and certain institutionalized configurations of political–economic power.

Ecological modernization depends upon and promotes a belief that economic activity systematically produces environmental harm (disruptions of 'nature') and that society should therefore adopt a proactive stance with respect to environmental regulation and ecological controls. Prevention is regarded as preferable to cure. This means that the ad hoc, fragmented, and bureaucratic approach to state regulation should be replaced by a far more systematic set of politics, institutional arrangements, and regulatory practices. The future, it is argued, cannot be expected to look after itself and some sorts of calculations are necessary to configure what would be a good strategy for sustainable economic growth and economic development in the long run. The key word in this formulation is 'sustainability'. And even though there are multiple definitions of what this might mean (and all sorts of rhetorical devices deployed by opponents to make the term meaningless or render it harmless since no one can possibly be in favour of 'unsustainability'), the concept nevertheless lies at the heart of the politics of ecological modernization. The rights of future generations and the question of appropriate temporality therefore move to the centre of discussion rather than being assumed away within market forces as typically occurs within the standard view.

This shift in emphasis is justified in a variety of ways. The irreversibility problem, in the standard view, becomes, for example, much more prominent, not only with respect to biodiversity but also with respect to the elimination of whole habitats, permanent resource depletion, desertification, deforestation, and the like. High orders of environmental risk are emphasized coupled with a rising recognition that unintended ecological consequences of human activity can be far-reaching, long lasting, and potentially damaging. U. Beck's (1992) formulation of the idea that we now live in a 'risk society' (largely a consequence of an accelerating pace of seemingly uncontrollable technological change) has proven a useful and influential adjunct to the discursive thrust to define a risk-minimizing politics of ecological modernization. There has also been growing recognition that ad hoc and after-the-fact practices can produce unbalanced and ineffective results.

The role of scientists in promoting the discursive shift from the standard view to ecological modernization was important (see Litfin (1994) and Hajer (1995) for recent case studies). It was science that revealed global problems (acid rain, global warming, and ozone holes) demanding wide-ranging collective action beyond nation-state borders, thereby posing a challenge (legal, institutional, and cultural) to the closed bureaucratic rationality of the nation-state. And some individual scientists pushed the knowledge of ecological systems and interrelatedness to the point where the unintended consequences of human activities could be seen to be far more widespread, irreversible, and potentially serious than had previously been recognized. This made the 'business as usual' and 'after the fact' approach of the standard view appear more and more inadequate. This kind of science provided crucial support to many environmental pressure groups, many of whom initially viewed scientific rationality with scepticism and distrust. The thesis of ecological modernization has now become deeply entrenched within many segments of the environmental movement. The effects, as we shall see, have been somewhat contradictory. On the one hand, ecological modernization provides a common discursive basis for a contested rapprochement between them and dominant forms of political–economic power. But on the other, it presumes a certain kind of rationality that lessens the force of more purely moral arguments (cf. the comments of Louis Gibbs cited above) and exposes much of the environmental movement to the dangers of political co-optation.

The general persuasiveness of the ecological modernization thesis rests, however, on one other radical discursive shift. This refuses to see the supposed trade-off between environmental concerns and economic growth in zero-sum terms. What are known as 'win–win' examples of ecological control are increasingly emphasized. Given the power of money, it is vital to show that ecological modernization can be profitable. Environmental care, it is argued, often contributes to efficiency (through more efficient fuel use, for example) and long-term preservation of the resource base for capital accumulation. If, furthermore, pollution is merely being moved around (from air to water to land) under standard practices, then aggregate efficiency is being impaired in the long run if, as is increasingly the case, there are fewer and fewer empty 'sinks' within which pollutants can costlessly be absorbed. And if, to take the parallel case of supposedly 'natural' resources, depletion is occurring too fast to allow for smooth market adjustment and measured technological change, then costly disruptions to economic growth may be in the wind. To some degree the search for 'win–win' solutions has also been prompted by environmental litigation, environmental impact legislation, and, in some sectors like those directly associated with occupational and consumer safety and health, by extraordinarily high compensation awards for injured parties (as, for example, with the case of asbestos liability that drove firms and some insurers—a group of celebrated 'names' of Lloyds of London—into bankruptcy). The costliness of recent clean-up efforts—the 'superfund' experience in the United States to clean up hazardous waste sites being perhaps the best example—has also pushed many to take a new look at prevention.

Environmental equity (distributive justice) has a stronger role to play in ecological modernization arguments. This is in part due to the inroads made by the environmental justice movement and various other movements around the world expressive of what Martinez-Allier (1990) calls 'the environmentalism of the poor'. But leaving these aside, co-operation is required to gain support for proactive environmental initiatives so that the question of environmental justice has to be integrated into the search for long-term sustainability, partly as a pragmatic adaptation to the internationalism of several key contemporary ecological issues: sovereign nation-states, including those that are poor, have to agree to a certain regulatory environment on, for example, carbon emissions and CFC use, and, furthermore, enforce its provisions. Negotiating with China and India is politically quite different from negotiating the location of a hazardous waste site in Mississippi. So some sort of configuration has to be envisaged in which ecological modernization contributes both to growth and global distributive justice simultaneously. This was a central proposition in the Brundtland Report (WCED 1987) for example. How, and if, that can be done is at the heart of deeply contentious debates. There are also signs of a discursive shift, perhaps fashioned as a response to the contentiousness of the distributive justice issue, in which economic development (improvement in human capacities and conditions) is seen as quite distinctive from economic growth (the increase in output of goods and services). If governments can be persuaded to take the former path then the competitive challenge to the hegemony of the advanced capitalist powers with respect to capital accumulation through economic growth will be lessened.

One side-consequence of these shifts is that environmental management is no longer seen to be the exclusive provenance of governments or the nation-state. The nation-state, while clearly still important, should be supplemented by strong international organizations as well as local governments. The general import of the Rio conference, for example, was to give far greater powers to international organizations (like the World Bank and the United Nations Environmental Programme) and to set up local government mandates for environmental quality. Many layers of government operating at many different scales should be implicated as partners in the search for better paths of environmental management. This move to construct some sort of hierarchy of powers tacitly recognizes the diverse spatial scales at which environmental issues can arise. While very little of this has actually been worked out in practice, a discursive shift away from the nation state towards some sort of recognition of the spatial scalar layering of environmental issues can certainly be detected. A wide range of forces in civil society (NGOs, pressure groups, and community agents) can then become involved. The public debate over 'values' has consequently become much more explicit; preparing the ground for a veritable industry of philosophical reflection devoted to 'environmental ethics'. And much more open and democratic as well as wide-ranging discussions of environmental issues become possible. It is precisely at this interface that the fine line between incorporation and open contestation again and again gets crossed and recrossed, with legal, scientific, and economic discourses, institutions, and practices becoming a deeply implicated and contested terrain.

In portraying the general characteristics of the ecological modernization thesis in this systematic way, I am exaggerating both its coherence and its difference from the standard view. The raggedness of the environmental–ecological debate the last twenty years defies any such simple characterization. But the debate in the public realm has been much more open to ecological modernization arguments than was previously the case. And as often happens with a public discourse in formation, all sorts of interventions and openings have occurred, through which quite a bit of radicalization has been achieved. Some radical environmental groups have been partially drawn to the ecological modernization thesis, sometimes as a tactic because it provides convenient and more generally persuasive public arguments with which to pursue other objectives, but sometimes as a matter of deeper conviction, viewing it as the only way to move a deeply entrenched capitalism towards ecological sanity and a modicum of global justice. And there is some evidence that the nascent European bureaucracy in Brussels saw ecological modernization as a means of empowerment against narrower national and corporate interests. Socialists, for their part, could take to the argument as a way of combining traditional commitments to growth and equity with rational planning under socialized control. Commoner's *Making Peace with the Planet Earth* (1990) and Leff's *Green Production: Toward an Environmental Rationality* (1995) can be read, for example, as left-wing versions of this thesis. I shall come back to this particular line of thinking by way of conclusion.

But the discourse would not have the purchase it evidently has had without a significant tranche of support from the heartland of contemporary political–economic power. The rising tide of affluence in the advanced capitalist countries after World War II increased middle-class interest in environmental qualities and amenities, 'nature' tourism, and deepened concerns about environmental dangers to health. While this lent an indelible bourgeois aesthetic and politics to much of the environmental movement, it nevertheless pushed environmental issues to the political agenda where they could not easily be controlled as a mere adjunct of bourgeois fashion. The health connection, as Hays (1987) points out, became particularly salient and peculiarly open-ended in relation to environmental concerns in the United States after 1950 or so. Systematic environmental concern for everything from landscape despoliation, heritage, and wilderness preservation, control of air and water quality, exposure to toxics, waste disposal, regulation of consumer products, and the like became much easier to voice given middle-class acceptance of such issues as fundamental to its own qualities of life. This aspect to the problem has been strongly emphasized by U. Beck (1992) who argues that the costs of the contemporary form of a high-environmental risk society are spread across the class spectrum thereby turning the environmental issue into a populist issue (even the bourgeois can get skin cancer and leukaemia). *The Limits to Growth* (Meadows *et al.*) published in 1972, which in many respects was a powerful warning shot to say that the standard view was inadequate, was supported by the Club of Rome (an influential group of bankers and industrialists) and the Brundtland Report (WCED) of 1987, which consolidated the ecological modernization discourse in important ways, bringing the question of 'sustainability' to the fore, was an effort supported by many government officials, industrialists, financiers, and scientists. And since that time, major world institutions, such as the World Bank, which previously paid no attention whatsoever to environmental issues, some corporations (like IBM and even Monsanto), and powerful establishment politicians, like Margaret Thatcher and Al Gore, have been converted to some version of the ecological modernization thesis. Even *The Economist* (3 June 1995: 57) now sees fit to celebrate 'a budding romance between greens and business' in an article entitled 'How to Make Lots of Money, and Save the Planet Too'.

There is a more sinister aspect to this argument, however. The severe recession of 1973–5, the subsequent slow-down in economic growth and rise of widespread structural unemployment made an appeal to some notion of natural limits to growth more attractive. Scapegoating natural limits rather than the internal contradictions of capitalism is a well-tried tactic. When faced with a crisis, said Marx of Ricardo, he 'takes refuge in organic chemistry' (see Harvey 1974). This particular way of thinking puts particular blame on population growth, again and again raising the spectre of Malthus, thereby reducing much of the ecological–environmental problem to a simple population problem. But this essentially reactionary political approach was paralleled in *The Limits to Growth* and the Brundtland Report by concerns for natural limits to capital accumulation (and, hence, for employment possibilities and rising standards of affluence worldwide). The rhetoric of 'sustainable development' could then be attached to the ideal of a growth economy that had to respect natural limits. Demands for higher wages or more rapid economic growth in poorer parts of the world were countered by appeal to certain immutable laws of nature; thus diverting attention from the far more mutable laws of entrenched class and imperialist privilege. The supposed sheer physical inability of the planet to support global populations with aspirations to a living standard of Sweden or Switzerland became an important political argument against even trying to spread the benefits of capitalist growth around.

The evident failures of capitalist modernization and resource management in many developing countries also made the rhetoric of ecological modernization more attractive. In many developing countries this meant a partial return to traditional methods as more ecologically sensitive and hence more efficient. The World Bank, for example, took to blaming the governments of Africa for the failure of its own development projects there and then sought to decentralize the process of development to see if indigenous methods led by indigenous peoples, with women cast in a much more central role, could work so as to pay off the accumulating debts built up precisely through World Bank-imposed western-style development.

Finally, many corporations, like IBM, saw a great deal of profit to be had from superior environmental technologies and stricter global environmental regulation. For the advanced capitalist nations, struggling to remain competitive, the imposition of strong environmental regulations demanding high-tech solutions promised not only a competitive advantage to their own industries but also a strong export market for the more environmentally friendly technology they had developed (the environmental clean-up in eastern Europe has proved particularly lucrative). If only a small fragment of corporate capital thought this way, it was nevertheless a significant dissident voice arguing for ecological modernization from within a powerful segment of the bourgeoisie. Global environmental management 'for the good of the planet' and to maintain 'the health' of planet earth could also be conveniently used to make claims on behalf of major governments and corporations for their exclusive and technologically advanced management of all the world's resources. So while a good deal of corporate capture of the ecological modernization rhetoric (particularly via 'green consumerism') could be found, there are also positive reasons for some segments of corporate capital to align themselves with a movement that emphasized certain kinds of technological change coupled with highly centralized global environmental management practices. The clean-up industry alone now has a value of some $200 billion within the OECD and, being heavily dependent upon proper regulation, forms a significant pressure group for regulatory action and ecological modernization (*The Economist*, 3 June 1995: 57).

As a discourse, ecological modernization internalizes conflict. It has a radical populist edge, paying serious attention to environmental–ecological issues and most particularly to the accumulation of scientific evidence of environmental impacts on human populations, without challenging the capitalist economic system head on. It does imply strict regulation of private property rights, however, and in so far as it leads to action it can *de facto*, through regulatory action, curb the possibilities for uncontrolled capital accumulation. Yet it is also a discourse that can rather too easily be corrupted into yet another discursive representation of dominant forms of economic power. It can be appropriated by multinational corporations to legitimize a global grab to manage all of the world's resources. Indeed, it is not impossible to imagine a world in which big industry (certain segments), big governments (including the World Bank), and establishment, high-tech big science can get to dominate the world even more than they currently do in the name of 'sustainability', ecological modernization, and appropriate global management of the supposedly fragile health of planet earth. This is precisely the shift that Sachs (1993: p. xv) fears:

As governments, business and international agencies raise the banner of global ecology, environmentalism changes its face. In part, ecology—understood as the philosophy of a social movement—is about to transform itself from a knowledge of opposition to a knowledge of domination. . . . In the process, environmentalism . . . becomes sanitized of its radical content and reshaped as expert neutral knowledge, until it can be wedded to the dominating worldview.

Class forces resolutely opposed to such a reshaping can be found at both ends of the political spectrum. Let us look first at the reaction of the libertarian right.

'Wise Use' and the Defence of Private Property

Ecological modernization is anathema to certain segments of capital (including important segments of the traditional petit bourgeoisie). There is a strong desire to smother it (together with anything other than the minimalist version of the standard view) in many quarters. While some corporations are favourably disposed towards it, most are not. By far the most powerful opposition derives from its impacts upon the rights of private property (particularly owners of raw materials and 'natural' resources). The whole idea of ecological modernization, and the planned government-led or collective interventions it presupposes, is anathema to the libertarian wing of conservative politics. And through the 'wise use' movement, particularly focused in the US west, it has found a libertarian equivalent of the environmental justice movement with which to attack not only ecological modernization but anything except minimalist appeal to the standard view.

The 'wise use' movement draws in fact on a long tradition of environmental activism—though, as we shall see, of a very special sort. The appropriation of the term 'wise use' is not merely an opportunistic rhetorical device with which to counter any form of governmental intervention or reg-ulation. The tradition has its origins in classical liberal theories, particularly those generally attributed to Locke, and their translation into political–economic practices most particularly in the United States with its tradition of Jeffersonian democracy. The argument is in part based on the inalienable right of individuals to mix their labour with the land in such a way as to 'make the earth fruitful and to multiply'. But it is also strongly based on the view that private property owners have every incentive in the world to main-tain and sustain the ecological conditions of productivity that furnish them with a living and that, left to their own devices, they will more likely pass on the land to their offspring in an improved rather than deteriorated con-dition. Arthur Young, an influential commentator on agricultural affairs in late eighteenth-century England, put it this way: 'on an annual rental a man will turn a garden into a desert: but give a man a fourteen year lease and he will turn a desert into a garden.'

This was, of course, exactly the sentiment that led William Lloyd to propose 'the tragedy of the common' thesis in 1833. And some commenta-tors on Hardin's (1968) influential restatement of that idea have treated it as a plea for private property arrangements as the best protection against those abuses of the commons which governments by their very nature are powerless to prevent. Even if Hardin does not himself follow that line of reasoning, it has not been hard for legal scholars and for theoreticians to argue that the taking away of private property rights without full compen-sation for environmental reasons is unjustified and that the wisest and best organizational form for ensuring proper use of the land is a highly decen-tralized property-owning democracy. Von Hayek, Nozick, and a whole host of contemporary economists and legal scholars (such as Epstein 1985) would agree.

The 'wise use' movement in the United States has its roots in a long tradition of opposition to the powers of the federal government to regulate private property. The so-called 'sage-brush rebellion' of western cattle-ranching interests against federal control over extensive tracts of land in the US west was just one incident in that history. It appeals to popular common sense and makes effective use of powerful anecdotes of personal injustice on the part of individuals caught in the regulatory thickets of government action. In treating the rights of private property as sacrosanct (and the spread of 'privatization' and 'deregulation' as social goods), the 'wise use' doc-trine gathers many powerful adherents from the corporate sector which, when coupled with a populist base, makes for a potent political force (see Echeverria and Eby 1995). It became dominant in the congress of the United States with the Republican victory of 1994, for example, though there is abundant evidence that it was gathering momentum in the courts as well as within various levels of government in the United States from Reagan's election in 1979 onwards.

The 'wise use' movement has two other arguments which it adds to its strong defence of private property against governmental constraints. The first is that the right to jobs (and hence economic development and capital accumulation) must take precedence over the 'rights of nature' (however the latter may be construed, if at all). The 'wise use' movement thrives on zero-sum arguments of the sort that pitted the fate of the spotted owl in the US north-west against employment opportunities in logging. And the second is that universal land-use rules necessarily do an injustice to local and private determination. Even the most sophisticated science allied with big government cannot come up with regulations sufficiently sensitive to cover all contingencies in all particulars.

Private property owners are judged in principle much more knowledgeable about their own particulars than state bureaucrats and scientists. In all of these respects, the 'wise use' movement has some strong arguments on its side. Keith Schneider (Echeverria and Eby 1995: 351), an environmental journalist of some repute, considers it as 'maybe one of the most important and interesting movements to arise in environmentalism in a long time' precisely because of its ability to question much of the environmental orthodoxy that has arisen in recent years. So although the movement has been powerfully co-opted and funded by corporate, industrial, and, perhaps most important of all, by commercial logging, ranching, and agribusiness interests, it has sufficient of a democratic and populist edge to deserve serious consideration.

The case against the 'wise use' movements is strong if not fatal to its pretensions. Even presuming that private property owners are paragons of bourgeois virtue and that they stay in place long enough to become deeply familiar with their local ecological conditions of production (a presumption that hardly applies to most land developers, resource extractors, and speculators), there is no ground to believe in principle that each owner is more knowledgeable than the collective. There is even less ground for believing that the territorial purview of the private owner bears any relationship whatsoever to the spatio-temporal scale of ecological processes varying from the microcosm of the field through regional questions concerning land use, amenities, resource allocations, water and air qualities, to global questions of biodiversity, climate warming, and the like. Since the pattern of property ownership is ecologically chaotic and socially lop-sided, there are absolutely no grounds for believing that appeal to its commonsensical wisdoms can allow for any wisdom at all with respect to environmental justice let alone ecologically sustainable development even in its most naked capitalistic form.

Environmental Justice and the Defence of the Poor

The environmental justice movement advances a discourse radically at odds with the standard view and ecological modernization. It is also profoundly at odds with the 'wise use' movement though for quite different reasons. Of all the discourses considered here, it has proven far less amenable to corporate or governmental co-optation. Five issues stand out:

1. Inequalities in protection against environmental hazards have been felt in very tangible ways in enough instances, such as Love Canal, to make compensation for and elimination of such inequalities a pressing material (largely health) issue for many. Putting the inequalities at the top of the environmental agenda directly challenges the dominant discourses (be they of the standard, ecological modernization, or 'wise use' variety).

2. 'Expert' and 'professional' discourses have frequently been mobilized by dominant forms of political-economic power to either deny, question, or diminish what were either known or strongly felt to be serious health effects deriving from unequal exposure. The resultant climate of suspicion towards expert and professional discourses (and the form of rationality they frequently espouse) underlies the search for an alternative rationality (even, if necessary, 'irrationality') with which to approach environmental hazards. While science, medicine, economics, and the law may remain important ingredients within the discourse of environmental justice, they are not therefore ever permitted to frame the arguments in toto. In this regard there is a similarity of sorts between the 'wise use' and the environmental justice movements.

3. The adoption of biocentric discourses that focus on the fate of 'nature' rather than of humans on the part of many environmental groups (albeit modified by incorporation of theses of ecological modernization) has prompted its own reaction. As D. Taylor (1992) notes:

The more established environmental organizations do fight issues of survival, and they use the survival theme to get the support of their members, but these are survival issues as they pertain to endangered species, national parks and preserves, threatened landscapes. . . . These survival debates are not linked to rural and urban poverty and quality of life issues. If it is discovered that birds have lost their nesting sites, then environmentalists go to great expense and lengths to erect nesting boxes and find alternative breeding sites for them; when whales are stranded, enormous sums are spent to provide them food and shelter, when forests are threatened large numbers of people are mobilized to prevent damage; but we have yet to see an environmental group champion the cause of homelessness in humans or joblessness as issues on which it will spend vast resources. It is a strange paradox that a movement which exhorts the harmonious coexistence of people and nature, and worries about the continued survival of nature (particularly loss of habitat problems), somehow forgets about the survival of humans (especially those who have lost their 'habitats' and 'food sources'). The environmental justice movement therefore puts the survival of people in general, and of the poor and marginalized in particular, at the centre of its concerns.

4. The marginalized, disempowered, and racially marked positions of many of those most affected, together with the strong involvement of women as dominant carers for the children who have suffered most from, for example, the consequences of lead-paint poisoning or leukaemia, have forced otherwise disempowered individuals to seek empowerment outside of prevailing institutions. The coupling of the search for empowerment and personal self-respect on the one hand with environmentalist goals on the other means that the movement for environmental justice twins ecological with social justice goals in quite unique ways. In so doing, the movement opens itself to distinctive positionalities from which injustice can differentially be measured. As Krauss (1994: 270) observes:

Women's protests have different beginning places, and their analyses of environmental justice are mediated by issues of class and race. For white blue-collar women, the critique of the corporate state and the realization of a more genuine democracy are central to a vision of environmental justice. . . . For women of colour, it is the link between race and environment, rather than between class and environment, that characterizes definitions of environmental justice. African American women's narratives strongly link environmental justice to other social justice concerns, such as jobs, housing, and crime. Environmental justice comes to mean the need to resolve the broad social inequities of race. For Native American women, environmental justice is bound up with the sovereignty of the indigenous peoples.

Such different positionalities create, as we shall see, interpretative tensions within the environmental justice movement across the themes of class, race, gender, and national identity. Bullard (1993: 21) summarizes evidence to show, for example, that people of colour are much more vulnerable to environmental hazards even when controlling for social status and class and concludes that the injustice is fundamentally a race and not a class problem.

5. Doing battle with the lack of self-respect that comes from 'being associated with trash' lends a very emotive symbolic angle to the discourse and highlights the racial and discriminatory aspects of the problem. This

ultimately pushes discussion far beyond the scientific evidence on, for example, health effects, cost-benefit schedules, or 'Parts per billion' to the thorny, volatile, and morally charged terrain of symbolic violence, 'cultural imperialism', and personalized revolt against the association of 'pollution' (in its symbolic sense of defilement and degradation) with dangerous social disorder and supposed racial impurities of certain groups in the population.

These conditions of production of an environmental justice movement in the United States account for some of its central features. To begin with, the focus on particular kinds of pollution—toxics and dangerous contaminants—loads the discussion towards symbolic questions, making clear that the issue is as much about 'claims and counter-claims to status' (cf. Douglas 1984: 3), as it is about pollution *per se*. This is what gives the movement so much of its moral force and capacity for moral outrage. But the corollary, as Szasz (1994) points out, is that the movement relies heavily upon symbolic politics and powerful media icons of pollution incidents. Toxics in someone's basement at Love Canal in Buffalo, New York, is a much more powerful issue from this perspective, even though it involves a very small number of people, than the diffuse cloud of ozone concentrations in major cities that affects millions every summer throughout much of the United States. In the case of Love Canal, there was an identifiable enemy (a negligent corporation), a direct and unmistakable effect (nasty liquids in the basement, sick children, and worried suburban mothers), a clear threat to public trust in government (the Board of Education was clearly negligent), a legal capacity to demand personal compensation, an undefinable fear of the unknown, and an excellent opportunity for dramatization that the media could and did use with relish. In the case of ozone concentration, the enemy is everyone who drives, governments have very little mandate to intervene in people's driving habits, the effects are diffuse, demands for compensation hard to mount, and the capacity for dramatization limited making for very little media coverage. The resultant bias in choice of targets permits critics to charge that the emphases of the environmental justice movement are misplaced, that its politics are based on an iconography and politics of fear, and that the movement has more to do with moral outrage than the science of impacts. Such criticisms—which are frequently made of Greenpeace as well—are often justifiable by certain standards (such as those espoused by mainstream environmentalists), but precisely for that reason are largely beside the point.

The refusal to cast discussion in monetary terms, to take another example, reflects an intuitive or experiential understanding of how it is that seemingly fair market exchange always leads to the least privileged falling under the disciplinary sway of the more privileged and that costs are always visited on those who have to bow to money discipline while benefits always go to those who enjoy the personal authority conferred by wealth. There is an acute recognition within the environmental justice movement that the game is lost for the poor and marginalized as soon as any problem is cast in terms of the asymmetry of money exchange (and particularly in terms of cost-benefit analysis). Money is always a form of social power and an instrument of discipline in social relations rather than a neutral universal equivalent with which to calculate 'welfare-enhancing benefits'.

This active denial of the neutrality of the monetary calculus perhaps accounts for the somewhat medieval tone of the declaration on environmental justice adopted at the 1991 conference (though, of course, cast in terms of contemporary technologies and possibilities). The affirmation of 'the sacredness of Mother Earth, ecological unity and the interdependence of all species, and the right to be free from ecological destruction' parallels in interesting ways Gurevich's (1985: 274) characterization of medieval justice as:

at one and the same time a moral and a cosmic principle, to which an human activity must be subordinated. Any departure from this principle is equivalent to transgression of the divine order of things and of natural law . . . social justice [is] that by which the harmony of the whole is sustained, and which denies none their due desserts.

I do not present this parallel in order to undermine, but rather to suggest that the principles of environmental justice, though cast in a mould somewhat unfamiliar to many of us, would be familiar to those upon whom what Benton (1993) calls 'the liberal illusion' has yet to do its insidious work. This illusion takes the following form:

In societies governed by deep inequalities of political power, economic wealth, social standing and cultural accomplishment the promise of equal rights is delusory with the consequence that for the majority, rights are merely abstract, formal entitlements with little or no de facto purchase on the realities of social life. In so far as social life is regulated by these abstract principles and in so far as the promise is mistaken for its fulfilment, then the discourse of rights and justice is an ideology, a form of mystification which has a causal role in binding individuals to the very conditions of dependence and impoverishment from which it purports to offer emancipation.

The environmental justice movement has, by and large, seen through this illusory state of affairs. But this means that it also has to do battle with the liberal illusion and its pervasive effects as well as with direct forms of ecological harm. In so doing, some have indeed been led into backward-looking praise for the medieval world (a mythical golden age of integration with nature when human societies trod so lightly on the earth that all was well between humans and nature) and sidewards looking admiration for those marginalized peoples who have not yet been fully brought within the global political economy of technologically advanced and bureaucratically rationalized capitalism.

The affirmation of the 'sacredness of Mother Earth' and other rhetoric of that sort is, I want to suggest, both problematic and empowering. It is empowering precisely because it permits issues to be judged in terms of moral absolutes, of good and evil, right and wrong. By posing matters in terms of the defilement, violation, or even 'rape' of a sacred Mother Earth, the environmental justice movement adopts a non-negotiable position of intense moral rectitude untouchable by legal, scientific, or other rationalistic discourses. It permits the assertion, in quasi-religious language, of the widespread view that the proper approach is to ask, in Lois Gibbs's world, 'what is morally correct?' rather than 'what is legally, scientifically, and pragmatically possible?'

It also permits, through the medium of social protest, the articulation of ideas about a moral economy of collective provision and collective responsibility as opposed to a set of distributive relations within the political economy of profit. While the 'moral economy' being proposed is definitely not that of the traditional peasant, the very grounding of the discourse in a language of sacredness and moral absolutes creates a certain homology between, say, struggles over exposure to environmental hazards in urban areas, nativist beliefs on the relation to nature, and peasant movements throughout the developing world such as that of the Chipko (cf. Guha 1993: 100) or the Amazon rubber-tappers. It is therefore not surprising to find that 'the fundamental right to political, economic, cultural and environmental self-determination of all peoples' is asserted as one of the principles of environmental justice.

It is precisely through this discursive strategy that links can then be found between the environmental justice movement as shaped within the specific conditions of the United States, and the broader movement that Martinez-Allier (1990) refers to as 'the environmentalism of the poor'. These movements fundamentally concern either the defence of livelihoods and of communal access to 'natural' resources threatened by commodification, state take-overs, and private property arrangements, or more dynamic movements (both *in situ* and migratory) arising as a response to ecological scarcities, threats to survival and destruction of longstanding ways of life (see Ghai and Vivian, 1995; Sachs, 1993). But, as with the environmental justice movement, the symbolic dimension, the struggle for empowerment, for recognition and respect, and above all for emancipation from the oppressions of material want and domination of others, inevitably has a powerful role to play, making the environmentalism of the poor focus upon survivability in all of its senses.

From this standpoint, it is not hard to understand the fierce critique of 'sustainable development' and 'ecological modernization' (in its corrupted form) launched by Sachs in this volume as well as elsewhere (1993):

The eco-cratic view likes universalist ecological rules, just as the developmentalist liked universalist economic rules. Both pass over the rights of local communities to be in charge of their resources and to build a meaningful society. The conservation of nature (should be) intimately related to rights of communal ownership, traditional ways of knowing, cultural autonomy, religious rituals, and freedom from state-centred development.

Doctrines of cultural autonomy and dispersion, of tradition and difference, nevertheless carry with them a more universal message which permits a loose alliance of forces around alternative strategies of development (or even, in some instances, growth) that focus as much upon diversity and geographical difference as upon the necessary homogeneities of global market integrations. What seems to be at work here is the conversion of ideals learned through intense ecologically-based militant particularism into some universal principles of environmental justice. The environmental justice movement, like other 'militant particularist' movements:

has tried to connect particular struggles to a general struggle in one quite special way. It has set out, as a movement, to make real what is at first sight the extraordinary claim that the defence and advancement of certain particular interests, properly brought together, are in fact the general interest.   (Williams 1989: 115)

This connection is nowhere more apparent than in the shift from 'Not-in-my-back-yard' politics to 'Not-in-Anyone's-Back Yard' principles in the United States:

Environmental philosophy and decision making has often failed to address the justice question of who gets help and who does not; who can afford help and who cannot; . . . why industry poisons some communities and not others; why some contaminated communities get cleaned up but others do not; and why some communities are protected and others are not protected . . . The grassroots environmental justice movement . . . seeks to strip away ideological blinders that overlook racism and class exploitation in environmental decision making. From this critical vantagepoint, the solution to unequal environmental protection is seen to lie in the struggle for justice for all Americans. No community, rich or poor, black or white, should be allowed to become an ecological "sacrifice zone." Saying "NO" to the continued poisoning of our communities of colour is the first step in this struggle. Yet our long-range vision must also include institutionalizing sustainable and just environmental practices that meet human needs without sacrificing the land's ecological integrity. If we are to succeed, we must be visionary as well as militant. Our very future depends on it.   (Bullard 1993: 206)

This is not, however, the only leap that the environmental justice movement is prepared to make. The environment itself gets redefined to include 'the totality of life conditions in our communities—air and water, safe jobs for all at decent wages, housing, education, health care, humane prisons, equity, justice' (Southern Organizing Committee for Economic and Social justice, 1992; cited in Szasz 1994: 151). And this leads straight back to the connection between environmental and social justice.

Principles of Justice and Environments of Difference

A comparison of environmental discourses and principles of social justice, suggests a crude set of pairings. Utilitarian theories of justice are strongly associated with the standard view. The intermingling of both such discourses in the advanced capitalist societies is fairly evident making this by far the most prevalent and hegemonic mode of thinking for regulating institutional behaviours, political action and material practices. Ecological modernization, particularly in terms of its concerns for the rights of future generations, seems more compatible with some sort of social contract view and I think it is significant that several attempts to adapt the Rawlsian version of the social contract have emerged in recent years (see Wenz 1988; de-Shalit 1995). 'Wise use' doctrine appeals directly to libertarian views and draws much of its strength precisely from that association. The environmental justice movement, by contrast, frequently invokes egalitarian principles (sometimes individualistic but more frequently communitarian) in its demands for a more equitable distribution of environmental advantages and burdens.

Each of these broadly anthropocentric theoretical positions, interestingly, has its biocentric analogue. The libertarian view, for example, produces strong doctrines of animal rights when extended onto the terrain of rights accorded to all 'subjects of a life' (Regan 1983). The utilitarian view can be extended to accord rights to as many species as possible in terms of their ability to flourish and to multiply. Radical egalitarianism across all species and habitats characterizes the deep ecology movement while the contractarian view suggests a strong appreciation for rights of the less well-off (endangered species) as well as a conservative approach to habitat transformation (justified only if it is to the benefit of the least advantaged species).

It is on this sort of terrain that we now find an essentially irresolvable debate on the proper form of environmental ethics unfolding. And the arguments can be bitter: for example, concern for whole ecosystems and habitats as against the rights of individual organisms is tantamount to fascism in Regan's view (cited in Benton 1993: 3). We are then left with a case of determining which is the most socially just theory of social justice. A case of lead paint poisoning in Baltimore City, for example, is not a conflict between just and unjust solutions but between different conceptions of justice. Libertarian views put the rights of private property owners (and their contractual position *vis à vis* consumers of housing services) at a premium and what happens between the parties is a private matter. Utilitarians would treat the problem as a public health nuisance that ought to be cleaned up insofar as it imposes intolerable burdens (while leaving open the Achilles' heel that the greatest happiness of the greatest number might be consistent with inflicting damage on a minority, particularly when the cost of doing otherwise is burdensome for the majority). Contractarians of a Rawlsian persuasion would take it more as a question of an inequality of exposure that benefits no one, and most certainly not the least privileged. If none of us knew (and Rawls presumes a 'veil of ignorance' as essential to the derivation of his theory) what our location or position in life might be (i.e. whether or not we would be in a lead paint environment) all parties would presumably choose to eliminate the hazard altogether. Egalitarians would treat differential exposure to lead paint hazards as an affront to their principles. But the egalitarian principle is not so helpful when it comes to allocating the cost of remediation. Should the poor pay for the clean up of their own rather dirty environments on an equal footing with the rich who live in cleanier circumstances? Nonfunded federal mandates with respect to clean water and sewage treatment in the United States, for example, will impose enormous financial burdens on older cities where the less affluent live, making this an intractable problem for environmental justice if the raw equality principle is adhered to rigorously.

These are all valid theoretical positions. Each can be subjected to philosophical critique. Benton (1993) thus provides a deep and trenchant analysis of animal rights and social justice theories, de-Shalit (1995) subjects the contractarian theory to a sympathetic critique and Wenz (1988) examines the whole spectrum of possible theories of environmental justice only to decide that 'each theory failed when taken by itself'. We are therefore confronted with a plurality of theories of justice, all equally plausible and all equally lacking in one way or other. We are, Wenz notes, 'attracted to using one theory in one kind of situation and a different theory in a different kind of situation' and in a conflict, such as that surrounding lead paint poisoning, different groups will resort to different concepts of justice to bolster their position (the property owners use the libertarian rhetoric and the defenders of children typically use a contractarian rhetoric). Wenz's answer to this situation is to abandon the search for coherency among moral judgements and for a singular theory applicable to all environmental questions. Instead, he proposes a much more flexible pluralistic theory, which combines principles from many separate theories applicable to a diversity of environmental issues arising at different scales. The difficulty with such a solution is evident: why one particular blend of principles rather than another? And what is to prevent the vaunted flexibility of some pluralistic discourse on environmental justice being perverted by acts of power to the material advantage of the already elite and powerful? Trade in toxics, as Summers argued, can indeed be welfare-enhancing for all, given certain suppositions about how to theorize just outcomes from trade. Class struggle is then over exactly which principles of justice shall prevail.

So while philosophers can operate as sophisticated underlabourers, clearing away much of the underbrush that clutters the way to defining more pristine principles of environmental justice, there is no way to define a philosophical and discursive answer to intense questions of social relations, power, beliefs and institutions in relation to environmental practices. 'Between equal rights, force decides,' Marx argued. And so it is with the diversity of currencies to measure that most ancient of all coin, that of social justice. It is therefore vital to move from 'a predisposition to regard social justice as a matter of eternal justice and morality, to regard it as something contingent upon the social processes operating in society as a whole'. The practice of the environmental justice movement has its origins in the inequalities of power and the way those inequalities have distinctive environmental consequences for the marginalized and the impoverished, for those who may be freely denigrated as 'others' or as 'people out of place'. The principles of justice it enunciates are embedded in a particular experiential world and environmental objectives are coupled with a struggle for recognition, respect, and empowerment.

But as a movement embedded in multiple 'militant particularisms', it has to find a way to cross that problematic divide between action that is deeply embedded in *place*, in local experience, power conditions and social relations to a much more general movement. And like the working-class movement, it has proven, in Williams's (1989: 115) words, 'always insufficiently aware of the quite systematic obstacles which stood in the way'. The move from tangible solidarities felt as patterns of social bonding in affective and knowable communities to a more abstract set of conceptions with universal meaning involves a move from one level of abstraction—attached to place—to quite different levels of abstraction capable of reaching across a space in which communities could not be known in the same unmediated ways. Furthermore, principles developed out of the experience of Love Canal or the fight in Warren County do not necessary travel to places where environmental and social conditions are radically different. And in that move from the particular to the general something was bound to be lost. In comes, Williams notes, 'the politics of negation, the politics of differentiation, the politics of abstract analysis. And these, whether we liked them or not, were now necessary even to understand what was happening'. And in the case of the environmental justice movement the constant search for media attention and an iconography of events around which to build a symbolic politics carries its own negative freight.

But it is exactly here that some of the empowering rhetoric of environmental justice itself becomes a liability. Appealing to 'the sacredness of Mother Earth', for example, does not help arbitrate complex conflicts over how to organize material production and distribution in a world grown dependent upon sophisticated market interrelations and commodity production through capital accumulation. The demand to cease the production of all toxins, hazardous wastes, and radioactive materials, if taken literally, would prove disastrous to the public health and well-being of large segments of the population, including the poor. And the right to be free of ecological destruction is posed so strongly as a negative right that it appears to preclude the positive right to transform the earth in ways conducive to the well-being of the poor, the marginalized, and the oppressed. To be sure, the environmental justice movement does incorporate positive rights particularly with respect to the rights of all people to 'political, cultural and environmental self-determination' but at this point the internal contradictions within the movement become blatant.

At this conjuncture, therefore, all of those militant particularist movements around the world that loosely come together under the umbrella of environmental justice and the environmentalism of the poor are faced with a critical choice. They can either ignore the contradiction, remain within the confines of their own particularist militancies—fighting an incinerator here, a toxic waste dump there, a World Bank dam project somewhere else, and commercial logging in yet another place—or they can treat the contradictions as a fecund nexus to create a more transcendent and universal politics. If they take the latter path, they have to find a discourse of universality and generality that unites the emancipatory quest for social justice with a strong recognition that social justice is impossible without environmental justice (and vice versa). But any such discourse has to transcend the narrow solidarities and particular affinities shaped in particular places—the preferred milieu of most grass-roots environmental activism—and adopt a politics of abstraction capable of reaching out across space, across the multiple environmental and social conditions that constitute the geography of difference in a contemporary world that capitalism has intensely shaped to its own purposes. And it has to do this without abandoning its militant particularist base.

The abstractions cannot rest solely upon a moral politics dedicated to protecting the sanctity of Mother Earth. It has to deal in the material and institutional issues of how to organize production and distribution in general, how to confront the realities of global power politics and how to displace the hegemonic powers of capitalism not simply with dispersed, autonomous, localized, and essentially communitarian solutions (apologists for which can be found on both right and left ends of the political spectrum), but with a rather more complex politics that recognizes how environmental and social justice must be sought by a rational ordering of activities at different scales. The reinsertion of the idea of 'rational ordering' indicates that such a movement will have no option, as it broadens out from its militant particularist base, but to reclaim for itself a non-coopted and non-perverted version of the theses of ecological modernization. On the one hand that means embracing and subsuming the highly geographically differentiated desire for cultural autonomy and dispersion, for the proliferation of tradition and difference within a more global politics, but on the other hand making the quest for environmental and social justice central rather than peripheral concerns.

For that to happen, the environmental justice movement has to radicalize the ecological modernization discourse itself. And that requires confronting the fundamental underlying processes (and their associated power structures, social relations, institutional configurations, discourses, and belief systems) that generate environmental and social injustices. Here, I revert to another key moment in the argument advanced in *Social Justice and the City* (Harvey 1973: 136–7): it is vital, when encountering a serious problem, not merely to try to solve the problem in itself but to confront and transform the processes that gave rise to the problem in the first place. Then, as now, the fundamental problem is that of unrelenting capital accumulation and the extraordinary asymmetries of money and political power that are embedded in that process. Alternative modes of production, consumption, and distribution as well as alternative modes of environmental transformation have to be explored if the discursive spaces of the environmental justice movement and the theses of ecological modernization are to be conjoined in a programme of radical political action. There are signs of such a transition occurring. Here, for example, is a recent argument from the Citizen's Clearing House for Hazardous Waste's journal *Everyone's Backyard*:

Environmental justice is a people-oriented way of addressing "environmentalism" that adds a vital social, economic and political element . . . the new Grassroots Environmental Justice Movement seeks common ground with low-income and minority communities, with organized workers, with churches and with all others who stand for freedom and equality . . . When we fight for environmental justice we fight for our homes and families and struggle to end economic, social and political domination by the strong and greedy. (cited in Szasz 1994: 153)

And Szasz (1994) concludes his thorough history of the movement as follows:

Movements take on greater historical significance when they move from the particular to the universal, when they expand out from their specific issues of origin and embrace a more global social change agenda. They take on greater historical significance when they not only mobilize participants to fight for their own interests but also provide a broader radicalizing experience . . . The hazardous wastes movement is making explicit gestures in this direction. It increasingly defines its environmental mission in terms of a larger critique of society; it makes common cause with other movements and says that, ultimately, they are all joined in the same struggle. It even envisions a future in which grass-roots environmentalism spearheads the reconstitution of a broad social justice movement.

Those of us who are still somewhat enamoured of rather traditional foundational values of socialism will, I think, say 'amen' to that. But there is a long and arduous road to travel to take the environmental justice movement beyond the phase of rhetorical flourishes, media successes, and symbolic politics, into a world of strong coherent political organizing and practical revolutionary action.

9

Images of Place in Green Politics: The Cultural Mirror of Indigenous Traditions

DOUGLAS TORGERSON

Greens want to defend nature, but what is *nature*? There is no green consensus on exactly how to understand and value nature, but there is a common focus on the rich complexities and astonishing interdependencies of the natural world. Nature is emphatically not something that can be—or should be—simplified and mastered through conceptual abstractions. At a minimum, greens hold that human activities need to take account of ecological complexity in order not to destroy humanity's niche in the ecosphere. At the same time, the green perspective throws into question the dichotomy between humanity and nature. Greens portray humans as fully natural beings, thereby promoting a re-evaluation of the entire human/nature relationship.

Resisting the instrumentalist and reductionist features of modern culture, greens champion the idea that ecological sensibility is needed to understand and defend nature. While the green perspective directly challenges the dichotomy between humanity and nature, the outlook often neglects the importance of cultural context. Greens at least need to be aware of such a cultural tension.

This neglect may not be immediately obvious, but it becomes clear once we look beyond general notions of nature and recognize that green political action commonly takes the form of defending *place*. The idea of place draws attention to a diversity of cultural meanings, particularly when one considers the distinctive images of place that animate indigenous cultures. From a modern, Eurocentric perspective these images provide a mirror that makes the importance of cultural context unmistakable.

The need for cultural sensibility arises most clearly in struggles where greens become allied with indigenous peoples in defence of place. However, the need is not just one of being sensitive in the interpretation of other cultures. Being reflective and sensitive is important also in the interpretation of one's own culture. This is especially the case for greens because green politics is inescapably a form of cultural politics.

Already evident in the promotion of ecological sensibility, the cultural character of green politics can also be seen in the green celebration of the potential for participatory politics. Green politics challenges technocratic institutions and policy processes, anticipating the possibility of informed public participation in open discourse. The challenge is to dominant oligarchical and bureaucratic forces that thrive on secrecy, deception, closed policy institutions, and a thin veneer of rationality. Green inclinations thus coincide with hopes for enhanced public discourse (see Dryzek 1997; Torgerson 1997, 1999; Dobson 1995; Eckersley 1988; Spretnak and Capra 1986).

Greens want consistency between means and ends, and they do not appear to recognize any potential inconsistency in defending place through political action. In practical terms, there certainly seems no choice but to engage in active political struggle. This essay is, indeed, written in sympathy with such struggle and with the potential for enhancing democratic citizenship. However, focusing on cultural complexities makes it obvious that the defence of place is not the same as the value of place. Looking to an indigenous context suggests that the two can be quite sharply at odds. Greens at least need to be aware of such a political tension.

While challenging much of Eurocentric modernity, greens also remain part of the cultural context that they challenge. To demonstrate the importance of cultural sensibility in green politics, this essay focuses on a context where cultural issues simply cannot be ignored—the defence against continuing Euro-Canadian intrusions into lands claimed by indigenous peoples. This focus draws attention to important problems that arise in alliances between the green movement and First Nations. At the same time, however, the focus also shows how cultural sensibility is needed in assessing the relationship between means and ends in green politics.

Ecological Sensibility: From Nature to Place

Ecological sensibility contains an aesthetic dimension and, at the same time, a moral position tending to displace the human centre of ethical concern in favour of the ecosphere. The shift away from human-centered concern to ecocentrism has not gained complete green assent, but ecocentrism has become a key influence on the way greens understand and value nature, to the extent of now being something of a 'litmus test' for greenness (B. P. Taylor 1991: 576).

The meaning of ecocentrism also remains a matter of contention. It can mean viewing human beings strictly as members of an ecological community (Leopold 1968). It can also mean recognizing the intrinsic value of non-human entities, or even expanding one's self beyond conventionally constricted bounds to develop a sense of identity with non-human nature (W. Fox 1990). There is also a distinct tendency for ecocentrism to leap from the particular to the universal. As Carolyn Merchant has insightfully suggested, ecocentrism anticipates an all-encompassing concern with 'the cosmos' (1992: 74).

A consequence of the ecocentric aim to displace the traditionally human centre of ethical concern is that the significance of human culture tends to be neglected. This is by no means to say that culture is altogether ignored. Rather, the focus on culture is inconsistent. The cultural dimension of understanding, valuing, and defending nature does not receive the attention necessary to promote cultural sensibility.

By John Rodman's sophisticated account, ecological sensibility is both aesthetic and moral. The natural world contains valuable 'structures and potentialities' which we can discern 'if we will but look' (1983: 89). Ecological sensibility gives rise to an impulse of resistance against an industrializing juggernaut that threatens diversity. While Rodman is especially insightful on the human/nature interchange and clearly speaks on behalf of cultural diversity, he ultimately leaves us, in a manner reminiscent of Thoreau, with an image of the individual human self standing in defence of nature (1977: 118). The cultural dimension of understanding, valuing, and defending nature—even though sometimes acknowledged—is at key points neglected (see Torgerson 1999: ch. 6).

Similarly, Christopher Manes is unsympathetic to Georg Lukács's famous statement that 'nature is a societal category' (Manes 1992: 339; Lukács 1971: 234; cf. Leiss 1974: 23). Manes is concerned that this idea simply reinforces the silencing of nature. He wants us to listen to nature, to its 'buzzing, howling, gurgling'. He thus shies away from cultural context. But he also clearly invokes it: 'Nature', he says, 'is silent in our culture . . .' Indeed, he relies not only upon the lessons of ecology but also upon shamanistic notions of an animal language—voiced especially by birds—that contains the secrets of the natural world. Leaving aside the perplexities of constructivism and objectivism (cf. Bernstein 1985), Manes's account of the voices of nature is inconsistent to the extent it assumes a nature in itself, observable apart from cultural mediation. Indeed, it was precisely such an idea of nature in general which allowed for the conception of an essentially homogeneous nature that, existing in itself apart from mind and spirit (*Geist, esprit*), becomes an object of domination.

The modern project of controlling nature through the agency of a rational subject rising above and away from it was vividly portrayed some years ago by the distinguished literary theorist Northrop Frye (1970: 224):

Civilization in Canada, as elsewhere, has advanced geometrically across the country, throwing down the long parallel lines of the railways, dividing up the farm lines into chessboards of square-mile sections and concession-line roads. There is little adaptation to nature: in both architecture and arrangement, Canadian cities and villages express rather an arrogant abstraction, the conquest of nature by an intelligence that does not love it.

The rationalized discourse of modernity, assuming its potential mastery of all things by calculation, systematically neglects or denies claims to irreducible difference, uniqueness, incommensurability. There is a prevalent image of the environment as uniform, 'indifferent space' that can be reduced to discrete units, each being commensurable and interchangeable, subject to rational comprehension and control as well as market exchange (Bachelard 1969: p. xxxii; Leiss 1974: 132, 118; Gowdy and Olsen 1994).

In *The Poetics of Space*, Gaston Bachelard anticipated a distinction between space and place, indicating an aesthetic dimension in the defence of place. He maintained (1969: p. xxxii) that 'space that has been seized upon by the imagination cannot remain indifferent space subject to the measures and estimates of the surveyor.' In contrast to 'indifferent space', there is 'eulogized space': it possesses 'human value', it 'has been lived in'—not neutrally—'but with all the partiality of the imagination'; it is space 'that may be defended against adverse forces, the space that we love'. This special space, in another word, is *place*.

Bachelard's focus on the aesthetics of place, however, only begins to suggest what is involved in the defence of place. Resistance in the name of defending place is not just a matter of aesthetics and, certainly, not just a matter of individual imagination and personal feeling. What is primarily involved in a defence of place is an effort to protect the culturally achieved meaningfulness of a particular way of life.

Green political practice is, indeed, often animated less by a concern with an all-encompassing whole than by a desire to defend particular valued places. Green politics, as Ronnie D. Lipschutz has argued, is characteristically grounded in the value of place (1996: 220): 'while there may be many rivers and creeks all over Europe and the United States, and groups dedicated to restoration of creeks and rivers in many of those places, one does not find these organizations dedicating themselves to some universalized creek or river.' Drawing significantly on the work of David Harvey (1989), Lipschutz indeed explicitly emphasizes that the 'identities constructed around environmentalism and Ecology are linked to specific places, rather than more abstract "space" . . .' (1996: 218). In practice, the ecological sensibility of the green movement is not only concerned with nature in general, but is also attuned to a defence of place.

Cultural Sensibility: The Defence of Place

How is place to be defended? In a context where prevailing power relations, closed policy deliberations, and narrowly constricted discourse are amenable to the advance of industrialization, the clear answer would appear to be more politics. The need for a cultural politics in defence of place seems obvious and inescapable. There seems nothing to lose and much to gain by speaking out, by giving voice to the value of a threatened place and provoking public debate about the desirability of industrialist initiatives. All this seems so obvious, in fact, that it is easy to miss something paradoxical.

Valuing place and defending it are clearly different, and they do not necessarily go together. This point clearly raises questions about means and ends in green politics, but it may take a considerable wrench of the imagination to recognize the paradox from the context of western culture.

The paradox can become quite evident and perplexing, however, when industrial projects face not only green resistance in defence of place, but also a diversity of First Nations, indigenous peoples who were there first and lay claim to threatened land as *their place*. A troubling aspect of the paradox is captured in the questions posed by Canadian anthropologist Hugh Brody in his book *Maps and Dreams* (1981: 97–8):

In a colonial situation, the colonized may find that any challenge or resistance to the new order is acutely difficult. In a culture where the wisest and most competent members regard outspokenness and adamance as foolhardy, childish, and profoundly self-defeating, how can a way of life protect itself, when its protection requires outspoken and adamant protest? . . . Can persons who have become dependent upon intruders, while keeping their real selves hidden from prying and moralistic eyes, come out into the open and demand that the invasion go no further? The answers to such questions are anything but simple.

The defence of place, even as it resists domination, can thus become part of a larger, subtle process of further colonization or assimilation.

Especially in the context of settler societies such as Canada, green politics is inescapably connected with issues and alliances involving indigenous peoples. Here green politics is removed from the cultural milieu that the European tradition of enlightened, radical politics could take for granted.

There appears to be some significant common ground between the green movement and aboriginal peoples. Certainly traditional aboriginal cultures are profoundly at odds with the concept of nature that guides modern civilization. For greens who oppose this concept and seek to promote an ecological sensibility, aboriginal cultures often seem to offer images and understandings—indeed a spiritual dimension—rich in the potential to guide and inspire (e.g. Callicott 1982).

Even an enthusiastic appreciation for aboriginal cultures, however, often continues to betray an Enlightenment propensity to ignore and obscure what really makes different cultures different. The Enlightenment, it is often pointed out, has much to answer for. This point extends beyond the dominant forces of modern civilization and includes all efforts inspired by the Enlightenment to 'change the world'. In green political thought (e.g. Dobson 1995) and related efforts to promote a democratic politics of radical social transformation (e.g. Carroll 1992), there is of course little left of Engels's contempt for 'primitive nonsense' (1890: 482) or of Marx's exaltation of 'man' as 'the sovereign of nature' (1853: 493). If anything, there is outrage at the way modern civilization has blatantly colonized and oppressed aboriginal peoples and their cultures, coupled with a respectful interest in learning.

Still, there has been an implicit tendency to reinforce a logic of assimilation. The case of a famous speech by Chief Seattle may serve as a cautionary tale: 'Every part of this earth is sacred to my people,' the current version of the speech reads. 'Every shining pine needle, every sandy shore, every mist in the dark wood, every clearing and humming insect is holy in the memory of my people.' Carolyn Merchant (1992: 122) quotes the speech and notes that its words have been 'repeated in hundreds of books, articles, classrooms and student papers' and 'represent an inspiration to return to a sane, respectful way of living within nature rather than against it'.[1] 'Yet', she continues, 'these words seem not to have been spoken by the great chief after all, but are a third- or fourth-hand version of an oral address delivered by Seattle in 1854, translated on the spot, by an unknown person' and later reconstructed, put into more polished English, and rewritten by white people: 'Many of the words which resonate with modern ecological consciousness are not the original words,' Merchant concludes, 'but contain phrases and flourishes designed to appeal to ecological idealism and the Christian religion.'

There are bigger issues here than deciding which sources should inspire an ecological sensibility. There is also a question of how those coming from a modern cultural world are to communicate with cultures that are radically different in their presuppositions and dispositions. This question is directly relevant to problems that have arisen from green–aboriginal relationships. However, when we move beyond the modern cultural world to focus on difference rather than similarity, we are also able to recognize clearly the paradox of defending place and its implications for means and ends in green politics.

Green Politics and First Nations: A Cultural Alliance?

Green politics in Canada has generally intersected with aboriginal struggles to defend valued places against industrialist incursions that would reduce them to indifferent space. The idea of commonality between environmentalists and aboriginal peoples came to the fore and gained credibility in Canada during the mid-1970s. In Canada modernity directly confronts vital cultural worlds, which not only contradict the presuppositions and values of modern culture, but also often offer significant opposition to industrial expansion.

Because of Canada's British legal tradition and past colonialist practices in the expropriation of land, there remain major unresolved land claims by First Nations peoples. From 1867 (the time of Confederation) the official Canadian policy had been one of wardship and assimilation. Continuing through the 1960s an assimilationist policy was widely taken for granted among government officials and policy-oriented social scientists as reflecting what was both desirable and inevitable. However, resistance to government policy by aboriginal peoples intensified in the late 1960s, as they pressed for a resolution of land claims, frequently maintaining a case for unextinguished title to resource-rich areas (see Doerr 1974; Kariya 1993). The value of aboriginal ways of life was clearly asserted in accounts of how these cultures are inextricably related with the land, with place.

This assertion especially gained visibility in response to industry proposals for petroleum pipelines and related transportation corridors across northern lands traditionally used by aboriginal peoples. In one celebrated case, the assertion of aboriginal interests converged with a rising tide of environmentalism, and the federal cabinet convened a public inquiry under Thomas Berger to investigate the environmental and social impact of the proposed development.

The Berger Inquiry, which subsequently received a good deal of international attention, was significant because it provided a model of a participatory practice to encourage the involvement of the citizenry, particularly aboriginal peoples. This was no accident. Berger took deliberate steps, obviously clashing with government preferences, to ensure that all parties to the inquiry had both access to relevant information and funding adequate to prepare a case.

What especially emerged during the inquiry was an expression of competing images of the land, as succinctly captured in the title of Berger's final report: *Northern Frontier, Northern Homeland*. The industry view was of indifferent space while the aboriginal view was of a loved place, expressed in aesthetic and spiritual terms. Berger—though stopping short of clearly recognizing spiritual significance—nonetheless concluded that for the aboriginal people, the land was 'the permanent source not only of their physical, but also of their psychological well being . . .' (1977: i. 108). The love of the land, coupled with the apparently egalitarian, community character of aboriginal life, resonated well with aspirations by many environmentalists. Indeed, the aboriginal cause could be portrayed as part of a larger struggle aiming for social transformation and radical democracy (Caloren 1978).

Hugh Brody, the anthropologist whose *Maps and Dreams* was quoted earlier, emerged as a significant participant in the Berger Inquiry, particularly in connection with the design and conduct of land use and occupancy studies to bolster aboriginal land claims. Later, he became involved in another study involving the clash between a pipeline proposal and an indigenous culture. His work on this study led to *Maps and Dreams*. This book draws the reader into a world that stands in marked contrast to the realm of open inquiry and discussion that seemed to prevail in the context of Berger: 'The Indians' use of the land, like every other aspect of their way of life, is little known and less understood by outsiders.' To a significant extent, Brody indicates, this is no doubt because outsiders are not really interested; but he also draws attention to 'the Indians' own inclination to remain hidden', a tendency he suggests is partly rooted in cultural heritage and is partly a response to cultural invasion (1981: 146).

Maps and Dreams is significant in giving pause to reconsider the impressions projected by the Berger Inquiry, or at least to question whether these impressions are reliable guides to all cases where environmentalists and aboriginals come together in a common cause. Just as we may recall the cautionary tale of Chief Seattle, so Brody's book presents striking evidence that vague, general references to aboriginal relationships with the land as involving psychological, aesthetic, or even spiritual dimensions may not only be insufficient, but may block understanding by translating everything back into the terms of outsiders. The terms of understanding shared among the aboriginal people in this case, Brody suggests, is of a kind that cannot be brought out into the open and discussed in a forum of public discourse, however fair and democratic. Brody gives the first hint of this when, as he gains greater intimacy with the people, things are revealed to him. He paraphrases one such revelation about 'old-timers', hunters 'famous for their powers and skills', who were 'great dreamers' (1981: 44):

They did not hunt as most people do now. They did not seek uncertainly for the trails of animals whose movements we can only guess at. No, they located their prey in dreams, found their trails, and made dream kills. Then, the next day, or a few days later, whenever it seemed auspicious to do so, they could go out, find the trail, re-encounter the animal, and collect the kill.

Later, there is a visit from officials of the inquiry. Following a formal discussion on the officials' terms, the aboriginal people invite them to view a 'dream map' (Brody 1981: 267):

The dream map was as large as the table top, and had been folded tightly for many years. It was covered with thousands of short, firm, and variously coloured markings . . . Abe Fellow and Aggan Wolf explained. Up here is heaven; this is the trail that must be followed; here is a wrong direction; this is where it would be worst of all to go; and over there are all the animals. They explained that all of this had been discovered in dreams.

Whenever a dream map is shown, a ceremony is to ensue. When it was time for the ceremony, however, the officials had already gone, leaving the people wondering whether anything had been understood.

Ecocentrism as Common Ground? The Case of Clayoquot Sound

Clayoquot Sound is an area of old growth temperate rainforest, located in Canada on the west coast of British Columbia's Vancouver Island. In recent years, clear-cut logging practices, sustainable development inquiries, and acts of mass civil disobedience have made the protection of the area something of an international *cause célèbre*. During the summer of 1993, in particular, opposition to clear-cut logging in the area saw dramatic episodes of civil disobedience and the largest mass arrests in Canadian history.

A green theorist and activist arrested during the civil disobedience campaign has described the 'struggle for Clayoquot' as 'part of a social phenomenon known as radical environmentalism, which signals the limits of technocratic society'. In elaborating this point, Loÿs Maingon (1994: 158, 177) goes on to describe 'radical environmentalism' as a cultural movement that is both 'ecocentric' and 'a social expression of dissent from the anti-democratic implications of technology': 'Radical environmentalism is a will to recover the democratic foundations of our cultural heritage which have been usurped by technocratic pseudo-culture.'

Maingon reports that a distinctive image of the forest emerged as 'a key piece of evidence' for the prosecution during the roughly forty mass trials following the arrests at Clayoquot. Here the prosecution—the Crown—relied upon a map from MacMillan Bloedel, a large forestry company operating in Clayoquot Sound (1994: 159):

It was a forestry map of MacMillan Bloedel's Tree Farm License 44. Simple, passive and apparently harmless, this map was essential to the Crown's case . . . The map represented the industry's and the government's understanding of what Clayoquot Sound is: a timber supply area for which MacMillan Bloedel holds cutting rights to extract the resource.

What the 'the evidentiary map of TFL 44', the company's Tree Farm License, left out, according to Maingon, were 'the cultural geographies of two other social groups': the Nuu-chah-nulth[2]—the First Nations people—and the radical environmentalists (1994: 160): 'The meaning of the watersheds of Clayoquot Sound to these two groups differs radically from the industry's meaning. For these groups, the watersheds represent the numinous power of cultural continuity dependent on the integrity of natural environments.'

The image of place reflected in the evidentiary map—one of indifferent space—surely stands in stark contrast to the images one would expect to inform the actions of either the Nuu-chah-nulth or the radical environmentalists. What is nonetheless striking is the way that what Maingon primarily characterizes as a struggle by radical environmentalists is revealed actually to include *two* 'social groups' and the way, moreover, that the stance of the Nuu-chah-nulth fuses with, even becomes assimilated to, that of radical environmentalism (1994: 165): 'First Nations people and environmentalists oppose the hegemony of technocratic corporate culture by appealing to their own group distinctiveness.'

This tendency is all the more remarkable because the author, who has done extensive work on nature and culture in relation to Western and First Nations cultures, makes it very clear that he 'cannot presume to speak for First Nations'. He nonetheless makes the following claim (1994: 161): 'It is essential that we understand that, for First Nations, the land and the people remain one. First Nations people consider their identity to be inextricably bound to the land.' 'The common ground between First Nations and environmentalists', furthermore (1994: 165), 'lies in the recognition of the earth as a living entity.' For both what is 'central' is 'the ecocentric character of their cultural beliefs' (1994: 177).

The context of Maingon's argument is no doubt significant. As one arrested for an act of civil disobedience, he is concerned to make a case for what he calls 'environmental group rights' (1994: 176). Here a connection with the indigenous traditions of the First Nations becomes crucial (1994: 177):

Given the parallels and precedents created by the legitimacy of First Nations' claims regarding right relation to the land, the aspirations of environmentalists ought to be approached *sui generis*. The *sui generis* aspect of the claim arises from the distinct relationship that environmentalists have with the land.

Here Maingon's reference is to the point, established in Canadian jurisprudence, that—as stated by Justice J. Lambert—'aboriginal title is *sui generis* . . . in a class or category of its own': 'The solution to further problems in relation to aboriginal title should be sought in a deeper understanding of the nature of aboriginal title itself, in aboriginal terms . . .' (Maingon 1994: 162).

The environmentalist opposition to industrial logging did often involve an ecocentric recognition of the ancient forests as being intrinsically valuable (see Friends of Clayoquot Sound 1989; Langer 1994; C. Young 1994).[3] But the understanding of aboriginal culture is not much enhanced by speaking of it as sharing an 'ecocentric character' with radical environmentalism. Although ecocentrism ventures beyond the cultural framework of modernity, it nonetheless proceeds from that framework. Ecocentrism is, as we have seen, a contested concept, and it draws influences from a diverse, rather eclectic, array of philosophical, religious, and cultural sources; but the key point of departure remains the modern science of ecology (see Dobson 1995: 5 ff.; Dryzek 1995; Merchant 1992: 74 ff.; W. Fox 1990; Rodman 1983; Lovelock 1979; Worster 1992; Leopold 1970). What Maingon overlooks is the ambivalence of ecocentrism: it has the potential both to challenge modern culture and to recast indigenous cultures in its terms.

Maingon's contention that there is an ecocentric common ground between environmental and aboriginal cultures begins with a focus on common opposition to a corporate map incorporating the shared perspectives of industry and government. The stark opposition portrayed here is one of an oppressive power structure meeting two forces of cultural resistance aligned against it. This power structure is shown as being destructive of the natural world and of the twin cultures that seek to dwell in harmony with it. Consequently, there is plausibility in the idea that there is something profoundly alike in the ways that these two sources of cultural resistance approach nature. However, this notion neglects the unique images of place arising from indigenous traditions.

Conspicuously absent from the summer 1993 acts of mass civil disobedience in Clayoquot Sound was organized participation or formal support by the First Nations (Burney 1996: 128 n. 27; cf. Blomley 1996). When he visited Clayoquot on behalf of the Environmental Defence Fund in 1993, Robert F. Kennedy, Jr. apparently solicited this support without success (Anderson 1993) and later spoke of the efforts of 'environmentalists and First Nations . . . to reconcile their respective visions . . .' (Kennedy 1994: p. vii).

The Nuu-chah-nulth had strongly aligned themselves with environmentalists in the early 1980s, particularly in the key move to block logging on Meares Island. But a partial victory in that case, won in court in 1985, concerned unresolved aboriginal land claims (Darling n.d.: 7). The Nuu-chah-nulth had also expressed quite a distinct view of the forest: it was their property. As Chief Moses Martin put it in the context of the Meares Island conflict (quoted in Burney 1996: 67–8), 'We object to any logging until our land claims are settled and until then we are your landlords.' While the environmentalist focus turned to the potential and problems of 'sustainable development' as a key concept in policy deliberations, the First Nations gave much more attention to reclaiming their land (C. Young 1994: 24; Burney 1996: 79).

Like the environmentalists, the Nuu-chah-nulth voiced opposition to the British Columbia government's attempt to impose a Clayoquot Sound logging decision in 1993. However, their focus was on the failure of the government to recognize their land claims and to engage with them on a government-to-government basis (Burney 1996: 108–9). Later that year, the provincial government announced that it was finally willing to extend recognition to Nuu-chah-nulth representatives and to enter into negotiations with them (Ingram 1994: 15). The result was an agreement whereby the Nuu-chah-nulth gained the status of participants in decisions on forest management, pending a resolution of land claims.

This came only a few months after hundreds of environmentalists had been arrested, tried, fined, and jailed; and it is no exaggeration to say that there was a sense of disappointment among many environmentalists, even a view that the First Nations had in effect largely abandoned the cause of environmental protection. Little of this was expressed openly. Environmentalists 'decided for the most part to keep their mouths shut', because they wanted to avoid 'telling First Nations people what is good for them' (Hatch

1994: 202). But there was nonetheless a concern that an agreement supposedly designed 'to grant native peoples a voice in the destiny of their own
lands' had in fact 'functioned as a way to buy more time while the area continues to be logged' (Ingram 1994: 22).

The shock experienced by some environmentalists over the independent
direction taken by the Nuu-chah-nulth may suggest that environmentalists
and aboriginals were, in fact, operating with quite different images of the
forest—and that what the forest means from aboriginal perspectives cannot
simply be subsumed under the notion of ecocentrism. Indeed, since the ear-
liest contact, Europeans had noted that the tribal peoples of the area had a
tenacious sense of property. To interpret this sense of property as being the
same as the European sense of property would, however, surely misconstrue
the nature of property relationships among these First Nations people. The
underlying concept of property is, as we have seen, indeed *sui generis*,
distinctly different.

Property at the time of contact was certainly something quite different
from the kind of property that could be acquired by the 'possessive individual' (Macpherson 1964) who emerged in conjunction with the European
market society and who anticipated the abstract, anonymous actors popu-
lating today's economic models. Property was, rather, part of an ensemble
of relationships constituting a ranked social order with hereditary chiefs
holding positions of prominence. Indeed, the traditional right to property—
'Hahoolthe'—was also the traditional right of chieftainship. The
Nuu-chah-nulth offered an explanation of the meaning of this concept in
a 1990 pamphlet on the 'Land Question' (Nuu-chah-nulth Tribal Council
1990: 3–4):

Our 'title' has existed continuously since before occupation by non-Indian society.
'Title' to Nuu-chah-nulth territories and resources is the property of our Hereditary
Chiefs and relates to more than just the land, sea, and their respective resources.
In our language, this title is called 'Hahoolthe,' the rights of chieftainship, which
would translate more into "ancestral title" and also includes ownership of songs,
dances and a full range of rights and responsibilities . . . Hahoolthe is passed from
generation to generation through our potlatch or feasting system; a system which
is very much alive today.

The 1990 Nuu-chah-nulth document on the 'Land Question' refers to a
concern not just with 'real estate', but with 'a total way of life', involving
'the authority of our chiefs' and 'spirituality' (1990: 11). The references to
spirituality remain rather general and readily accord with the presuppositions of cultures rooted in the European tradition. However, anthropological accounts of the aboriginal cultures in the area suggest that the terms of

the Nuu-chah-nulth document implicitly allude to quite different notions of spirituality.

Both Hahoolthe and the potlatch ceremonies through which it was transmitted and sustained involved relationships that extended beyond the social context to a wider world comprising both 'natural' and 'spiritual' aspects. As part of his Hahoolthe, a chief—as E. Y. Arima (1983: 69) indicates—'also inherited the knowledge and rituals for managing the supernatural realm'.

The traditional concept of property, that is, pertained to a 'general conception of the universe as a pantheon of spirits, great and small' (Arima 1983: 146). Arima emphasizes that the apparently natural creatures in this world were part of a spiritual realm, and the creatures the people ate 'were more than food' for them (1983: 19): 'To the West Coast people living creatures were not just what they appeared to be but were also characters in myths, talking and acting like people, each with a certain personality.' In other words, 'the West Coast world was very much one running on spirit power' (Arima 1983: 146).

The tradition of Hahoolthe, upon which Nuu-chah-nulth land claims are based, would appear to involve no vague ecocentrism—or conception of nature simply as a living entity—but a clearly delineated realm of individualized spirits, interacting both with human beings and among themselves, sometimes in a kindly fashion, but also through conflict and a contest for power (Arima 1983: 152).

What does this spiritual dimension of the culture mean? Can it be made consistent with ecocentrism? Can it even inform and enrich an ecological sensibility? Clearly, these questions involve complex matters of interpretation, and there can be no simple or easy answers to them. What, moreover, *did* spiritual practices mean before aboriginal traditions were subjected to systematic colonial assault? What does the spiritual tradition mean today for the surviving aboriginal people? Does it—did it—mean only one thing? Are there differences of interpretation or efforts to employ the practice in different ways? An answer to any of these questions would, of course, require an intimate understanding of the aboriginal cultures and the impact of colonization.

Any attempt to gain such an understanding, however, simply points to further puzzles, which raise questions about how a changing culture can be understood by anyone who is alien to it. A cultural practice is not something that remains static, opening itself in full transparency under the gaze of the objective observer, but is something vital and dynamic: the outward appearance and inner meaning both may shift significantly with a changing context. In the case of the potlatch—once suppressed as a 'heathenish custom' but now revived—there is a world that is simply 'unknown' to white outsiders (La Violette 1961: 39, 97, 146). Contemporary aboriginal culture does not lay itself open for investigation.⁴

It true that the Nuu-chah-nulth have mobilized with considerable effectiveness to defend their place, but it is also obvious that in doing so they have employed an alien idiom of legal rights and property relations (e.g. 'we are your landlords'). They have not advanced their land claims in a way that would overtly clash with the dominant culture. In this context, they have not sought to reveal fully what the places of Clayoquot Sound mean to them. Nor should they necessarily do so. They have long been subjected to the disapproving supervision of rationalistic and moralistic colonizers, and there is little reason for them to have confidence that a full revelation of their images of place would hold much sway in the arguments of a public forum.

More egalitarian power relations, if they were to be achieved, would not necessarily make such revelation more appropriate to a public forum. In recent years, the Nuu-chah-nulth have effectively argued for the importance of their 'traditional ecological knowledge', but it is notable that even here they have not accentuated the spiritual content of their traditional understandings and have, moreover, insisted that some aspects of traditional knowledge must remain secret (R. T. Smith 1997; cf. Freeman 1995).

The case of Clayoquot Sound indicates that much about indigenous images of place remains uncertain and unknown. Enhancing cultural sensibility is no simple matter. Even Maingon, a culturally sensitive observer, still conceptualizes indigenous images of place in a way that tends to assimilate them to the ecocentrism of radical environmentalists like himself. Even a sympathetic and sensitive inquiry into indigenous images of place runs the risk, moreover, of intruding into a world that can be sustained only by being left alone. Cultural understandings, finally, cannot always be put forward in an open and explicit fashion. Often too much tacit context is lost, too much eludes explicit statement, having to be indirectly suggested and inferred to be really understood. Too much of indigenous cultural meanings often seem lost in translation to the presuppositions of the modern cultural world.

Conclusion: Means and Ends in Green Politics

Political projects like to feel confident, to be assured about both their means and ends. Green politics is no exception, and indeed clearly aspires to a unity

of theory and practice. The key idea—largely drawn from the Enlightenment heritage—is that the green movement must have a clear direction and
sense of moral purpose, a coherent strategy and identity, in order to advance
its cause in a determined way (Torgerson 1999: ch. 2). By many accounts,
ecological sensibility appears to fill the bill, at least in the sense of providing
an impetus to determined resistance against the industrialist assault
on nature (e.g. Rodman 1977). A call for cultural sensibility, however,
complicates the situation by introducing greater uncertainty into the relationship between means and ends.

The interests of the green movement do obviously coincide in many
respects with the interests of aboriginal peoples. At a minimum, both have
a significant interest in challenging the forces of industrialism—forces that
are not only economic and governmental, but broadly cultural as well. These
forces typically draw power from a technocratic domain of closed policy
deliberations, conducted through the idiom of conventional policy discourse
and reinforced by industrialist assumptions. In that regard, the promotion of
participatory politics clearly makes sense for environmentalists and aboriginals shut out of the established policy process. Here there is a potential
opportunity for disadvantaged interests and perspectives to be stated in clear,
strong voices.

To accentuate the common cause that tends to ally environmentalists and
aboriginals, however, is also to indicate that green politics cannot elude the
paradox of defending place. This difficulty would be misconstrued if it were
viewed as simply a matter of resolving the practical challenges that greens
face in achieving a good working relationship with aboriginal allies. For the
problem also involves a more subtle cultural level that is to be found apart
from connections between greens and aboriginals.

The very act of defending place is bound to have a cultural effect. For
example, greens have sometimes sought to protect valued places by having
them designated World Heritage Areas (WHA) under the United Nations.
This may seem benign enough, but it should be recognized that designating
and maintaining a WHA requires attention to officially established criteria.
Focusing attention in this way tends to reconstruct the meaning of a place—
i.e. the act changes the place by changing its cultural significance. Thus
it is that greens who have attempted to establish WHAs for ecocentric
reasons have found it necessary to speak instead in terms of human
interests (Hay 1994).

Conventional public discourse tends to exclude whatever cannot be
clearly and explicitly stated, whatever cannot stand up and be counted
in accredited terms. Green images of place, at the very least, do not necessarily seek to come out into the open in order to grab the spotlight, to

engage in political conflict, to speak in the public realm, or to argue about public policy (see Cole 1993). The cultural dimension of green politics thus cannot rely entirely upon disenchanted discourse, but must be nourished and promoted through a wider range of expression and communication.

How can political struggle and open public discourse adequately encourage the kinds of expression needed to sustain ecological sensibility and the values of place?

Iris Marion Young (1996, 1987) has significantly maintained that publicly relevant communication ought to extend beyond conventional modes of public discourse. She explicitly suggests the alternative of 'heterogeneous publics of passion, play and aesthetic interest' so that even 'the practice of such discussion' serves to affirm 'the proper place of passion and play in public'. Young thus indicates the possibility for public discourse to include 'guerilla theatre and costumes' as well as 'chants, music, song, dancing'. All these gestures serve, as she puts it, 'to make political points' (1987: 75; cf. 1996: 129).

Is it even possible to defend place through political struggle? The problem has been suggested at this broader level by Ariel Salleh from an ecofeminist perspective which she directly connects to the struggles of indigenous peoples. Conceiving the key green goal as a non-patriarchal, 'nurturant world,' she draws attention to cultures in which the very word for 'tribe' is the same as the word for 'land' and 'animals' and 'trees of the land'. 'But how', she asks, 'can one "fight" for a nurturant world? Can the voice of those whose daily labour is to nourish and to bond actually be heard as a "political" voice?' (1997: 49, 54).

The paradox of defending place is actually part of a larger paradox of cultural politics. When politicized, culture changes. The deliberate attempt to defend a traditional culture or to create a new ecocentric one thus runs the risk of defeating itself: certain cultural possibilities can wither when politicized. It is entirely conceivable for a defence of place—through its own political and cultural dynamics—to undermine the very culture that gives a place its unique meaning and value.

An image of place, to defend itself, must speak out, must come out into the open, into the forum. However, can such an image survive the public glare? Can it be translated into the appropriate language, be made to speak out properly? While these questions may become particularly pressing in the struggles of indigenous peoples, the difficulty is not only one for the colonized and their traditions. Even if it largely remains invisible, the problem also besets all who inhabit the modern world, including those who promote ecological sensibility. If greens wish to enhance ecological sensibility, they need at the same time to promote a cultural sensibility that values place. This indicates not only a need for effective political action, but also a need to protect and nurture a cultural domain beyond the clash and glare of politics.[5]

10

Partnership Ethics and Cultural Discourse: Women and the Earth Summit

CAROLYN MERCHANT

The women's tent at the 1992 Earth Summit in Rio de Janeiro bustled with activity.[1] Stands of colourful scarves and saris from India, intricately decorated bowls and wooden utensils from the Pacific islands, and woven bags from Africa lined the tent's entryway. Tables of literature on population, women's rights, forest restoration, agriculture, and water purification surrounded the huge central amphitheatre, its rows of chairs occupied by hundreds of brightly dressed women from all over the world. A microcosm of the world's women, their collective problems, achievements, and energy, the tent was christened Planeta Fêmea (the female planet) by the Brazilian Women's Coalition. The Coalition had organized the women's component of the Global Forum, the NGO conference running parallel to the Earth Summit. Tape-recorders, translation headsets, and microphones hummed with the sounds of human voices emanating from the speakers' table in front. The speakers' words, processed into many languages and common understandings, were finally interpreted by those eagerly listening to the reading of the final women's documents arrived at after months of preparatory conferences and two hot, exciting weeks of negotiations in Rio (Darcy de Oliveira and Corral 1992, 1993).

The Earth Summit altered the discourse of environmentalism in significant ways. Sustainability, introduced in the 1987 Brundtland Report—*Our Common Future*—and enacted in the Rio agreements, became a new and accepted code word for development. After Rio, sustainability meant both development as usual and development as environmental and social change. Discourse shifted from promoting the idea of an environmental crisis to a debate on how to implement long-term sustainability. How would the various cultural meanings associated with the term 'sustainable development' be interpreted in North–South negotiations over funding. The debate fostered a new cultural politics of how humanity should live with nature.

How can and should society be restructured to create an enduring relationship with the non-human world?

After Rio, a new democratic praxis began to emerge that encompassed feminism, environmental justice, multicultural concerns, and North–South conflicts. Most important, the new discourse had to be congruent with a new environmental ethic that recognized the global movements for women's welfare and social justice and the global environmental movement for sustainability. A new cultural politics and a new environmental ethic arising out of women's experiences and needs can provide an ethic of sustainability. Many of the goals and gains of feminists are central to that new discourse and ethic. Women's interests and nature's interests intertwine. The goal is a sustainable partnership with the natural world.

Partnership as a word is experiencing a renaissance in the discourse of the business and environmental communities. Successful environmental partnerships, focused on resolving policy conflicts surrounding local issues, are forming among corporations, local communities, government agencies, and environmental organizations. Trees, rivers, endangered species, tribal groups, minority coalitions, and citizen activists may all find representation, along with business, at the negotiating table. The partnership process offers a new approach to collaboration, one in which non-human nature itself can be a partner (Long and Arnold 1994; MIBE 1994 a, b, and c, Beckenstein et al. 1995).

In the new discourse, partnership can refer not only to humans and social processes, but also to natural entities and natural processes. Domestic partners with legal status may include not only married couples, but also stable relationships between men and women, women and women, and men and men. The international Rio environmental conference, the Cairo population conference, and the Beijing women's conference, by building on the idea of partnership, help to liberate cultural politics from the constraints of older contestable modes of development underlying industrial society and the spread of global capitalism. But the term partner can also refer to gnat-catchers, coho salmon, grizzly bears, checkerspot butterflies, and even the unpredictable activities of nature. An ethic of partnership may offer guidelines for moving beyond the rhetoric of environmental conflict and toward a discourse of co-operation.

Rio's Planeta Fêmea, a remarkable event by one of the most diverse groups of women yet assembled on a global scale, put forward the human dimensions of a partnership ethic. The need for a new ethic had been building out of the experiences of women in Third World countries for over a decade through the recognition that women and nature together bore the brunt of malconceived development programmes. Women all over the globe in both the North and the South began to insist that women's issues and environmental issues be addressed in the same context. Allowed to attend development conferences, but not involved in policy formation and planning, women saw vital questions affecting their livelihoods, resources, and security ignored and neglected. Realizing that women's concerns would not be a part of the preparation for the Earth Summit unless they themselves seized the initiative, they drew on their experiences, history, and political skills to place their issues on the agenda. Women's issues became integral to a new global discourse of sustainability. But while women succeeded in many of their aspirations for inclusion in the process and great strides have been taken in the post-Rio and post-Cairo years, concrete results remain difficult to evaluate. Even with some hopeful changes, much remains the same and much work remains to be done.

Planeta Fêmea was the culmination of more than a decade of advancement on the roles of women in environment and development. While women had barely been acknowledged in development programmes in the 1960s, their contributions to agriculture in Third World households gained recognition as part of a Women in Development (WID) approach in the 1970s (Braidotti *et al.* 1994: 78–80, Boserup 1970). The United Nations Decade on Women, which concluded with a 1985 conference in Nairobi, brought women into development through access to education, resources, and grants that would help to eliminate poverty. As development agencies began to incorporate gender analysis into their programmes in the late 1980s, women's concerns were added onto mainstream agency approaches in a shift to Gender and Development (GAD). An explicit environmental strand in development, Women, Environment, and Development (WEDO) gradually emerged from the United Nations Conference on the Human Environment in Stockholm in 1972 and within the subsequent United Nations Environmental Programme (UNEP). After the completion of the 1987 United Nations' report, *Our Common Future*, chaired by Norwegian Prime Minister Gro Harlem Brundtland, and in preparation for the 1992 Earth Summit in Rio de Janeiro, the emphasis changed to sustainable development, or development that meets the needs of the present without compromising those of future generations (Braidotti *et al.* 1994: 86–7; Charlton 1984; Dankelman and Davidson 1988; Sontheimer 1988; Shiva 1989; Ofusu-Amaah 1991; Henshall Momsen 1991; Rodda 1993).

In order to present the needs and policy recommendations of women at the Earth Summit, two back-to-back conferences were held in Miami, Florida in November 1991. Here the discourse of partnership enters the working vocabulary of women positioning themselves to engage in sustainable relationships with the earth. The first conference, the Global

Assembly of Women and the Environment–Partners in Life, presented environmental case studies of the ways in which women throughout the world were managing and conserving resources to achieve sustainability. The second, the World Women's Congress for a Healthy Planet, attended by 1,500 women from 83 countries, presented case studies of the impacts of past development projects on women and the environment to an international tribunal of female judges. Through an outstanding exercise in co-operation and consensus, the conference formulated the Women's Action Agenda 21 (an agenda for the twenty-first century), to be brought to the Earth Summit. A discourse of sustainable partnerships became central to that agenda (Braidotti *et al.* 1994: 90–2; WIPAC 1991).

A prominent plank in the Miami Women's Action Agenda to which a session was devoted at the Earth Summit's Planeta Fêmea conference was the 'Code of Environmental Ethics and Accountability'. The code asserted that 'the women's global environmental model is cooperative rather than competitive, values women's roles, work, and participation, and acknowledges the responsibility that accompanies power and is owed to future generations'. Drawing on the work of women economists, such as Marilyn Waring's *If Women Counted*, it made a number of specific recommendations for economic and ethical accountability, such as including the full value of women's labour, the value of environmental resources and pollution, and the intrinsic value of biodiversity in national accounting systems and international trade (Waring 1988, IPAC 1991). Here the discourse of a sustainable partnership among women, men, and the earth takes form.

The Earth Summit's Planeta Fêmea conference, organized in cooperation with the Women's Environment and Development Organization (WEDO) in New York City, co-chaired by former US Congresswoman Bella Abzug, was attended by representatives from women-and-environment organizations from all over the world. A constant stream of well-known female heads of state and local governments flowed through the women's tent, as ideas were exchanged between grassroots groups and women of state-power. After examining and debating the themes of the Miami Women's Action Agenda 21, the women's tent adopted the 'Global Women's Treaty for NGOs Seeking a Just and Healthy Planet', which was incorporated into the Global Forum's final NGO treaty. Partnership was a key concept in the new agenda. Living with nature is essential to the health of both humanity and that of the blue planet.

At the official Earth Summit in Rio Centro, the second document to emerge from the women's preparatory process was also adopted. 'The Global Action for Women Towards Sustainable and Equitable Development', was included as chapter 24 of UNCED's final document, *Agenda*

21 (the 500-page agenda for the twenty-first century ratified at the Earth Summit). Additionally, women's interests were part of the Rio Declaration—the Earth Summit's 27-point proclamation replacing the intended Earth Charter that was to have enunciated far-reaching ethical principles on human–human and human–environment relations. Item 20 of the Rio Declaration stated that 'women have a vital role in environmental management and development. Their full participation is therefore essential to achieve sustainable development' (cf. Grubb *et al.* 1993: 137).

The women's 'Code of Environmental Ethics and Accountability' exemplifies the first prong of what I have called a partnership ethic of earth-care; the second, as we shall see, is the autonomy of nature itself as partner. A ethic of partnership is formed from women's experiences in the post-Rio/Cairo/Bejing era and from treating nature as a living subject. What are the three most prominent forms of environmental ethics underlying the discourse at the Earth Summit and how does a partnership ethic emerge from that discourse?[2]

Forms of Environmental Ethics

A partnership ethic differs from the three major forms of environmental ethics that currently dominate human–environment relations—egocentric, homocentric, and ecocentric. Each ethic reflects a different discourse stemming from conflicts among underlying modernist institutions. The 1992 Earth Summit in Rio de Janeiro illustrates the underlying assumptions of the three ethical frameworks and their associated discourses. The egocentric ethic is exemplified by GATT (General Agreement on Tariffs and Trade); the homocentric by UNCED and its *Agenda 21* programme; and the ecocentric by many environmental organizations involved in sustainable development. While conflicts arise from the different discourses associated with the institutional arrangements of capitalism, the state, and environmentalism, a new transcendent ethic of partnership may help to resolve them. The concept of partnership arising out of women's social and environmental experiences and nature's inherent worth and activity should include both human–human and human–nature relationships and interactions.

Egocentric Ethics

The Uruguay round of GATT, which began in 1986 and by 1994 was concluded and undergoing ratification, assumes a free market model of world trade and an egocentric ethic. Based on the idea of trickle-down economic benefits, an egocentric ethic is the idea that what is good for the individual, or the corporation acting as an individual, is good for society as a whole. Here a discourse of individual freedom to act in one's own self-interest, rhetoric that lies at the very heart of modernism, promotes human actions in which nature is represented as mere 'raw material'. Nature comprises resources that can be turned into commodities for trade. It consists of free goods from an inexhaustible tap whose wastes go into an inexhaustible sink. Based on the model of a factory, nature is conceptualized as a dead machine, isolated from its environment, whose parts are manipulated for assembly line production. Resource depletion (the tap) and environmental pollution (the sink) are not part of the profit–loss accounts, hence there is no account-ability to or for nature. Because the individual, or individual corporation, is free to profit, there are no ethical restraints on nature's 'free' goods or on free trade. The result is the Hobbesian Good Society, an egocentric ethic, and a discourse rooted in individual gain.

GATT's egocentric ethic eliminates barriers to trade and with it environ-mental and consumer-safety measures, despite the possibility of environ-mental side-agreements. For example, in 1990, the United States, in response to a consumer boycott of tuna caught in drift nets that trapped and killed dolphins, enacted an embargo on Mexican tuna. Mexico protested and a GATT review panel ruled that no country can restrict imports on the basis of methods of production, essentially invalidating a US law protecting dolphins (the Marine Mammal Protection Act) (cf. Greijn 1992). GATT harmonizes environmental and consumer safety standards to the lowest common denominator worldwide. It increases corporate control and decreases local control. Communities and resources are forced to comply with the demands of the global market. This approach essentially removes control from local communities, homelands, and indigenous and tribal peoples over their own resources. In addition, tropical and temperate old-growth forests suffer along with marine mammals and other com-ponents of local ecosystems. GATT further externalizes environmental costs and penalizes sustainable technologies that attempt to internalize costs. Again the discourse of profit maximization legitimates individual and corporate actions to treat nature as a passive backdrop to human achievement. Living with nature is not even an admissible term in the debate.

GATT's egocentric ethic promotes Trans-National Corporations (TNCs) and limits democracy in these industries. The successful completion of GATT's Uruguay Round is the dream of the self-made man, the darling of Reagan–Bush–Thatcher economics, and the ethic of capitalist patriarchy.

The Women's NGO treaty, adopted by the Global Forum, contains an indictment of GATT as a major cause of environmental degradation.[3]

Homocentric Ethics

In contrast to GATT's egocentric ethic, the ethic of UNCED's sustainable development programme is a homocentric ethic. Here new terms of discourse enter the vocabulary of national representatives. A utilitarian ethic based on the precept of the greatest good for the greatest number promotes a discourse whose terms of debate are in potential conflict with those of individualism. Developed by Jeremy Bentham and John Stuart Mill in the nineteenth century, utilitarian ethics became the conservation ethic of Theodore Roosevelt and Gifford Pinchot during the Progressive Era in the early twentieth century with the addition of the phrase 'for the longest time'. The idea of 'the greatest good for the greatest number for the longest time', is a public-interest, social-interest ethic that considers conservation of natural resources to be consistent with the needs and interests of the majority over those of the individual. In Bentham and Mill's formulations it promotes the general good, the greatest happiness for the greatest number, and freedom from pain and suffering. In its purest form, it is the ethic of federal and state agencies, acting free of political forces and private lobbyists on behalf of the people for the common good. The utilitarian calculus of benefits and costs, rather than the bottom line of profits, guides the ethical choices made. In reality, however, the discourse of homocentric ethics is always in conflict with the egocentric discourse of private individuals and lobbyists who promote monopoly-capitalist interests. Conflicts of interest stem from underlying institutions and are expressed in the rhetoric of GATT versus the rhetoric of UNCED.

For the homocentric ethic of UNCED, as for the egocentric ethic of GATT, nature is viewed primarily as a resource for humans and as a source of commodities. But in contrast to GATT, the United Nations is dedicated to promoting the general good of all nations and all peoples in the world community. Its policies reflect the principle of the greatest good for the greatest number. Like the Progressive Era's conservation ethic, UNCED's sustainable development ethic adds the principle of the longest time. Sustainable development is development that fulfills the needs of the present generation without compromising the needs of future generations. This principle brings future generations into the accountibility calculus. The Earth Summit's goal is to promote greater democracy for more people for a longer time by developing and conserving resources sustainably. Yet a cultural politics of social good conflicts with a cultural politics of individual good, expressed through opposing homocentric and egocentric discourses, interests, and ethics.[4]

Ecocentric Ethics

Many (but not all) environmentalists attending the Earth Summit, subscribed to the assumptions of a third ethic—ecocentrism. Here a new discourse of what is good for non-human entities enters the conversation. Developed by ecologist Aldo Leopold, who formulated the land ethic in the 1940s, and elaborated as ecocentric (and biocentric) ethics by environmental philosophers over the past three decades, ecocentrism includes the entire biotic and abiotic world. Leopold's land ethic had expanded the human community to include 'soils, waters, plants, animals, or collectively the land'. 'A thing is right', Leopold said, 'when it tends to preserve the integrity, beauty, and stability of the biotic community. It is wrong when it tends otherwise.' Ecocentrism, as elaborated in the 1970s and 1980s, went a step further to assert that all things have intrinsic worth—value in and of themselves—not just instrumental or utilitarian value. Because biota have evolved over millennia, all organisms have a right to exist and should be preserved for future generations. Biodiversity is necessary not only for utilitarian and humanitarian reasons (for maintaining the present and future health of the entire biosphere, for enhancing the quality of life, and for aesthetic enjoyment), but for its own sake. Ecocentrism expands the good of the human community to embrace and include within it the good of the biotic community. From an ecocentric point of view, accountability must include the rights of all other organisms, as well as humans, to continue to exist (cf. Leopold 1949, Baird Callicott 1989, Holmes Rolston 1986).

Ethical dilemmas occur when real world situations produce conflicts among the three forms of ethics. Acting on the basis of GATT's egocentric ethic, with the goal of maximizing profits through free trade in natural resources, transnational corporations harvest rainforests for timbers and turn cut-over areas into range lands for grazing cattle. Acting on the basis of ecocentric ethics, with the goal of saving rainforests and endangered species, environmentalists engineer debt-for-nature swaps that preserve and value whole ecosystems. Both ethics, however, can negatively affect communities of indigenous peoples by forcing them out of long-inhabited areas onto marginal lands, where they increase their populations to obtain the labour to survive, or migrate to cities where they end up jobless and homeless. In this example, the social-interest ethic of these communities to fulfil their basic needs conflicts with the egocentric ethic of transnational corporations and the ecocentric ethic of nature preservationists. From one point of view nature is victimized at the expense of people, from another people are victimized at the expense of nature (Gilliam 1994).

The three dominant forms of environmental ethics all have conceptual and practical shortcomings. Egocentric ethics are criticized for privileging the few at the expense of the many (narcissistic, cut-throat individualism), homocentric ethics for privileging majorities at the expense of minorities (tyranny of the majority, environmental racism), and ecocentric ethics for privileging the whole at the expense of the individual (holistic fascism) (cf. Regan 1983: 262, Baird Callicott 1994: 53, 1989: 92–4). Egocentric and homocentric ethics are often lumped together as anthropocentrism (by deep ecologists, for example). But this approach masks the role of economics and particularly of capitalism, placing the onus on human hubris and domination rather than the capitalist appropriation of both nature and labour. Moreover, it fails to recognize the positive aspects of the social-justice approach of homocentric ethics. On the other hand, the ecocentric approach of many environmentalists suggests the possibility of incorporating the intrinsic value of nature into an emancipatory green politics (cf. Eckersley 1992).

Partnership Ethics

An alternative that transcends many of these problems is a partnership ethic. A partnership ethic sees the human community *and* the biotic community in a mutual relationship with each other. It states that 'the greatest good for the human and the non-human communities is to be found in their mutual, living interdependence'.

A partnership ethic draws on the principles and advantages of both the homocentric social-interest ethic and the ecocentric environmental ethic, while rejecting the egocentric ethic associated with capitalist exploitation of people and nature. The term partnership avoids gendering nature as a mother or a goddess (sex-typing the planet), avoids endowing either males or females with a special relationship to nature or to each other (essentialism), and admits the anthropogenic, or human-generated (but not anthropocentric, or human-centred) nature of environmental ethics and metaphor. A partnership ethic of earthcare means that both women and men can enter into mutual relationships with each other and the planet independently of gender. It does not hold women responsible for 'cleaning up the mess' made by male-dominated science, technology, and capitalism, or individual men responsible for creating it.

Just as egocentric ethics is grounded in the principle of self-interest, homocentric ethics in the concept of utility, and ecocentric ethics in intrinsic value, so partnership ethics is grounded in the concept of relation. A relation is a mode of connection. This connection may be between people or kin in the same family or community, between men and women, between people, other organisms, and inorganic entities, or between specific places and the rest of the earth. A relation is also a narrative; to relate is to narrate. A narrative connects people to a place, to its history, and to its multi-levelled meanings. It is a story that is recounted and told, in which connections are made, alliances and associations established. A partnership ethic of earthcare is an ethic of the connections between a human and a non-human community. The relationship is situational and contextual within the local community, but the community is also embedded in and connected to the wider earth, especially national and global economies.[5]

A partnership ethic has the following precepts:

1. Equity between the human and non-human communities.
2. Moral consideration for humans and non-human nature.
3. Respect for cultural diversity and biodiversity.
4. Inclusion of women, minorities, and non-human nature in the code of ethical accountability.
5. Ecologically sound management is consistent with the continued health of both the human and non-human communities.

A partnership ethic goes beyond egocentric and homocentric ethics in which the good of the human community wins out over the good of the biotic community (as in egocentric and homocentric ethics). It likewise transcends ecocentric ethics in which the good of the biotic community may take precedence over the good of the human community. In contrast to Leopold's extensionist ethic, in which the community is extended to encompass non-human nature, partnership ethics recognizes both continuities and differences between humans and non-human nature. It admits that humans are dependent on non-human nature and that non-human nature has preceded and will postdate human nature. But also it recognizes that humans now have the power, knowledge, and technology to destroy *life as we know it* today.

For millennia, nature held the upper hand over humans. People were subordinate to nature and fatalistically accepted the hand that nature dealt. Since the seventeenth century, the balance of power has shifted and humans have gained the upper hand over nature. We have an increasing ability to destroy nature as we know it through mechanistic science, technology, capitalism, and the Baconian hubris that the human race should have dominion over the entire universe. In the late twentieth century, however, the environmental crisis and developments in postmodern science and philosophy have called into the question the efficacy of the mechanistic world-view, the idea of Enlightenment progress, and the ethics of unrestrained development as a means of dominating nature.

A partnership ethic calls for a dynamic balance in which both humans and nonhuman nature are equal partners, neither having the upper hand, yet interacting cooperatively with each other. Both humans and nature are active agents. Both the needs of nature to continue to exist and the basic needs of human beings must be considered. As George Perkins Marsh put it in 1864, humanity should 'become a co-worker with nature in the reconstruction of the damaged fabric', by restoring the waters, forests, and bogs 'laid waste by human improvidence or malice'. While thunderstorms, tornados, volcanos, and earthquakes represented nature's power over humanity to rearrange elementary matter, humans equally had the power 'irreparably to derange the combinations of inorganic matter and of organic life, which through the night of aeons she had been proportioning and balancing' (Perkins Marsh 1864: 35, 36).

In the 1970s Herbert Marcuse conceptualized nature as an opposing partner, emphasizing the differences, as well as the continuities that people share with nature. Nature is an ally, not mere organic and inorganic matter—a 'life force in its own right', appearing as 'subject-object'. Nature as subject 'may well be hostile to man, in which case the relation would be one of struggle; but the struggle may also subside and make room for peace, tranquility, fulfillment'. A non-exploitative relation would be a 'surrender, "letting-be," acceptance'. (Marcuse 1972: 65, 69)

Partnership Ethic and Environmental Politics

A partnership ethic draws on both homocentric, social-interest ethics and ecocentric ethics. The human dimension, the idea of a partnership among human groups, is reflected in both the preamble to UNCED's *Agenda 21* of 'a global partnership for sustainable development' and in the opening paragraph of the 'Rio Declaration on Environment and Development' proclaiming that the conference met 'with the goal of establishing a new and equitable global partnership through the creation of new levels of cooperation among states, key sectors of societies, and people'. Article 7 of the Rio Declaration asserts that 'States shall cooperate in a spirit of global partnership to conserve, protect, and restore the health of the the Earth's Ecosystem'. The concept of partnership is also called forth in the title of the Miami 'Global Assembly of Women and the Environment—Partners in Life' (cf.

Grubb 1993: 101, 87). The document from the second Miami conference, the World Women's Congress for a Healthy Planet, exemplifies ways of actually putting the human side of the partnership into practice.

First, as they would apply to the sphere of production, the Women's Action Agenda 21 and its Code of Environmental Ethics and Accountability hold (among other things) that:

- Fulfilment of basic needs takes precedence over profit.
- Depletion and pollution are part of individual and corporate accounts and should be paid by the producer and polluter.
- Resources should be replenished, environments restored, and biodiversity maintained by all industries and businesses, especially transnational corporations.
- Air, water, and soil should be left clean and healthy.
- Corporations, institutions, organizations, states, and nations are accountable to the public.
- Environmental audits and impact assessments must be made for all proposals before funding.

Second, as they would apply to the sphere of reproduction, the Women's Action Agenda 21 and its Code of Environmental Ethics and Accountability hold (among other things) that:

- Voluntary birth control should be managed by women for women. Contraception should be safe and legal.
- Reproductive healthcare and family planning should be available to all women.
- Education, sex education, job education, and old age security should be available to all women.
- Men should participate in childcare.

The women's code of ethics thus exemplifies the human dimension of an active partnership. But a partnership ethic also recognizes nature as subject and actor leading to a new consciousness of and discourse about nature. Living with and communicating with nature as a partner, rather than a passive resource, opens the possibility of a non-dominating, non-hierarchical mode of interaction between humanity and nature. Rather than speaking about nature as a machine to be manipulated, a resource to be exploited, or an object to be studied and transformed, nature becomes a subject. Nature's voice is heard through winds and waves, sounds and smells, and the changing play of shadows on hillsides. As in any partnership, nature will sometimes win out; in other cases, humanity's needs will receive greater consideration. But both will have equal voice and both voices will be heard.

The new postmodern sciences of ecology, chaos, and complexity theory help to make this partnership possible.

Postmodern science reconstructs the relationship between humans and nature. While mechanistic science assumes that nature is divided into parts and that change comes from external forces (a billiard ball model), ecology emphasizes nature as continuous change and process. Chaos theory goes a step further, suggesting that the human ability to predict the outcome of those processes is limited. Disorderly order, the world represented by chaos theory, becomes a component of the partnership ethic (cf. Hayles 1990, 1991; Abraham 1994; Waldrop 1992).

While a certain domain of nature can be represented by linear, deterministic equations, and is therefore predictable (or can be subjected to probabilities, stochastic approximations, and complex systems analysis), a very large domain can be represented only through nonlinear equations that do not admit of solutions. The closed systems and determinism of classical physics described by Isaac Newton and Pierre Simon Laplace gives way to a postclassical physics of open complex systems and chaos theory. These theories suggest that there are limits to the knowable world. This is not the same as saying there is a non-knowable noumenal world behind the phenomena. It says there is a real, material, physical world, but a world that can never be totally known by means of mathematics. It is a world that is primarily chaotic and unpredictable and therefore cannot be totally controlled by science and technology. Science can no longer perform the god-trick—imposing the view of everything from nowhere. It cannot offer the totalizing viewpoint associated with modernism, the Enlightenment, and mechanistic science. The real world is both orderly and disorderly, predictable and unpredictable, controllable and uncontrollable, depending on context and situation.[6]

Chaos theory challenges two basic assumptions of ecology as it developed in the 1960s and 1970s and formed the basis of environmental management: the ideas of the balance of nature and the diversity–stability hypothesis. The historical concept of a balance of nature which humans could disrupt implied that people could repair damaged ecosystems with better practices. The idea that biodiversity led to ecosystem stability meant that species conservation and ecological restoration could improve ecosystem health. Yet chaos theory suggests that natural disturbances and mosaic patches that do not exhibit regular or predictable patterns are the norm rather than the aberration. Moreover, the seemingly stable world that is the object of socially-constructed representations can be destabilized by human social practices (as when pesticides produce mutant insects or antibiotics produce resistant bacteria). Such theories undercut assumptions of stability at the root of

Leopold's land ethic and holism as a foundation for ecocentrism. They reinforce the idea that predictability, while still useful, is more limited than previously assumed and that nature, while a human construct and a representation, is also a real, material, autonomous agent. A postclassical, postmodern science is a science of limited knowledge, of the primacy of process over parts, and of imbedded contexts within complex, open ecological systems.[7]

This disorderly, ordered world of non-human nature must be acknowledged as a free autonomous actor, just as humans are free autonomous agents. But nature limits human freedom to dominate and control it, just as human power limits nature's and other humans' freedom. Science and technology can tell us that an event such as a hurricane, earthquake, flood, or fire is likely to happen in a certain locale, but not when it will happen. Because nature is fundamentally chaotic, it must be respected and related to as an active partner through a partnership ethic.

If we know that an earthquake in Los Angeles is likely in the next 75 years, a utilitarian, homocentric ethic would state that the government ought not to license the construction of a nuclear reactor on the faultline. But a partnership ethic would say that, we, the human community, ought to respect nature's autonomy as an actor by limiting building and leaving open space. If we know there is a possibility of a 100-year flood on the Mississippi River, we respect human needs for navigation and power, but we also respect nature's autonomy by limiting our capacity to dam every tributary that feeds the river and build homes on every flood plain. We leave some rivers wild and free and leave some flood plains as wetlands, while using others to fulfil human needs. If we know that forest fires are likely in the Rockies, we do not build cities along forest edges. We limit the extent of development, leave open spaces, plant fire-resistant vegetation, and use tile rather than shake roofs. If cutting tropical and temperate old-growth forests creates problems for both the global environment and local communities, but we cannot adequately predict the outcome or effects of those changes, we need to conduct partnership negotiations in which non-human nature and the people involved are equally represented.

Each of these difficult, time-consuming ethical and policy decisions will be negotiated by a human community in a particular place, but the outcome will depend on the history of people and nature in the area, the narratives they tell themselves about the land, vital human needs, past and present land-use patterns, the larger global context, and the ability or lack of it to predict nature's events. Each human community is in a changing, evolving relationship with a non-human community that is local, but also connected to

global environmental and human patterns. Each ethical instance is historical, contextual, and situational, but located within a larger environmental
and economic system.

Consensus and negotiation should be attempted as partners speak
together about the short and long-term interests of the interlinked human
and nonhuman communities. Seated at the table, participating in the discourse, are not only representatives of human concerns, but also those of
non-human entities. The meetings will be lengthy and may continue over
many weeks or months. As in any partnership relationship, there will be give
and take as the needs of each party are expressed, heard, and acknowledged.
If the partners identify their own egocentric, homocentric, and ecocentric
ethical assumptions and agree to start anew from a partnership ethic
of mutual obligation and respect, there is hope for consensus. A partnership
ethic does not mean that all dams must be blasted down, electrical production forfeited, and irrigation curtailed for the sake of redwoods or
salmon. It means that the vital needs of humans and the vital needs of trees
and fish along with their mutually-linked terrestrial and aqueous habitats
must both be given equal consideration. Indeed there is no other choice, for
failure means a regression from consensus, into contention, and thence into
litigation.

A partnership ethic offers new approaches to relationships between business and the environment that can transcend the egocentric ethic's emphasis on the domination of nature and the get-ahead individualistic mentality.
Environmental partnerships are 'voluntary collaborations among organizations working toward a common objective'. Partnerships are formed, often
among formerly contesting parties, to solve a specific problem and to
avoid the acrimony and costs of litigation. Furthermore, the co-operative
agreement that emerges from the process is one to which all parties have
agreed and in which they have a stake. Hence the outcome may have the
prospect of lasting longer than one settled through a courtroom battle
(MIBE 1994a: 3).

For example, a manufacturing company in the midwestern United States
is approached by a wildlife conservation organization about creating a
wildlife reserve on 3,200 acres of company-owned grounds. The company
has recently decided not to use the area for a formerly planned expansion.
Employees are enthusiastic about developing the land for jogging, wildlife
viewing, photography, and perhaps limited seasonal fishing and hunting.
Schools and local Audubon societies are eager to have an educational wildlife
viewing area. The business and the conservation organization agree to form
a voluntary partnership and begin to hold regular meetings with the specific
goal of 'protecting, restoring, and enhancing the 3,200 acres as a wildlife

conservation area with recreational facilities'. Seated at the table (located away from each of the partners' home grounds) are not only company representatives, wildlife biologists, planners, and employees who wish to hunt and fish, but also people who speak on behalf of deer and trout.[8] The discourse begins by asking questions:

1. Will the partnership project solve or significantly impact a problem?
2. Are the goals consistent with the company's mission and objectives?
3. Are co-operation and collaboration needed to do the project?
4. Do the partners all have a reason to participate in the partnership?
5. Has the partnership indentified all groups needed for the project to succeed?
6. Will the partnership be voluntary and equitable? (MIBE 1994a: 11–12)

After much discussion, the partners decide that a wildlife area will be established on the 3,200 acre plot for a minimum of twenty years. The company's image will be enhanced within the community; employees will have an area for jogging and hiking; wildlife viewing areas will be set aside. The interests of deer and fish have been heard and, after an intensely passionate discussion, their needs for survival are made compatible with limited hunting and fishing through a well-defined management plan. The conservation group has acquired an addition to a migratory bird flyway, an educational site for school children, a refuge for birdwatchers, and a recreational area for the surrounding community. While it has not set aside the area in perpetuity, it has achieved a green zone in place of potential concrete and pollution and time to become involved in and respond to a longer-term company and community planning-process (MIBE 1994a: 12).

The following are some examples of successful partnership negotiations and how has business participated in them:

• On the Cooper River, near Charleston, SC, the Wildlife Habitat Enhancement Council (WHEC) worked with the Amoco and DuPont Chemical companies to develop wildlife management programmes on company lands. Landholders in the vicinity then developed a 'wildlife corridor' running 10 miles between the two companies (MIBE 1994b: 11).
• In 1989, a group of leading corporations that use CFCs as solvents collaborated with each other and the US Environmental Protection Agency in order to become CFC-free in advance of the time-lines established by regulaton. Several companies have used the new technologies to replace CFC use in plants in developing countries (Long and Arnold 1994: 5).

- In the Columbia River Basin, where salmon runs have declined from 16 million per year in the 1800s to less than two million in the early 1990s, the Northwest Power Planning Council (NPPC) initiated a partnership negotiating group comprising American Indian tribes, environmental groups, corporations, and agencies to plan and implement harvesting reductions, habitat restoration, hatchery projects, water flow changes, and other means of enhancing the salmon's survival (Long and Arnold 1994: 5).
- The East Bay Conservation Corps of the San Francisco Bay Area formed a partnership with public agencies that resulted in funds for developing an environmental ethic in minority and lower income youth through a summer programme employing young people to assist with public land maintenance work. (MIBE 1994b: 32).

In these examples, the partnership process focuses mainly on human–human interactions, but it opens the way for the inclusion of persons representing non-human entities and the chaotic patterns of nature. Partnerships are a new form of co-operative discourse aimed at reaching consensus rather than creating winners and losers. Partnerships can be formed between women and women, men and men, women and men, people and nature, and North and South to solve specific problems and to work toward a socially just, environmentally sustainable world.

The partnership process draws on many of the skills and goals long advocated and practised by women's groups. While not essentialist (i.e. the position that co-operation is an essential trait of being female), partnership discourse is nevertheless rooted in many women's social experiences and attitudes toward problem-solving. But this co-operative discourse does not claim that women have a special knowledge of nature or a special ability to care for nature. Nor is it a case of 'some' women speaking for 'all' women or for 'other' women who are capable of speaking for themselves. Here women and minorities participate in the process. But 'nature', which often speaks in a different voice, is also heard at the table.

In addition to feminist discourse, a partnership ethic draws on social and socialist ecology in making visible the connections between economic systems, people, and the environment in an effort to find new economic forms that fulfil basic needs, provide security, and enhance the quality of life without degrading the local or global environment. Finally, a partnership ethic draws on work in the sciences of chaos and complexity that suggest possibilities for non-dominating relationships between humans and non-human nature.

Implementing a Partnership Ethic

Many difficulties exist in implementing a partnership ethic. The free market economy's growth-oriented ethic that uses both natural and human resources inequitably to create profits presents the greatest challenge. The power of the global capitalist system to remove resources, especially those in Third World countries, without regard to restoration, reuse, or recycling is a major roadblock to reorganizing relations between production and ecology. Even as capitalism continues to undercut the grounds of its own perpetuation by using renewable resources, such as redwoods and fish, faster than the species' or stock's own recruitment, so green capitalism attempts to slow down the decline by submitting to some types of regulation and recycling. Ultimately new economic forms will need to be found that are compatible with sustainability, intergenerational equity, and a partnership ethic (Merchant 1997).

Another source of resistance to a partnership ethic is the property rights movement, which in many ways is a backlash against both environmentalism and ecocentrism. The protection of private property is integral to the growth and profit-maximization approaches of capitalism and egocentrism and to their preservation by government institutions and laws. While individual, community, or common ownership of 'appropriate' amounts of property is not inconsistent with a partnership ethic, determining what is sustainable and hence appropriate to the continuation of human and nonhuman nature is both challenging and important (Merchant 1997).

Still other problems stem from the meaning of the term sustainable development and its relationship to power. Defined by the Brundtland Report as 'development which meets the needs of the present without compromising the ability of future generations to meet their own needs' and as 'meeting the basic needs of all and extending to all the opportunity to satisfy their aspirations for a better life', sustainable development can be used either to mean sustained economic growth or fulfilment of basic needs. Secondly, sustainable development cast as a partnership between North and South obscures existing, uneven power-relationships. The debt burden of Third World countries, imbalances between the G-7 and G-77 nations, the role of militarism, the export of military technology and toxic wastes, and the power of aid organizations such as the World Bank, the IMF (International Monetary Fund), and the economic power vested in TNCs and GATT are all implicated by their egocentric, self-interested ethical and power relationships.

Rather than sustainable development, which reinforces dominant approaches to development, women's environmental groups, and many other NGOs, have substituted the term 'sustainable livelihood.' Sustainable livelihood is a people-oriented approach that emphasizes the fulfilment of basic needs—health, employment, and old-age security, the elimination of poverty, and women's control over their own bodies, methods of contraception, and resources (Braidotti *et al.* 1994, WCED 1987: 43–4).

Another problem for the implementation of partnership ethics may come from relationships among women's groups themselves. For example, some women of the South criticize the consumption-oriented lifestyles of many of those in the North and of elites in the South. At the same time, women of the South point out the burden on poor women stemming from Third World indebtedness to the North; the effects on women's bodies of poor health and nutrition, involuntary sterilization, and 'population control' programmes; and the effects of environmental exposures to pesticides and toxics from cash crop production by TNCs.

From this perspective, the poor woman of the South is in a privileged position to criticize maldevelopment and the many northern environmental groups who blame the environmental crisis on women's reproduction of large numbers of children. Moreover, if a woman's body is her primary environment, the desperate need for food, water, and fuel just to stay alive would seem to preclude the possibility of a partnership with non-human nature. Women of the South focus instead on subsistence, healthcare, and security as the primary needs. The approach of the South is not inconsistent with partnership ethics, however, and a reconciliation of North–South differences might be achieved from other perspectives.[9]

From the perspective of socialist ecofeminism, for example, the key causes of the crisis are the twin impacts of production on ecology and of production on reproduction. Production oriented toward profit-maximization sanctioned by the egocentric ethic undercuts the conditions for its own perpetuation by destroying the environment from which it extracts 'free' resources. Production threatens biological reproduction by driving people onto marginal lands and into urban areas where they produce children as a labour asset to survive, while also threatening social reproduction by creating homelessness, poverty, crime, and political instability. Historically produced colonialism and capitalism in First World/Third World relations results in the expansion of profit-oriented market economies at the expense of basic-needs oriented local/subsistence economies. An analysis of the role of colonial and capitalist forms of production in the larger system of historically generated power relations can illuminate common problems and suggest new strategies for change.

Thus to place the blame for the environmental crisis on the evolution of domination and Western dualism (as do some social ecologists and social ecofeminists) or on anthropocentrism (as do deep ecologists), or on the primacy of power relations and enlightenment rationality (as do some post-modernists) is insufficient. These approaches tend to ignore or downplay the critical role played by capitalism (as well as state socialism). They can be helpful, however, when integrated into an economic analysis of the capital-ist exploitation of people and nature. The emphasis placed by many envi-ronmental groups on 'overpopulation' in the South and 'overconsumption' in the North neglects the crucial role of production that underlies and unites both causes of degradation. Instead, reduction of production for profit and its reorientation towards fulfilment of basic needs and human security would go a long way towards creating sustainable livelihoods and stablizing populations.

A framework based on the dialectical, historical, structural, and systemic relations among the conceptual levels of ecology, production, reproduction, and consciousness can integrate these approaches into a comprehensive analysis and propose strategies for revolutionary transformation. Such strategies would analyse past and present power relations, identify the weak points in the system, and draw on the energy and vision of new social/ecology movements and NGOs to bring about a sustainable world.

If the goals of economic production were reoriented toward the repro-duction of human and non-human life (rather than the reverse as is presently the case), many of the problems that promote exponential population growth, unlimited economic expansion, and environmental degradation would wither away. Such an ecological revolution could realize the goals of the Global Forum's Planta Fêmea by implementing a partnership ethic of earthcare and a movement toward a sustainable world for the new millennium.

As philosopher Max Horkheimer put it, in 1947, when he called for the revolt of nature: 'Once it was the endeavor of art, literature, and philoso-phy to express the meaning of things and of life, to be the voice of all that is dumb, to endow nature with an organ for making known her sufferings, or we might say, to call reality by its rightful name. Today nature's tongue is taken away.' Through a partnership ethic, discourse and reality can merge into sustainability. Nature, along with women and minorities, will speak in a different voice (Horkheimer 1947: 101, 115).

Endnotes

CHAPTER 1: SUSTAINABLE DEVELOPMENT AS CULTURAL
CHALLENGE: ON THE POLITICAL ANATOMY OF AN OXYMORON

1. Susan George (1992) used the boomerang as metaphor for North–South relations.
2. Entry 'underdeveloped' in *The Oxford English Dictionary*, 1989, xviii. 960. Extensive inquiries into the history of the development discourse can be found in Sachs (1992). For the history of the word 'development' see H. W. Arndt (1981).
3. See for instance Rajni Kothari (1993) with the telling title *Growing Amnesia: An Essay on Poverty and Human Consciousness*.
4. For an overview over the international discussion see: McCormick (1989), Harbordt (1991), Moll (1991).
5. World Commission on Environment and Development (1987:8).
6. Examples include Clark and Munn (1986), *Scientific American* (1989), Rambler *et al.* (1989), and, in a different spirit, also Lovelock (1979).

CHAPTER 2: THE NORTH AS / AND THE OTHER:
ECOLOGY, DOMINATION, SOLIDARITY

1. The vision got an early expression in Harry Martinson's poem 'Aniara' (Swedish original published in 1956; Martinson was awarded the Nobel prize for literature in 1958).
2. Indeed, these are on the level of Kantian *a priori* categories, namely, uniform Newtonian space-time and straightforward causality. But as Zizek (1993: 84) pointed out, the Kantian antinomies ultimately lead to the opposite: '[T]here is no way for us to imagine in a consistent way the universe as a Whole; that is, as soon as we do it, we obtain two antinomical, mutually exclusive versions of the universe as a Whole.' The antinomical versions are sense data vs. the thing in itself. Through his Copernican revolution Kant demonstrated that to think anything at all, humans have to ground their thinking on assumptions that are ultimately unfounded.
3. For neo-Malthusian ecologists this question certainly ought to matter. We know that the continents actually do differ from each other because ecological processes on different continents are to a large extent uncoupled from each other (Haila and Levins 1992: 183–8). So, when does it make sense to add up what happens on different continents to a single formula? Does it

make sense to calculate the 'global impact' of kangaroos, or polar bears? If not, why does it make sense to calculate the 'global impact" of the human population, for instance, of pre-Neolithic hunter-gatherers who, according to Ehrlich (1993) used on average 300 watts of energy? The very idea of doing so reveals the underlying zero-sum-game logic. Why should the activities of gathering, hunting, eating, excreting, reproducing, and dying (and, hence, submitting one's body to the affective care of decomposer organisms) as performed by pre-Neolithic humans be any different from the same activities as per-formed by kangaroos or polar bears? The argument is fundamentally obscure.

Although there may be some human effects that in the present day need to be estimated on the global scale, this does not entail that everything humans have ever done is estimable in the same way. As a matter of fact, the very assumption that the estimation of global human effects is reasonable even today, is controversial (P. J. Taylor and Buttel 1992; Wynne 1994). One problem here is that most 'global effects' are due to local activities which occur, in actual fact, in very variable forms across the globe—think of forest destruction—but are 'added up' to the global scale.

4. 'A world doomed to starvation, inequality, oppression and superstition . . . is totally different from a world in which affluence and liberty are at least possible, and within which there is genuine knowledge, independent of any one tradition and independent of them all' (Gellner 1997).

5. In an interview 'A Marxist biologist in the United States', made during a winter night in 1982 in Finnish Lapland and published in *Tiede & edistys* 1983(1) (in Finnish).

6. An earlier and shorter version of this chapter, entitled 'The North as/and the Other', was published in the catalogue of an exhibition 'Strangers in the Arctic', curated by Pori Art Museum in 1996 (shown in Copenhagen and Helsinki-Pori in 1996, and Toronto in 1997). As part of the preparation the curator Marketta Seppälä, our son Teemu, and myself made a trip to Yakutsk together with Jimmie Durham, and to the Ural Mountains together with Jussi Kivi. On an earlier trip to Magadan, Chukotka, and Kolyma in 1992 we were joined by Lauri Anttila, Marianne Heske, and Ian McKeever (Haila and Seppälä 1995). These trips would not have been possible without the help of our friends and hosts Gennadij Germogenov (Institute of Biology, Yakutsk), Aleksej Estafjev (Institute of Biology, Syktyvkar), and D. I. Berman (Institute of Biological Problems of the North, Magadan).

7. Naming as a means of taking into possession was an older habit; the Norse used it, too, in Greenland and 'Vinland'.

8. There certainly was a great variety of attitudes toward strangers or barbarians in the classical world, including also the myth of the 'noble savage' (Lovejoy and Boas 1935). Among the Greek gods the unstable boundary between civilization and wildness was guarded and negotiated by Dionysos and Artemis

(Vernant 1991; Harrison 1992). However, it seems the development of the relation of 'otherness' requires a more stable political community than what was possible in Antiquity. After all, conceptions of the 'other' tell primarily about their beholders.

Let us note, too, that an important historical prerequisite for the evolution of a political community with a collective identity was a shared, codified language. The first grammar in any modern European language, Elio Antonio de Nebrija's *Gramática Castellana*, was published in Spain on 18 August 1492, fifteen days after Columbus had set sail toward the New World (Illich and Sanders 1989).

9. Hence, Polanyi (1944: 113) remarked that Malthus's doctrine was 'a paradigm which is not dependent upon empirical support'.

10. '[F]or Hegel nature as a whole implies mind in the same way in which the bud implies the leaf; nature must first of all be itself, so our conception of it is true and not illusory; but it is only being itself provisionally; it is going to stop being itself and turn into mind, as the bud is only being itself in order to stop being bud and turn into a leaf.' This is the idea of nature as a 'real abstraction' (Collingwood 1945: 130).

11. Again, however, with important variation across nations. Benedict Anderson (1991) hardly mentions 'nature' at all in his account of the origin and spread of nationalism.

12. The 'conquest' of the South Pole offers a perfect analogy (Katz and Kirby 1991).

13. A relevant example in the European tradition is the supplementation in the early modern period of traditional Greek geometry and arithmetics with the algorithmic style of reasoning which was mediated to Europe from India by Arab authors (Hacking 1992).

14. This claim is arguable. Certainly economic forces, commercialization, and increasing dependence on the markets and modern technology have had a tremendously destructive influence on the cultures of northern peoples from early on. However, 'internal colonialism' (Dryzek and Young 1985), for all the havoc it brings about, is less disastrous than purposeful elimination. Besides, another critical aspect is dignity. Jimmy Durham—a Cherokee activist—was impressed by what he experienced as dignified pride among our native hosts in Yakutia.

15. There is some specific evidence to support this conclusion; for instance, John Wiens (1996) concluded that seabird populations damaged by the Exxon Valdez disaster in the northern Pacific recovered remarkably quickly because they are adapted to harsh and fluctuating natural conditions.

16. But then we also have to *unlearn* most of what we have 'learned' on these matters; as Jimmie Durham writes, 'In school I learned of heroic discoveries / Made by liars and crooks. The courage / Of millions of sweet and true people / Was not commemorated' (Durham 1993: 11).

17. The Yakuts are of Turkic origin from Inner Asia. By the time of the Russian

colonization of eastern Siberia they were well established in the lowlands of the Lena and Tungus Rivers (Forsyth 1994).

18. While in Yakutia we made several excursions from the capital by cars. During one of the trips the temperature was $-54°C$ (in early January, 1996). The excursions were made by two vehicles, just in case. A real feeling of safety, however, came from the conviction that if something actually happened, nobody would in these conditions pass by and leave us stranded on the roadside.

CHAPTER 3: NATURE IN SPIRITUAL TRADITIONS: SOCIAL AND CULTURAL IMPLICATIONS FOR ENVIRONMENTAL CHANGE

1. It is noteworthy that the official Agenda 21 for global environmental change bears no mention of religious organizations or spirituality in its goals and strategies for change (Sitarz 1993).
2. Perhaps the most vocal critic has been social ecologist, Murray Bookchin (1994) who advocates a strictly secular ecological theory which has no place for the 'spiritualism' proposed by 'ecomystics', 'ecotheists' and deep ecologists.
3. I am indebted to Don Wolfe of Case Western Reserve University for these words and thoughts on the spiritual dimension of environmental thinking and writing.

CHAPTER 6: MAPPING COMPLEX SOCIAL-NATURAL RELATIONSHIPS: CASES FROM MEXICO AND AFRICA

I acknowledge the collaboration of Ravil Garcia-Barrios, Yryo Haila, Derek Hall and Chris London while developing the ideas in this chapter. Ann Blum, Chuck Dyke, Frank Fischer, Maarten Hajer, and Jesse Ribot also provided valuable comments on drafts.

1. I use the term process in this paper in the sense of sequences of events that persist or are repeated sufficiently long for us to notice them and need to explain them. This contrasts with a sense of process as a basic underlying causal structure that allows people to explain events as instances of the process or as noisy deviations from it.
2. A neologism *intra*secting processes might better convey the processes' inseparability.
3. The combination of differentiation, historical contingency and structuredness distinguishes political ecology from more particularist and sceptical-of-theory approaches that otherwise share many qualities (Vayda 1996).
4. Such discontinuities and transitions often rely on the sense of process that I want to avoid; see n. 2.
5. Heterogeneous constructionism is similar to the 'heterogeneous engineering' of sociologist of science John Law, and to the related approaches of Michel Callon

and Bruno Latour. Heterogeneous constructionism places more emphasis, however, on explanation. See P. J. Taylor (1995) for a discussion of differences.

6. Although some of these resources will be real, material, and perhaps unmodifiable aspects of the world, heterogeneous constructionism is not a realist philosophy of science. The difficulty of modifying science always depends on how such 'natural' resources are linked by people in the making of science to other resources, including 'social' ones. For this reason, heterogeneous constructionism is not philosophical relativism either (P. J. Taylor 1995).

7. For more recent assessments see Berkes *et al.* (1989); McCay and Jentoft (1997).

8. Unattributed page numbers in this section refer to Picardi (1974).

9. See Little (1988) for a historical review of comparable changes in East African pastoralism.

10. In contrast, Little (1985, 1988) describes the differentiation of Il Chamus pastoralists in an area of Kenya whose ecology is similar to the West African Sahel. Having suffered prolonged droughts during the 1970s and into the 1980s, poor herders engaged in risky, but inexpensive, dryland (rainfed) farming in order to survive. Wealthy herders subject to the same drought could afford the labour and capital to engage in irrigated agriculture and thus reduce the need to sell livestock for grain during dry periods. After a drought, the rich herder-agriculturalists could rebuild their herds more rapidly; some of the poor became their hired labourers. The differentiation among pastoralists has been accentuated by rich herders commanding greater influence in land claims when states have initiated privatization of landholdings. Now that there has been an increase in cultivation and wage-earning activities, labour for herding has become a limiting consideration. Rich herders can pay for their herds to be grazed on better land some distance away from settlements, while the poor, who must make use of wage-earning opportunities, graze their herds near their households. As a result, environmental degradation, where apparent, lies close to population concentrations—not, contrary to the tragedy of the commons view of nomadic pastoralism, out on the range.

11. For example, Brokensha *et al.* (1977) point to labour demands rather than range area limiting pastoralists' herd expansion and Little (1985) connects environmental degradation with accumulation and impoverishment.

12. This is amplified by the full analysis of Picardi's modeling that uses nine contrasts (P. J. Taylor 1992).

13. The map-makers, to date, have been drawn from the fields of ecology and natural resources in two workshops of six or seven researchers: (i) ecologists at the University of Helsinki, where I collaborated with ecologist and philosopher, Yrjö Haila (see Ch. 2); and (ii) resource ecologists/economists at the University of California at Berkeley. Almost all were advanced graduate students with several years of research experience, self-selected by their willingness to commit time to reflect on their current research and possible future directions. Further details of the procedures adopted in these workshops are given in P. J. Taylor and Haila (1989).

14. In addition to the idiosyncrasy of maps, in P. J. Taylor (1990) I discuss the following issues: the relationship of mapping to modelling; the need for narration to accompany the diagrammatic representations; the reliability of self-reported information in the workshop setting; the representativeness of self-selected participants; the lack of a temporal dimension in most of the actual maps and in the metaphor of mapping itself; and the individual-centredness of maps.

15. One direction I am exploring in my teaching is to formulate *critical heuristics*— propositions that are simple enough to communicate, but disturb the simple analyses and always point to the need for further work to address the complexity of particular cases (Hall and Taylor 1998, Taylor 1999). For example, the first item in the list of eight implications of political ecology would become: 'Consider how the analysis of causes and the implications of the analysis changes if undifferentiated units were replaced by unequal units subject to further differentiation as a result of their linked economic, social and political dynamics.' The other items in the list of implications of political ecology in the first section, the alternatives or counterfactuals refered to in the second section, and the issues about mapping raised at the end of this chapter can all be rephrased in a similar way as critical heuristics that would be applicable to all three projects in this essay.

CHAPTER 7: SECURITY AND SOLIDARITY: TOWARD AN ANTI-REDUCTIONIST ANALYSIS OF ENVIRONMENTAL POLICY

1. Or, if there is a threshold (as the notion of carrying capacity implies), into a move towards that threshold.

2. For a thorough exposition of this argument for the social nature of human needs and wants see Douglas and Ney (1997).

3. The ecocentric critique of anthropocentrism is nothing if not swingeing. 'It is an intensely disturbing idea, that men should not be the master of all, that other suffering might be just as important. And that individual suffering—animal or human—might be less important than the suffering of species, ecosystems, the planet. It is disturbing in a way that an idea like, say, Marxism is not. It is not all *that* radical to talk about who is going to own the factories, at least compared with the question of whether there are going to *be* factories' (McKibben 1990: 167).

4. A formulation that accommodates both ecocentric and anthropocentric positions *and* their contradiction.

5. This distinction between *can* compensate and *do* compensate is far from trivial. The explicit intention in the Marsyangdi Project, for instance, was that those who were displaced would be compensated but it did not happen. Nor is it just a matter of ineffective institutional co-ordination. Embedded in the seemingly value-free notion of economic efficiency is an idea of fairness that is not shared by all those

who are affected. This is the idea that those who put most in should get most out, and this means that, in those situations where there *is* a Pareto improvement, the carrying out of the compensation that is possible will quite likely destroy the incentive structure that generated the improvement in the first place.

6. Alternatively, to free it, Rousseau-wise, from the chains that for too long have weighed it down. Man, on this argument, is essentially caring and co-operative, and it is only the overlay of exploitative institutions that has made him appear self-seeking. So here are two 'contradictory certainties'—two myths of human nature—each of which, I will be arguing, is shaped by (and in its turn upholds) a particular form of social solidarity.

7. A thing is right, according to the earth ethic, when it tends to preserve the integrity, community and beauty of the natural environment. It is wrong when it tends otherwise (Leopold 1970).

8. Complexity (both natural and social) and its implications are explored in Thompson and Trisoglio (1997).

9. One suggestion that I heard recently is 'hospitality'. This nicely captures the way in which markets and hierarchies, in coming together around the idea of sustainable development, have excluded the egalitarian concern with caring, sharing and community. This exclusion then results in the fatalization of those, like the Didis, who, up until then, were making a tenuous (and hospitable) go of things. Fatalization, essentially, is the destruction of social capital: a process which, surely, has to be the opposite of what development is supposed to be.

10. This section summarizes the analysis of land uses in mountain ecosystems that is set out in Price and Thompson (1997).

11. Venerable they certainly look, but their origins may not in fact be lost in the mists of time. Prakash (1997) has observed the creation of one such commons-managing institution (in the Indian Himalaya)—it happened, literally, over-night—and we have all heard of the apocryphal American university that announced that 'With effect from tomorrow, it will be a tradition to . . .'.

12. 'Cultural' because each of these solidarities shapes (and, in its turn, is strength-ened by) a distinctive set of certainties (about how the world is and people are) which contradicts those that are shaped by the other certainties. Humans, indi-vidualists know, are *self-seeking*; hierarchists know they are *malleable* (born in sin but redeemable by firm and nurturing institutions); egalitarians know they are *caring and co-operative* until corrupted by coercive institutions (markets and hier-archies); fatalists know they are *fickle*. Physical nature, individualists know, is *benign* (capable of bouncing back from whatever insults we deliver); hierarchists know that it is *perverse/tolerant* (stable within discoverable limits, unstable beyond those limits); egalitarians know it is *ephemeral* (so intricately intercon-nected that any severing of any of those connections may result in the collapse of the entire system); fatalists know that it is *capricious* (operates without rhyme or reason).

These social constructions of reality—cultural theorists call them *myths of nature*—do not require their holders to insist that water flows uphill, or that the sun goes round the earth; they are all contained within the uncertainty that surrounds pretty well all policy issues (global warming, for instance, mad cow disease, deforestation and nuclear power, to mention just a few). See Part I of Thompson, Ellis, and Wildavsky (1990) and Schwarz and Thompson (1990).

13. The recognition (starting in the 1970s) that environmental problems constitute a crisis and, in so doing, reveal fundamental omissions in the workings of our main institutional arrangements (see Hajer 1995). Where radical environmentalists call for a whole new way of doing things, ecological modernisers believe these omissions can be rectified without such drastic recourse.

14. This evidence is assembled in Thompson, Warburton, and Hatley (1986) and in Ives and Messerli (1989).

15. Not all of them; many large forests remote from the farmed areas remain under their control.

CHAPTER 9: IMAGES OF PLACE IN GREEN POLITICS: THE CULTURAL MIRROR OF INDIGENOUS TRADITIONS

1. Bahro (1983: 159) describes the speech as 'one of the few more or less mandatory cultural treasures of the green-alternative movement'.

2. Nuu-chah-nulth is the collectively adopted name of a number of tribes. Nootka, an older term coined and used by anthropologists (e.g. Kenyon 1980; Arima 1983), is not welcomed by the Nuu-chah-nulth.

3. It should be noted that the force of the resistance also arose from economic interests, particularly the interests of the tourist trade (Darling, n.d.: 13). I thank Leanne Burney, a participant–observer in the Clayoquot Sound case, for sharing with me material from her research and for answering many questions. In the following discussion, I have also relied heavily on her insightful thesis (Burney 1996). She does not bear any responsibility, of course, for my treatment of the case.

4. On this and related points, I am indebted to insights offered me by Gary Potts, former Chief of the Teme-Augama Anishnabi in Ontario.

5. This is not to deny the importance and value of politics (see Torgerson 1999).

CHAPTER 10: PARTNERSHIP ETHICS AND CULTURAL DISCOURSE: WOMEN AND THE EARTH SUMMIT

1. This chapter draws on material that appeared in Carolyn Merchant (1996).

2. On egocentric, homocentric, and ecocentric ethics see, 'Environmental Ethics and Political Conflict', (Merchant 1992: 63–82).

3. The Global Women's Treaty contained the following paragraph: 'We recognize the failure of governments to either address the true causes of the planetary

crisis or reach agreement on urgent action to save our planet. We believe that the chief causes lie in militarism, debt and structural adjustment and trade policies being promoted by multinational corporations and international financial and trade institutions such as the International Monetary Fund, the World Bank, and the General Agreement on Tariffs and Trade (GATT). The policies of these institutions are causing the degradation of human and natural environments, leading to the growing impoverishment of the majority of the world's people, perpetuating the inequity of the existing world order, and contributing to the continuing and intensified pressure on natural resources. We condemn these policies and call for the immediate adoption of altenative policies based on principles of justice, equity, and sustainability.' (Cf. *Global Assembly of Women and the Environment*, No. 4 (July 1992), p. 8.)

4. The Preamble to UNCED's Agenda 21 states: '[the] integration of environment and development concerns and greater attention to them will lead to the fulfillment of basic needs, improved living standards for all, better protected and managed ecosystems and a safer, more prosperous future. No nation can achieve this on its own; but together we can—in a global partnership for sustainable development.' Quoted in Grubb *et al.* (1993: 101).

5. The idea of a partnership between women and men as the basis for a new society, but without explicit attention to environmental ethics, has been developed by Riane Eisler (1988). The concept of relation as a foundation for ecofeminism and the relational self has been developed by Val Plumwood (1993). On the connections between ethics and narrative, see Jim Cheney (1989). On the importance of seeing the local community as connected to a global capitalist system see, James O'Connor (1991).

6. On the god-trick of seeing everything from nowhere, see Haraway (1991: 183–201, esp. 189, 191, 193, 195).

7. For the diversity–stability hypothesis, see Odum (1953, 1969). On shortcomings of equilibrium theories in ecology, see Reice (1994). On the history and disruption of the balance of nature theory see, Botkin (1990); Pickett and White (1985). On the problem of a stable world behind socially constructed representations, see Bird (1987). On the history of chaos theory in ecology see Worster (1990).

8. In constructing this example I have drawn on a hypothetical case presented in Management Institute for Business and Environment (1994*a*: 11–12), but I have added representatives of affected natural entities.

9. Environmental groups from the South include DAWN (Development Alternatives with Women for a New Era), headed by Peggy Antrobus of Barbados, Vandana Shiva's Research Foundation for Science, Technology, and Resource Development, in Dehra Dun India, and the Regional Assemblies of women of Africa; the West Asia/Arab World; Asia/Pacific; and Latin America/Caribbean comprising the Global Assembly of Women and the Environment—Partners in Life. Cf. Braidotti *et al.* (1994: 116–22, 134, 166–7).

References

ABRAHAM, R. (1994). *Chaos, Eros, and Gaia*, San Francisco: Harper and Row.

ADAMS, C. J. (ed.) (1993). *Ecofeminism and the sacred*, New York: Continuum.

AGARWAL, A., and NARAIN, S. (1989). *Towards Green Villages: A Strategy for Environmentally Sound and Participatory Rural Development*, New Delhi: Centre fo Science and Environment.

ALLEN, J. (1991). *Biosphere 2: The Human Experiment*, London: Verlag kann ich nicht mehr rekonstruieren.

ALTVATER, E. (1992). *Der Preis des Wohlstands*, Münster: Westfälisches Dampfboot.

ANDERSON, B. (1991). *Imagined Communities. Reflections on the Origin and Spread of Nationalism*, rev. edn. London: Verso.

ANDERSON, C. (1993). 'Kennedy, Natives To Join Hands', *The Province*, 1 August 1993, repr. in A. Champagne and R. MacIssac (eds.), *Clayoquot Mass Trials: Defending the Rainforest*, Gabriola Island, BC: New Society Publishers.

ARIMA, E. Y. (1983). *The West Coast People: The Nootka of Vancouver Island and Cape Flattery*, Victoria: British Columbian Provincial Museum.

ARMSTRONG, K. (1993). *A History of God: The 4,000-year Quest of Judaism, Christianity and Islam*, New York: Ballantine Books.

ARNDT, H. W. (1981). 'Economic Development: A Semantic History', *Economic Development and Cultural Change*, 26: 463–84.

BACHELARD, G. (1969). *The Poetics of Space*, tr. Maria Jolas. Boston: Beacon Press.

BADINER, A. H. (ed.) (1990). *Dharma Gaia: A Harvest of Essays in Buddhism and Ecology*. Berkeley, Calif.: Parallax Press.

BAERSELMAN, F., and VERA, F. (1990). 'Zorgen voor de natuur van morgen', *Panda*, May 1990.

BAHRO, R. (1983). *Building the Green Movement*, tr. Mary Tyler. London: Heretic Books.

——(1994). *Avoiding Social and Ecological Disaster: The Politics of World Transformation*. Bath, UK: Gateway Books.

BAILEY, C., FAUPEL, C., and GUNDLACH, J. (1993). 'Environmental politics in Alabama's Blackbelt', in Bullard (1993).

BAIRD CALLICOTT, J. (1982). 'Traditional American Indian and Western European Attitudes Toward Nature: An Overview', *Environmental Ethics*, 4: 5–31.

—— (1989). *In Defense of the Land Ethic: Essays in Environmental Philosophy*, Albany: State University of New York Press.

—— (1994). 'Moral Monism in Environmental Ethics Defended', *Journal of Philosophical Research*, 19: 51–60.

—— and AMES, R. T. (eds.) (1989). *Nature in Asian traditions of Thought:*

Essays in Environmental Philosophy, Albany, NY: State University of New York Press.

BECK, B. (1995). 'Reintroduction, Zoos, Conservation, and Animal Welfare', in B. Norton *et al.* (eds.), *Ethics on the Ark; Zoos, Animal Welfare, and Wildlife Conservation*, London, 155–164.

BECK, U. (1992). *Risk Society: Towards a New Modernity*, London: Sage.

—— (1996). 'Risk Society and the Provident State', in S. Lash, B. Szerszynski, and B. Wynne (eds.), *Risk, Environment & Modernity: Towards a New Ecology*, London: Sage.

BECKENSTEIN, A. R. *et al.* (1995) *Stakeholder Negotiations: Exercises in Sustainable Development*, Chicago: Richard D. Irwin.

BELLAMY, C. (1996). 'How Nature is Inflaming the Wars of the World', *The Independent* (London) 29 October.

BENTON, T. (1993). *Natural Relations: Ecology, Animal Rights and Social Justice*, London: Verso.

BERGER, T. (1977). *Northern Frontier, Northern Homeland: The Report of the Mackenzie Valley Pipeline Inquiry*, 2 vols., Ottawa: Supply and Services Canada.

BERKES, F., FEENY, D., McCAY, B., and ACHESON, J. (1989). 'The Benefits of the Commons', *Nature*, 340: 91–3.

BERNSTEIN, RICHARD (1985). *Beyond Objectivism and Relativism: Science, Hermeneutics and Praxis*, Philadelphia: University of Pennsylvania Press.

BERRY, T. (1988). *The Dream of the Earth*, San Francisco: Sierra Club Books.

—— (1990). *Ideas: The Age of Ecology Series*. Transcript of an interview with David Cayley, Toronto: Canadian Broadcasting Corporation.

—— (1993). 'Into the Future', in F. Hull (ed.), *Earth & Spirit: The Spiritual Dimension of the Environmental Crisis*, New York: Continuum, 34–41.

BEYER, P. (1992). 'The Global Environment as a Religious Issue: A Sociological Analysis', *Religion*, 22: 1–19.

BHATT, R. (1989). 'Lakshmi Ashram: A Gandhian Perspective in the Himalayan Foothills', in J. Plant (ed.), *Healing the Wounds: The Promise of Ecofeminism*, Santa Cruz, Calif.: New Society Publishers, 168–73.

BILIMORIA, D., COOPERRIDER, D. L., KACZMARSKI, K., KHALSA, G., SRIVASTVA, S., and UPADHAYA, P. (1995). 'The Organization Dimensions of Global Change: No Limits to Cooperation', *Journal of Management Inquiry*, 4(1): 71–90.

BIRD, E. A. R. (1987). 'The Social Construction of Nature: Theoretical Approaches to the History of Environmental Problems', *Environmental Review*, 11 no. 4 (Winter): 255–64.

BLAIKIE, P. (1985). *The Political Economy of Soil Erosion in Developing Countries*, London: Longman.

BLOMLEY, N. (1996). ' "Shut the Province Down": First Nations Blockades in British Columbia, 1984–1995', *BC Studies*, 111: 5–35.

BLUMBERG, M., and GOTTLIEB, R. (1989). *War on Waste: Can America Win its Battle with Garbage*, Washington, DC: Island Press.

Böhme, G. (1992). *Natürlich Natur—Über Natur im Zeitalter ihrer technischen Repro-duzierbarkeit*, Frankfurt a/M: Suhrkamp.

Bookchin, M. (1994). *Which Way for the Ecology Movement?*, San Francisco: AK Press.

Boserup, E. (1970). *Women's Role in Economic Development*, New York: St Martin's Press.

Botkin, D. B. (1990). *Discordant Harmonies*, New York: Oxford University Press.

Braidotti, R. *et al.* (1994). *Women, the Environment, and Sustainable Development*, London: Zed Books.

Bramwell, A. (1989). *Ecology in the 20th century*, New Haven: Yale University Press.

Braudel, F. (1980). *On History*, London: Weidenfeld and Nicolson.

Brody, Hugh (1981). *Maps and Dreams: Indians and the British Columbia Frontier*, Vancouver: Douglas and McIntyre.

Brokensha, D. W., Horowitz, M. M., and Scudder, T. (1977). *The Anthropology of Rural Development in the Sahel: Proposals for Research*, Binghamton, NY: Institute for Development Anthropology.

Brown, L. R. (1981). *Building a sustainable society*, New York: W.W. Norton & Co.

—— (ed.) (1991). *The WorldWatch reader on global environmental issues*. New York: W.W. Norton & Company.

Brulle, R. J. (1995). 'Environmentalism and Human Emancipation', in S. M. Lyman (ed.), *Social Movements: Critiques, Concepts, Case-Studies*, London: MacMillan Press, 309–28.

Bryant B., and Mohai, P. (eds.) (1992). *Race and the Incidence of Environmental Hazards*, Boulder, Colo.: Westview Press.

Bullard, R. (1990). *Dumping in Dixie: Race, Class, and Environmental Quality*, Boulder, Colo.: Westview Press.

—— (ed.) (1993). *Confronting Environmental Racism: Voices from the Grassroots*, Boston: South End Press.

—— (ed.) (1994). *Unequal Protection: Environmental Justice and Communities of Color*, San Francisco: Sierra Club.

Burney, Leanne (1996). *Sustainable Development and Civil Disobedience: The Politics of Environmental Discourse in Clayoquot Sound*, MA Thesis, Trent University, Peterborough, Ont.

Cairns, J. (1995). 'Achieving Sustainable Use of the Planet in the Next Century: What Should Virginians Do?', *Virginia Issues & Answers*, 2 no. 2 (Summer): 2–5.

Caloren, F. (1978). 'Getting Berger in Focus: The Revolutionary Struggle of the Native People of the Northwest', *Our Generation* 12: 3.

Carroll, J. E., Brockelman, P., and Westfall, M. (eds.) (1997). *The Greening of Faith: God, the Environment, and the Good Life*, Hanover, NH: University of New Hampshire.

Carroll, W. (ed.) (1992). *Organizing Dissent: Contemporary Social Movements in Theory and Practice*, Toronto: Garamond Press.

CARSON, R. (1963). *Silent Spring*, London: Hamish Hamilton (first published 1962).

CASTELLS, M. (1997). *The Power of Identity*, Oxford: Blackwell.

CERNEA, M. M. (1988). 'Involuntary Resettlement in Development Projects: Policy Guidelines in World Bank-Financed Projects', *World Bank Technical Paper*, No. 80, Washington, DC: World Bank.

CHAPMAN, G. P. (1985). 'Environmental Myth as International Politics: The Problem of the Bengal Delta', in G. P. Chapman and M. Thompson (eds.), *Water and the Quest for Sustainable Development in the Ganges Valley*, London: Mansell, 163–86.

CHAPPLE, C. K. (1993). 'Hindu Environmentalism: Traditional and Contemporary Resources', in M. E. Tucker and J. A. Grim (eds.), *Worldviews and Ecology*, Lewisburg, Pa.: Bucknell University Press, 113–23.

CHARLTON, S. E. M. (1984). *Women in Third World Development*, London: Westview Press.

CHENEY, J. (1987). 'Eco-feminism and Deep Ecology', *Environmental Ethics*, 9(2): 115–45.

—— (1989). 'Postmodern Environmental Ethics: Ethics as Bioregional Narrative', *Environmental Ethics*, 11: 117–34.

CHENG, C-Y. (1986). 'On the Environmental Ethics of the Tao and the Ch'i', *Environmental Ethics*, 8(4): 351–70.

CLARK, W. C., and MUNN, R. E. (eds.) (1986). *Sustainable Development of the Biosphere*, Cambridge: Cambridge University Press.

CHERNOV, Y. I. (1985). *The Living Tundra*, Cambridge: Cambridge University Press.

COBB, C., and COBB, J. (eds.) (1994). *The Green National Product: A Proposed Index of Sustainable Economic Welfare*, New York: University Press of America.

COBB, J. B. JR., and GRIFFIN, D. R. (1976). *Process Theology*. Philadelphia, Pa.: Westminister Press.

COLE, R. (1993). 'Ecotones and Environmental Ethics: Adorno and Lopez', in J. Bennett and W. Chaloupka (eds.), *In the Nature of Things: Language, Politics, and the Environment*, Minneapolis: University of Minnesota Press.

COLLINGWOOD, R. G. (1945). *The Idea of Nature*, Oxford: Clarendon Press.

COMMONER, B. (1990). *Making Peace with the Planet*, New York: Pantheon.

CROMBIE, A. C. (1988). 'Designed in the Mind: Western Visions of Science, Nature and Humankind', *History of Science*, 24: 1–12.

DALY, H. E., and COBB, J. B., (1989). *For the Common good: Redirecting the Economy toward Community, the Environment, and a Sustainable Future* (2nd ed., updated and expanded, 1994), Boston, Mass.: Beacon Press.

DANEEL, M. (1994). 'African Independent Churches Face the Challenge of Environmental Ethics', in D. G. Hallman (ed.), *Ecotheology: Voices from south and north*, Maryknoll, NY: Orbis Books, 248–63.

DANKELMAN, I., and DAVIDSON, J. (1988). *Women and Environment in the Third World: Alliance for the Future*, London: Earthscan.

DARCY DE OLIVEIRA, R., and CORRAL, T. (eds.) (1992). *Terra Femina*, Rio de Janeiro: Companhia Brasileira de Artes Gráficas.

—— —— (1993). *Planeta Fêmea: A Publication of the Brazilian Women's Coalition*, Rio de Janiero: IDAC.

DARLING, C. R. (n.d.). *In Search of Consensus: An Evaluation of the Clayoquot Sound Sustainable Development Task Force Process*. UVic Institute for Dispute Resolution, University of Victoria, Victoria, BC.

DAY, D. (1989). *The Environmental Wars: Reports From the Front Lines*, New York: St. Martin's Press.

DEAR, P. (1995). *Discipline & Experience. The Mathematical Way in the Scientific Revolution*, Chicago: The University of Chicago Press.

DELCOURT, H. R., and DELCOURT, P. A. (1991). *Quaternary Ecology. A Palaeoecological Perspective*, London: Chapman and Hall.

DEPARTMENT OF ENVIRONMENTAL SCIENCE, POLICY, and MANAGEMENT (1996). *Graduate Study, 1997–1998*, Berkeley: University of California.

DEPARTMENT OF FISHERY and WILDLIFE (1996). *Fishery and Wildlife*, Fort Collins: Colorado State University.

DEPARTMENT OF FOREST SCIENCE (1996). *Forest Science*, Fort Collins: Colorado State University.

DEPARTMENT OF NATURAL RESOURCE, RECREATION and TOURISM (1996). *Natural Resource, Recreation and Tourism*, Fort Collins: Colorado State University.

DE-SHALIT, A. (1995). *Why Posterity Matters: Environmental Policies and Future Generations*, London: Routledge.

DEUDNEY, D. (1995). 'In Search of Gaian Politics: Earth Religion's Challenge to Modern Western Civilization', in B. R. Taylor (ed.), *Ecological Resistance Movements: The Global Emergence of Radical and Popular Environmentalism*, Albany, NY: State University of New York Press, 282–99.

DEVALL, B. (1990). 'Ecocentric Sangha', in A. H. Badiner (ed.), *Dharma Gaia: A Harvest of Essays in Buddhism and Ecology*, Berkeley, Calif.: Parallax Press, 155–64.

—— and SESSIONS, G. (1985). *Deep Ecology*. Salt Lake City: Peregrine Smith Books.

DIXIT, A. (1994). 'Water Projects in Nepal. Lessons From Displacement and Rehabilitation', *Water Nepal*, 4.1: 74–85.

DOBSON, A. (1995). *Green Political Thought*, London: Routledge.

DOERR, A. D. (1974). 'Indian Policy', in G. Bruce Doern and V. Seymour Wilson (eds.), *Issues in Canadian Public Policy*, Toronto: Macmillan.

DOUGLAS, M. (1984). *Purity and Danger: An Analysis of the Concepts of Pollution and Taboo*, London: Routledge and Kegan Paul.

—— and NEY, S. (1997) *Missing Persons*, London: UCL Press.

—— and WILDAVSKY, A. (1982). *Risk and Culture: An Essay on the Selection of Technological and Environmental Dangers*, Berkeley: University of California Press.

DRENGSON, A., and INOUE, Y. (eds.) (1995). *The Deep Ecology Movement: An Introductory Anthology*, Berkeley, Calif.: North Atlantic Books.

DRYZEK, J. S. (1995). 'Political and Ecological Communication', *Environmental Politics*, 4: 13–30.

DRYZEK, J. S. (1997). *The Politics of the Earth: Environmental Discourses*, Oxford: Oxford University Press.

—— and YOUNG, O. (1985). 'Internal Colonialism in the Circumpolar North: The Case of Alaska', *Development and Change*, 16: 123–45.

DUKE NICHOLAS SCHOOL OF THE ENVIRONMENT (1996a). *Bulletin*, Durham: Duke University.

—— (1996b). *Employment Profile Letter*, Durham: Duke University.

DURHAM, J. (1993). *Columbus Day: Poems, Drawings and Stories about American Indian Life and Death in the Nineteen-Seventies*, 2nd edn., Albuquerque, N. Mex.: West End Press.

DURNING, A. (1992). *How Much Is Enough?*, London: Earthscan.

DWIVEDI, O. P. (1996). '*Satyagraha* for conservation: Awakening the spirit of Hinduism', in R. S. Gottlieb (ed.), *This Sacred Earth: Religion, Nature, Environment*, New York: Routledge, 151–63.

DYKE, C. (1988). *The Evolutionary Dynamics of Complex Systems: A Study in Biosocial Complexity*, Oxford: Oxford University Press.

ECHEVERRIA, J., and EBY, R. (eds.) (1995). *Let the People Judge: Wise Use and the Private Property Rights Movement*, Washington, DC: Island Press.

ECKERSLEY, R. (1988). 'Green Politics: A Practice in Search of a Theory?', *Alternatives: Perspectives on Society, Technology and Environment*, 15(4): 52–61.

—— (1992). *Environmentalism and Political Theory: Toward an Ecocentric Approach*, Albany: State University of New York Press.

Ecologist, The (1992). *Whose Common Future?*, London: Earthscan.

EGRI, C. P., and FROST, P. J. (1991). 'Shamanism and Change: Bringing back the Magic in Organizational Transformation', in R. W. Woodman and W. A. Pasmore (eds.), *Research in Organizational Change and Development*, vi, Greenwich, Conn.: JAI Press, 175–221.

EHRENFELD, D. (1978). *The Arrogance of Humanism*, New York: Oxford University Press.

EHRLICH, P. R. (1993). 'The Scale of the Human Enterprise', in D. A. Saunders, R. J. Hobbs, and P. R. Ehrlich (eds.), *Nature Conservation 3: The Reconstruction of Fragmented Ecosystems*, Chipping Norton, NSW: Surrey Beatty & Sons, 3–8.

—— and HOLDREN, J. (1974). 'Impact of Population Growth', *Science*, 171: 1212–17.

—— and EHRLICH, A. H. (1990). *The Population Explosion*, New York: Simon & Schuster.

EISLER, R. (1987). *The Chalice and the Blade: Our History, our Future*, San Francisco: Harper & Row.

EL SERAFY, S. (1991). 'The Environment as Capital', in R. Costanza (ed.), *Ecological Economics: The Science and Management of Sustainability*, New York: Columbia University Press, 168–75.

ENGELS, F. (1890). Letter to Conrad Schmidt of 27 October, in Karl Marx and Frederick Engels, *Correspondence, 1846–1895*, ed. and tr. Dona Torr, London: Lawrence and Wishart, 1936.

EPSTEIN, R. (1985). *Takings: Private Property and the Power of Eminent Domain*, Cambridge, Mass.: Harvard University Press.

FAGAN, B. M. (1991). *Ancient North America: The Archaeology of a Continent*, New York: Thames and Hudson.

FARHADI, R. (1989). 'Islam and Ecology as Taught by the Quar'an', *Ecology Center Newsletter*, 18(12): 6–7.

FISCHER, F. (1990). *Technocracy and the Politics of Expertise*, London: Sage.

—— (1995). Environmental Policy and Risk-Benefit: The Green Critique of Technocratic Ideology, in: F. Fischer, *Evaluating Public Policy*. Chicago: Nelson-Hall, pp. 175–203.

—— and BLACK, M. (eds.) (1995). *Greening Environmental Policy—The Politics of a Sustainable Future*, London: Paul Chapman.

—— and FORESTER, J. (1993). *The Argumentative Turn in Policy Analysis and Planning*, Durham: Duke University Press.

FORRESTER, J. W. (1969). *Urban Dynamics*, Cambridge, Mass.: MIT Press.

FORSYTH, J. (1994). *A History of Peoples of Siberia: Russia's North Asian Colony 1581–1990*, Cambridge: Cambridge University Press.

FOUCAULT, M. (1977). *Language, Counter-Memory and Practice*, Ithaca, NY: Cornell University Press.

—— (1980a). *The History of Sexuality*, New York: Vintage.

—— (1980b). *Power/Knowledge: Selected Interviews & Other Writings, 1972–1977*, New York: Pantheon.

—— (1991). 'Governmentality', in G. Burchell, C. Gordon, and P. Miller (eds.), *The Foucault Effect: Studies in Governmentality*, Chicago: University of Chicago Press.

—— (1994). *The Order of Things: An Archaeology of the Human Sciences*, New York: Vintage (previously published London: Tavistock, 1970).

Fox, M. (1988–9). 'My Final Statement before being Silenced by the Vatican', *Earth Island Journal*, (Winter): 50.

—— (1994). *The reinvention of work: A new vision of livelihood for our time*. San Francisco: Harper San Francisco.

Fox, W. (1990). *Toward a Transpersonal Ecology: Developing New Foundations for Environmentalism*, Boston, Mass.: Shambhala.

FREEMAN, M. M. R. (1995). 'The Nature and Utility of Traditional Ecological Knowledge', in C. Gaffield and P. Gaffield (eds.), *Consuming Canada: Readings in Environmental History*, Toronto: Copp Clark.

FRIENDS OF CLAYOQUOT SOUND (1989). 'The Battle for Clayoquot Sound', *Canadian Dimension*, 23(5): 27–9.

FRITSCH, B., SCHMIDHEINY, S., and SEIFRITZ, W. (1993). *Towards an Ecological Sustainable Growth Society*, Berlin: Springer.

FROSCH, R. A. (1996). 'Towards the End of Waste: Reflections on a New Ecology', *Daedalus*, 124 no. 3 (Summer): 201–11.

FROST, P. J., and EGRI, C. P. (1994). 'The Shamanic Perspective on Organizational Change and Development', *Journal of Organizational Change Management*, 7(1): 7–23.

FRYE, N. (1971). *The Bush Garden: Essays on the Canadian Imagination*, Toronto: Anansi.

FUJIMURA, J. H. (1987). 'Constructing "Do-able" Problems in Cancer Research: Articulating Alignment', *Social Studies of Science*, 17: 257–93.

GAARD, G. (1993). 'Ecofeminism and Native American Cultures: Pushing the Limits of Cultural Imperialism?', in: G. Gaard (ed.), *Ecofeminism: Women, Animals, Nature*, Philadelphia, Pa.: Temple University Press, 295–314.

GADGIL, M., and GUHA, R. (1992). *This Fissured Land: An Ecological History of India*, Berkeley, Calif.: University of California Press.

GARCÍA-BARRIOS, R. and GARCÍA-BARRIOS, L. (1990). 'Environmental and Technological Degradation in Peasant Agriculture: A Consequence of Development in Mexico', *World Development*, 18(11): 1569–85.

GELLNER, E. (1992). *Reason and Culture: The Historic Role of Rationality and Rationalism*, Oxford: Blackwell.

—— (1997). 'Reply to Critics', *New Left Review*, 221 (Jan./Feb.): 81–118.

GEORGE, S. (1992). *The Debt Boomerang*, London: Pluto

GHAI, D., and VIVIAN, J. (eds.) (1995). *Grassroots Environmental Action: People's Participation in Sustainable Development*, London: Routledge.

GIBBONS M. *et al.* (1994). *The New Production of Knowledge: The Dynamics of Science and Research in Contemporary Societies*, London: Sage.

GIBBS, L. (1982). *Love Canal, my story*, Albany, NY: State University of New York Press.

GILLIAM, H. (1994). 'The Real Price of Free Trade', *This World, San Francisco Examiner*, 2 Jan.: 13–14.

GIMBUTUS, M. (1982). *The Goddesses and Gods of Old Europe, 6500–3500 BC*, Berkeley, Calif.: University of California Press.

GLACKEN, C. (1967). *Traces on the Rhodian Shore: Nature and Culture in Western Thought from Ancient Times to the End of the Eighteenth Century*, Berkeley, Calif.: University of California Press.

GOLDMAN, M. (1998). 'Introduction', in M. Goldman (ed.) *Privatizing Nature: Political Struggles for the Global Commons*, London: Pluto.

GORE, A. (1992). *Earth in the Balance: Ecology and the Human Spirit*, Boston: Houghton Mifflin.

GOTTLIEB, R. S. (ed.). (1996). *This Sacred Earth: Religion, Nature, Environment*, New York: Routledge.

GOWDY, J. M. and OLSEN, P. R. (1994). 'Further Problems with Neoclassical Environmental Economics', *Environmental Ethics*, 16: 161–71.

GREENWAY, J. C. (1967). *Extinct and Vanishing Birds of the World*, New York: Dover.

GREIDER, W. (1992). *Who will Tell the People?*, New York: Simon and Schuster.

GREIJN, H. (1992). 'GATT, Environment, and Development', *Earth Island Journal*, 7 (June): 11–12.

GRENE, M. (1974). *The Understanding of Nature: Essays in the Philosophy of Biology*, Dordrecht, Holland: D. Reidel.

GROSSMAN, K. (1994). 'The People of Color Environmental Summit', in Bullard (1994).

GROVE, R. H. (1994). *Green Imperialism: Colonial Expansion, Tropical Island Edens and the Origins of Environmentalism, 1600–1860*, Cambridge: Cambridge University Press.

GRUBB, M. *et al.* (1993). *The Earth Summit Agreements: A Guide and Assessment*, London: Earthscan.

GUHA, R. (1989). *The Unquiet Woods: Ecological Change and Peasant Resistance in the Himalayas*, Berkeley, Calif.: University of California Press.

GUREVICH, A. (1985). *Categories of Medieval Culture*, London: Routledge.

HAAS, P. (1990). 'Obtaining International Environmental Protection through Epistemic Consensus', *Millenium*, 19: 347–63.

—— (1996). 'Is "Sustainable Development" Politically Sustainable?', *The Brown Journal of World Affairs*, 3(2): 239–240.

HACKING, I. (1991). 'A Tradition of Natural Kinds', *Philosophical Studies*, 61: 109–26.

—— (1992). '"Style" for Historians and Philosophers', *Studies in History and Philosophy of Science*, 23: 1–20.

HADSELL, H. (1995). 'Profits, Parrots, Peons: Ethical Perplexities in the Amazon', in B. R. Taylor (ed.), *Ecological Resistance Movements: The global Emergence of Radical and Popular Environmentalism*, Albany, NY: State University of New York Press, 70–87.

HAILA, Y. (1994). 'Preserving Ecological Diversity in Boreal Forests: Ecological Background, Research, and Management', *Annales Zoologici Fennici*, 31: 203–17.

—— (1995). 'Natural Dynamics as a Model for Management: Is the Analogue Practicable?', in A.-L. Sippola, P. Alaraudanjoki, B. Forbes, and V. Hallikainen (eds.), *Northern Wilderness Areas: Ecology, Sustainability, Values*, Rovaniemi: Arctic Centre Publications 7: 9–26.

—— (1998). 'Assessing Ecosystem Health across Spatial Scales', in D. J. Rapport, R. Costanza, P. R. Epstein, C. Gaudet, and R. Levins (eds.), *Ecosystem Health*, Malden, Mass.: Blackwell, 81–102.

—— and HEININEN, L. (1995). 'Ecology: A New Discipline for Disciplining?', *Social Text*, 42 (Spring): 153–71.

—— and LEVINS, R. (1992). *Humanity and Nature. Ecology, Science and Society*, London: Pluto Press.

—— and SEPPÄLÄ, M. (eds.) (1995). *Ikijää–Permafrost–Merzlota*. Pori: Pori Art Museum.

HAJER, M. A. (1995). *The Politics of Environmental Discourse: Ecological Modernization and the Policy Process*, Oxford: Oxford University Press.

—— (1996). 'Ecological Modernization as Cultural Politics', in: S. Lash, B. Szerszynski, and B. Wynne (eds.), *Risk, Environment & Modernity: Towards a New Ecology*, London: Sage.

HALIFAX, J. (1979). *Shamanic Voices: A Survey of Visionary Narratives*, New York: E. P. Dutton.

HALIFAX, J. (1990). 'The Third Body: Buddhism, Shamanism, & Deep Ecology', in A. H. Badiner (ed.), *Dharma Gaia: A Harvest of Essays in Buddhism and Ecology*, Berkeley, Calif.: Parallax Press, 20–38.

HALL, D. A. and TAYLOR, P. J. (1998). 'Political Ecology and the Changing Nature of Social theory', Unpublished paper presented to the 5th. Pori workshop on environmental policy, Pori, Finland, August 1998.

HALLMAN, D. G. (1994). 'Ethics and Sustainable Development', in D. G. Hallman, *Ecotheology: Voices from south and north*, Maryknoll, NY: Orbis Books, 264–83.

HARAWAY, D. (1991). 'Situated Knowledges', in: *Simians, Cyborgs, and Women: The Reinvention of Nature*, New York: Routledge.

HARBORDT, H. J. (1991). *Dauerhafte Entwicklung statt globaler Selbstzerstörung*, Berlin: Sigma.

HARDIN, G. (1968). 'The Tragedy of the Commons', *Science*, 162: 1243–8.

HARRISON, R. P. (1992). *Forests: The Shadow of Civilization*, Chicago: The University of Chicago Press.

HARVEY, D. (1973). *Social Justice and the City*, London: Edward Arnold.

—— (1974). 'Population, Resources, and the Ideology of Science', *Economic Geography*, 50: 256–77.

—— (1989). *The Condition of Postmodernity: An Inquiry into the Origins of Cultural Change*, Oxford: Blackwell.

—— (1993). 'The Nature of Environment: The Dialectics of Social and Environmental Change', *Socialist Register*, 1–51.

—— (1995). 'Militant Particularism and Global Ambition: The Conceptual Politics of Place, Space, and Environment in the Work of Raymond Williams', *Social Text*, 42: 69–98.

—— (1997). *Justice, Nature and the Geography of Difference*, Oxford: Basil Blackwell.

HATCH, C. (1994). 'The Clayoquot Protests: Taking Stock One Year Later', in A. Champagne and R. MacIssac (eds.), *Clayoquot Mass Trials: Defending the Rainforest*, Gabriola Island, BC: New Society Publishers.

HAWKEN, P. (1993). *The Ecology of Commerce: A Declaration of Sustainability*, New York: Harper Business.

HAY, P. (1994). 'The Politics of Tasmania's World Heritage Area: Contesting the Democratic Subject', *Environmental Politics*, 3: 1–21.

HAYLES, N. K. (1990). *Chaos Bound: Orderly Disorder in Contemporary Literature and Science*, Ithaca, NY: Cornell University Press.

—— (ed.) (1991). *Chaos and Order: Complex dynamics in Literature and Science*, Chicago: University of Chicago Press.

HAYS, S. (1959). *Conservation and the Gospel of Efficiency—The Progressive Conservation Movement 1890–1920*, 1979 edn., New York: Atheneum.

—— (1987). *Beauty, Health and Permanence—Environmental Politics in the United States, 1955–85*, Cambridge: Cambridge University Press.

HENSHALL MOMSEN, J. (1991). *Women and Development in the Third World*, London: Routledge.

HILDYARD, N. (1993). 'The Foxes in Charge of the Chickens', in W. Sachs (ed.), *Global Ecology*, London: Zed Books, 22–36.

HOBSBAWM, E. (1994). *The Age of Extremes: A History of the World, 1914–1991*, New York: Pantheon.

HOFFRICHTER, R. (ed.) (1993). *Toxic Struggles: The Theory and Practice of Environmental Justice*, Philadelphia: New Society Publishers.

HOLMES ROLSTON III, (1986). *Philosophy Gone Wild: Essays in Environmental Ethics*, Buffalo, NY: Prometheus Books.

HOMER-DIXON, T. F., BOUTWELL, J. H., and RATHJENS, G. W. (1993). 'Environmental Change and violent conflict', *Scientific American*, Feb.: 38–45.

HORKHEIMER, M. (1947). *The Eclipse of Reason*, New York: Oxford University Press.

HUGHES, J. D. (1975). *Ecology in Ancient Civilizations*, Albuquerque, N. Mex.: University of New Mexico Press.

HULL, F. (ed.) (1993). *Earth & Spirit: The Spiritual Dimension of the Environmental Crisis*, New York: Continuum.

ILLICH, I., and SANDERS, B. (1989). *ABC: The Alphabetization of the Popular Mind*, London: Penguin.

INGOLD, T. (1993). 'Globes and Spheres. The Topology of Environmentalism', in K. Milton (ed.), *Environmentalism: The View from Anthropology*, London: Routledge, 31–42.

INGRAM, G. B. (1994). 'The Ecology of a Conflict', in A. Champagne and R. MacIssac (eds.), *Clayoquot Mass Trials: Defending the Rainforest*, Gabriola Island, BC: New Society Publishers.

IVES, J. D. and MESSERLI, B. (1989). *The Himalayan Dilemma: Reconciling Development and Conservation*, London and New York: Routledge.

JAMISON, A. (1996). 'The Shaping of the Global Environmental Agenda: The Role of Non-Governmental Organizations', in Lash, Szerszynski, and Wynne (1996: 224–45).

JANCAR-WEBSTER, B. (ed.) (1993). *Environmental Action in Eastern Europe: Responses to Crisis*, Armonck, NY: M. E. Sharpe.

KAPLAN, R. (1990). 'The Coming Anarchy', *Atlantic Monthly*, 279.2 (Feb.): 45–58.

KARIYA, P. (1993). 'The Department of Indian Affairs and Northern Development: The Culture-Building Process within an Institution', in J. Duncan and D. Ley (eds.), *Place/Culture/Representation*, London: Routledge.

KATZ, C., and KIRBY, A. (1991). 'In the Nature of Things: The Environment and Everyday Life', *Transactions of the Institute of British Geographers*, 16: 259–71.

KAZA, S. (1993). 'Acting with Compassion: Buddhism, Feminism, and the Environmental Crisis', in C. J. Adams (ed.), *Ecofeminism and the Sacred*, New York: Continuum, 50–69.

KEHR, K. (1993). 'Nachhaltig denken. Zum sprachgeschichtlichen Hintergrund und zur Bedeutungsentwicklung des forstlichen Begriffs der Nachhaltigkeit', *Schweizerische Zeitschrift für Forstwesen*, 144: 595–605.

KELLER, E. F. (1985). *Reflections on Gender and Science*, New Haven: Yale University Press.

KELLERT, S. R. (1993). 'The Biological Basis for Human Values of Nature', in S. R. Kellert and E. O. Wilson (eds.), *The Biophilia Hypothesis*, Washington, DC: Island Press, 42–69.

KELLY, S. (1993). 'The Path of Place', in F. Hull (ed.), *Earth & Spirit: The Spiritual Dimension of the Environmental Crisis*, New York: Continuum, 105–13.

KENNEDY, R. F., Jr. (1994). 'Foreword', in A. Champagne and R. MacIssac (eds.), *Clayoquot Mass Trials: Defending the Rainforest*, Gabriola Island, BC: New Society Publishers.

KENYON, S. (1980). *The Kyquot Way: A Study of a West Coast (Nootkan) Community*, Ottawa: National Museums of Canada.

KEOHANE, R. O., and OSTROM, E. (1995). Editorial Introduction to *Local Commons and Global Interdependence*, London: Sage, 1–26.

KHALSA, G. S., and KACZMARSKI, K. (eds.) (1996). 'The United Religions Initiative Summit Conference Summary, 24–28 June 1996', San Francisco: The United Religions Initiative.

KINGSLAND, S. E. (1985). *Modelling Nature*, Chicago: University Press of Chicago.

KINSLEY, D. (1994). *Ecology and Religions*, Englewood Cliffs, NJ: Prentice-Hall.

KLOSTERMAIER, K. K. (1989). 'Spirituality and Nature', in K. Siviraman (ed.), *Hindu Spirituality: Vedas through Vedanta*, New York: Crossroads, 319–37.

KOLB, D. (1986). *The Critique of Pure Modernity: Hegel, Heidegger, and After*, Chicago: The University of Chicago Press.

KOTHARI, R. (1993). *Growing Amnesia: An Essay on Poverty and Human Consciousness*, New Delhi: Penguin.

KRAUSS, C. (1994). 'Women of Color in the Front Line', in Bullard (1994).

KWA, C. L. (1986). 'Representations of Nature in Cybernetic and Evolutionary Ecology', in P. Weingartner and G. Dorn (eds.), *Foundations of Biology*, Vienna: Hoelder-Pichler-Tempsky, 167–89.

LANGER, V. (1994). 'It Happened Suddenly (Over a Long Period of Time): A Clayoquot History', in H. Breen-Needham *et al.* (eds.), *Witness to Wilderness: The Clayoquot Sound Anthology*, Vancouver: Arsenal Pulp Press.

LAO TZU. (1988). *Tao Te Ching*, tr. Stephen Mitchell, New York: Harper & Row.

LASH, S., SZERSZYNSKI, B., and WYNNE, B. (eds.) (1996). *Risk, Environment & Modernity—Towards a New Ecology*, London: SAGE.

LAU, D. C. (tr.) (1963). *Lao Tzu: Tao Te Ching*, New York: Penguin Books.

LA VIOLETTE, F. E. (1961). *The Struggle for Survival: Indian Cultures and the Protestant Ethic in British Columbia*, Toronto: University of Toronto Press.

LAW, J. (ed.) (1991). *A Sociology of Monsters: Essays on Power, Technology and Domination*, London: Routledge.

LEFF, E. (1995). *Green Production: Toward an Environmental Rationality*, New York: Guilford.

LEFORT, C. 1983. 'La Question de la démocratie', in Ph. Lacoue-Labarthe and J.-L. Nancy (eds.), *Le Retrait du politique*, Paris: Galilée.

LEHTINEN, A. A. (1991). 'Northern Natures: A Study of the Forest Question Emerging within the Timber-Line Conflict in Finland', *Fennia* 169: 57–169.

LEISS, W. (1974). *The Domination of Nature*, Boston: Beacon Press.

LEOPOLD, A. (1970). *A Sand County Almanac, with Essays in Conservation from Round River* (originally Oxford University Press, 1949), New York: Ballantine Books.

LEOPOLD, R. (1996). *de Volkskrant*, 21 May.

LERNER, M. (1994). *Jewish Renewal: A Path to Healing and Transformation*, New York: G. P. Putnam's Sons.

LEVINE, A. (1982). *Love Canal: Science, Politics, and People,* Lexington, Mass.: Heath and Co.

LEVINS, R. (1996). 'Ten Popositions on Science and Antiscience', in A. Ross (ed.), *Science Wars*, Durham: Duke University Press, 180–91.

LINNEROOTH-BAYER, J., and FITZGERALD, K. B. (1996). 'Conflicting Views on Fair Siting Processes', *Risk, Health, Safety and* Environment, 7.1: 119–34.

LIPSCHUTZ, R. D. (1996). *Global Civil Society and Global Environmental Governance: The Politics of Nature from Place to Planet*, Albany, NY: SUNY Press.

LITTLE, P. (1985). 'Social Differentiation and Pastoralist Sedentarization in Northern Kenya', *Africa*, 55: 243–61.

—— (1988). 'Land Use Conflicts in the Agricultural/Pastoral Borderlands: The Case of Kenya', in P. Little, M. Horowitz, and A. Nyerges (eds.), *Lands at Risk in the Third World: Local Level Perspectives*, Boulder, Colo.: Westview, 195–212.

LITFIN, K, (1994). *Ozone Discourses: Science and Politics in Global Environmental Cooperation*, New York: Columbia.

LONG, F. J., and ARNOLD, M. (1994). *The Power of Environmental Partnerships*, Fort Worth, Tex.: Dryden Press.

LOVEJOY, A. O., and BOAS, G. (1935). *Primitivism and Related Ideas in Antiquity*, Baltimore: Johns Hopkins University Press.

LOVELOCK, J. (1979). *Gaia—A New Look at Planet Earth*, Oxford: Oxford University Press.

LUKÁCS, G. (1971). *History and Class Consciousness*, tr. Rodney Livingstone, London: Merlin Press.

LUKE, T. W. (1995). 'On Environmentality: Geo-Power and Eco-Knowledge in the Discourses of Contemporary Environmentalism', *Cultural Critique*, 31 (Fall): 57–81.

—— (1997). *Ecocritique: Contesting the Politics of Nature, Economy, and Culture*, Minneapolis: University of Minnesota Press.

LYOTARD, J.-F. (1984). *The Postmodern Condition: A Report on Knowledge*, Minneapolis: University of Minnesota Press.

LYOTARD, J.-F. (1988) *The differend*, Manchester: Manchester University Press.

McCarney, P. (1995). 'Urban Research in the Developing World: Four Approaches to the Environment of Cities', in E. Stren (ed.), *Urban Research in the Developing World*, Toronto: University of Toronto Press.

McCay, B., and Jentoft, S. (1997). 'Market or community failure? Critical perspectives on common property research', *Human Organization*, 57: 21–9.

McCormick, J. (1986), 'The Origins of the World Conservation Strategy', *Environmental Review*, 10: 177–87.

—— (1989). *Reclaiming Paradise: The Global Environmental Movement*, Bloomington: Indiana University Press.

McFague, S. (1993). *The Body of God: An Ecological Theology*, Philadelphia: Augsburg Fortress.

McGovern, T. H. (1994). 'Management for Extinction in Norse Greenland', in C. L. Crumley (ed.), *Historical Ecology: Cultural Knowledge and Changing Landscapes*, Santa Fe: School of American Research Press, 127–54.

McGrane, B. (1989). *Beyond Anthropology: Society and the Other*, New York: Columbia University Press.

MacIsaac, R., and Champagne, A. (1994). *Clayoquot Mass Trials: Defending the Rainforest*, Gabriola Island, BC: New Society Publishers.

McKibben, B. (1990). *The End of Nature*, London: Viking.

Macpherson, C. B. (1964). *The Political Theory of Possessive Individualism: Hobbes to Locke*, Oxford: Oxford University Press.

Maingon, L. (1994). 'Clayoquot: Recovering from Cultural Rape', in Tzeporah Berman *et al.*, *Clayoquot and Dissent*, Vancouver: Ronsdale Press.

Malone, T. F. (1986). 'Mission to Planet Earth: Integrating Studies of Global Change', *Environment*, 28(8): 6–11, 39–41.

Maloney, C. (1990). 'Environmental and Project Displacement of Population in India: Development and Deracination', *Field Staff Reports*, Universities Field Staff International and Natural Heritage Institute, California.

Manes, C. (1990). *Green Rage: Radical Environmentalism and the Unmaking of Civilization*, Boston, Mass.: Little, Brown and Company.

—— (1992). 'Nature and Silence', *Environmental Ethics*, 14: 339–50.

Mann, Ch. C., and Plummer, M. L. (1995). 'Are Wildlife Corridors the Right Path?', *Science*, 270: 1428–30.

Marcuse, H. (1972). 'Nature and Revolution', in *Counterrevolution and Revolt*, Boston: Beacon Press.

Martin, D. (1993). 'The Joining of Human, Earth, and Spirit', in F. Hull (ed.), *Earth & spirit: The spiritual dimension of the environmental crisis*, New York: Continuum, 43–57.

Martinez-Allier, J. (1990). 'Ecology and the Poor: A Neglected Dimension of Latin American History', *Journal of Latin American Studies*, 23: 621–39.

—— (1995). 'Political Ecology, Distributional Conflicts, and Economic Incommensurability', *New Left Review*, 211: 70–88.

MARX, K. (1853). 'The British Rule in India', in K. Marx and F. Engels, *Selected Works*, i, Moscow: Progress Publishers, 1969.

—— (1967). *Capital*, Vol. i, New York: International Publishers.

MEADOWS, D., MEADOWS, D., RANDERS, I., and BEHRENS, W. (1972). *The limits to growth*, New York: Universe.

MERCHANT, C. (1980). *The death of nature: Women, ecology, and the scientific revolution.* New York: Harper & Row.

—— (1992). *Radical ecology: The search for a livable world.* New York: Routledge.

—— (1996). *Earthcare: Women and the Environment*, New York: Routledge.

—— (1997). 'Fish First!: The Changing Ethics of Ecosystem Management', *Human Ecology Review* (Spring).

MIBE (Management Institute for Business and Environment) (1994*a*). *Environmental Partnerships: A Field Guide for Governmental Agencies*, Fort Worth, Tex.: Dryden Press.

—— (1994*b*). *Environmental Partnerships: A Business Handbook*, Forth Worth, Tex.: Dryden Press.

—— (1994*c*). *Environmental Partnerships: A Field Guide for Nonprofit Organizations and Community Interests*, Forth Worth, Tex.: Dryden Press.

MILTON, K. (1996). *Environmentalism and Cultural Theory*, London: Routledge.

MOLL, P. (1991). *From Scarcity to Sustainability: Future Studies and the Environment: the Role of the Club of Rome*, Frankfurt: Peter Lang.

MORRIS, A. D., and MUELLER, C. M. (eds.) (1992). *Frontiers in Social Movement Theory*, New Haven: Yale University Press.

MORTON, J. P. (1993). 'Environment and Religion: The Evolution of a New Vision', in F. Hull (ed.), *Earth & Spirit: The Spiritual Dimension of the Environmental Crisis*, New York: Continuum, 119–132.

NAESS, A. (1988). 'Identification as a Source of Deep Ecological Attitudes', in M. Tobias (ed.), *Deep Ecology*, San Marcos, Calif.: Avant Books, 256–70.

NASH, R. (1982). *Wilderness and the American Mind*, 3rd edn., New Haven: Yale University Press.

—— (1989). *The Rights of Nature: A History of Environmental Ethics*, Madison, Wis.: The University of Wisconsin Press.

NASR, S. H. (1968). 'Islam and the Earth', *The Encounter of Man and Nature*, London: Allen & Unwin.

Natuurbeleidsplan (1989). Ministerie van LNV, Den Haag: SDU Uitgeverij.

Natuurontwikkeling (1989). Ministerie van LNV, Den Haag: SDU Uitgeverij.

NICHOLSON, S. (ed.) (1989). *The Goddess Re-awakening: The Feminine Principle Today*, Wheaton, Ill.: Quest Books.

NIJPELS, E. (1995). *de Volkskrant*, 25 Feb.

Nota Landschap (1992). Ministerie van LNV, Den Haag: LNV.

NUU-CHAH-NULTH TRIBAL COUNCIL (1990). *Nuu-chah-nulth Land Question: Land Sea and Resources*, Port Alberni, BC, September (pamphlet).

O'CONNOR, J. (1991). 'Socialism and Ecology', *Capitalism, Nature, Socialism*, 2(3): 1–12.

ODUM, E. P. (1953). *Fundamentals of Ecology*, Philadelphia: Saunders.

—— (1969). 'The Strategy of Ecosystem Development', *Science*, 164: 262–70.

OELSCHLAEGER, M. (1994). *Caring for Creation: An Ecumenical Approach to the Environmental Crisis*, New Haven: Yale University Press.

OFOSU-AMAAH, W. (ed.) (1991). *Asia-Pacific Regional Assembly: Women and Environment: Partners in Life*, Washington, DC.: WorldWide Network.

OLWIG, K. R. (1996). 'Environmental History and the Construction of Nature and Landscape: The Case of the "landscaping" of the Jutland Heath', *Environment and History*, 2: 15–38.

PALMER, M. (1991). *The Elements of Taoism*, Rockport, Mass.: Element.

PASSMORE, J. (1980). *Man's Responsibility for Nature. Ecological Problems and Western Traditions*, London: Duckworth.

PEET, R., and WATTS, M. (eds.) (1996a). *Liberation Ecologies*. New York: Routledge.

—————— (1996b). 'Introduction', in R. Peet and M. Watts (eds.), *Liberation Ecologies*, New York: Routledge.

PEPPER, D. (1993). *Eco-socialism: From Deep Ecology to Social Justice*, London: Routledge.

PERKIN, H. (1996). *The Third Revolution: Professional Elites in the Modern World*, London: Routledge.

PERKINS MARSH, G. (1864). *Man and Nature*, New York: Charles Scribner's.

PICARDI, A. C. (1974). 'A Systems Analysis of Pastoralism in the West African Sahel', in W. W. Seifert and N. Kamrany (eds.), *A Framework For Evaluating Long-Term Strategies For The Development Of The Sahel-Sudan Region*, Cambridge, Mass.: MIT Center for Policy Alternatives.

PICKETT, S. T. A., and WHITE, P. S. (eds.) (1985). *The Ecology of Natural Disturbance and Patch Dynamics*, Orlando, Fla.: Academic Press.

PLUMWOOD, V. (1993). *Feminism and the Mastery of Nature*, London: Routledge.

POLANYI, K. (1944). *The Great Transformation: The Political and Economic Origins of Our Time*, New York: Rinehart & Co.

POPE JOHN PAUL II (1990). 'The Ecological Crisis: A Common Responsibility', repr. in Gottlieb (1996: 230–7).

PRAKASH, S. (1998). 'Fairness, Social Capital and the Commons', in M. Goldman (ed.), *Privatizing Nature: Political Struggles for the Global Commons*, London: Pluto, 167–97.

PRICE, M. F., and THOMPSON, M. (1997). 'The Complex Life: Human Land Uses in Mountain Ecosystems', *Global Ecology and Biogeography Letters*, 6: 77–90.

RAMBLER, M., MARGULIS, L., and FESTER, R. (eds.) (1989). *Global Ecology: Towards a Science of the Biosphere*, San Diego: Academic Press.

RAWLS, J. (1971). *A Theory of Justice*, Cambridge, Mass.: Harvard University Press.

REGAN, T. (1983). *The Case for Animal Rights*, Berkeley, Calif.: University of California Press.

REICE, S. R. (1994). 'Nonequilibrium Determinants of Biological Community Structure', *American Scientist*, 82 (Sept.–Oct.): 424–35.

REILLY, W. K. (1990). 'The Environmental Benefits of Sustainable Growth', *Policy Review* (Fall): 16–21.

RENNER, M. (1996). *Fighting for Survival: Environmental Decline, Social conflict and the New Age of Insecurity*, New York and London: Norton for Worldwatch Institute.

RICH, B. (1993). *Mortgaging the Earth: The World Bank, Environmental Impoverishment and the Crisis of Development*, Boston: Beacon Press.

ROBERTS, E. (1990). 'Gaian Buddhism', in A. H. Badiner (ed.), *Dharma Gaia: A Harvest of Essays in Buddhism and Ecology*, Berkeley, Calif.: Parallax Press, 147–54.

RODDA, A. (1993). *Women and the Environment*, London: Zed Books.

RODMAN, J. (1977). 'The Liberation of Nature?', *Inquiry*, 20: 83–125.

—— (1983). 'Four Forms of Ecological Consciousness Reconsidered', in D. Scherer and T. Attig (eds.), *Ethics and the Environment*, Englewood Cliffs, NJ: Prentice-Hall.

RODWELL, J. M. (tr.)(1994). *The Koran*, London: Everyman.

ROSZAK, T. (1969). *The Making of a Counter Culture*, New York: Anchor Books.

—— GOMES, M. E., and KANNER, A. D. (eds.) (1995). *Ecopsychology: Restoring the Earth, Healing the Mind*, San Francisco: Sierra Club Books.

RUETHER, R. R. (1993). 'Ecofeminism: Symbolic and Social Connections of the Oppression of Women and the Domination of Nature', in C. J. Adams (ed.), *Ecofeminism and the Sacred*, New York: Continuum, 13–23.

SACHS, W. (ed.) (1992). *The Development Dictionary: A Guide to Knowledge as Power*, London: Zed Books.

—— (ed.) (1993). *Global Ecology: A New Arena of Political Conflict*, London: Zed Books.

—— (1994). 'The Blue Planet. An Ambiguous Modern Icon', *The Ecologist*, 24: 170–5.

—— LOSKE, R., and LINZ, M. (eds.) (1997). *Greening the North: A Postindustrial Blueprint for Ecology and Equity*, London: Zed Books.

SALE, K. (1993). *The Green Revolution: The American Environmental Movement 1962–1992*, New York: Hill and Wang.

SALLEH, A. (1997). *Ecofeminism as Politics: Nature, Marx and the Postmodern*, London: Zed Books.

SCHAMA, S. 1995. *Landscape and Memory*, London: Harper Collins Publishers.

SCHMIDHEINY, S. (1992). *Changing Course: A Global Business Perspective on Development and the Environment*, Cambridge, Mass.: MIT Press.

SCHMIDT-BLEEK, F. (1994). *Wieviel Umwelt braucht der Mensch?*, Berlin and Basel: Birkhäuser.

SCHNEIDER, K. (1993). 'Plan for Toxic Dump Pits Blacks against Blacks', *New York Times* 13 Dec., A12.

SCHUMACHER, E. F. (1973). *Small is Beautiful: A Study of Economics as if People Mattered*, London: Sphere Books Ltd.

SCHWARZ, M., and THOMPSON, M. (1990). *Divided We Stand: Re-defining Politics, Technology and Social Choice*, Philadelphia: University of Pennsylvania Press.

SCHWARZ, M., and PAUL, S. (1992). 'Resource Mobilization versus the Mobilization of People: Why Consensus Movements Cannot be Instruments of Social Change', in A. D. Morris and C. M. Mueller (eds.), *Frontiers in Social Movement Theory*, New Haven: Yale University Press, 205–223.

SCHWARZ, W., and SCHWARZ, D. (1987). *Breaking Through*, Bideford: Green Books.

Scientific American (1990). *Managing Planet Earth: Readings from Scientific American*, New York: Freeman.

SCOTT, J. C. (1976). *The Moral Economy of the Peasant: Rebellion and Subsistence in Southeast Asia*, New Haven: Yale University Press.

SEED, J., MACY, J., FLEMING, P., and NAESS, A. (1988). *Thinking like a Mountain: Towards a Council of All Beings*, Philadelphia: New Society Publishers.

SEWALL, L. (1995). 'The Skill of Ecological Perception', in T. Roszak, M. E. Gomes, and A. D. Kanner (eds.), *Ecopsychology: Restoring the Earth, Healing the Mind*, San Francisco: Sierra Club Books, 201–15.

SHIVA, V. (1989). *Staying Alive: Women, Ecology and Development*, London: Zed Books.

SHRADER-FRECHETTE, K. S., and McCOY, E. D. (1993). *Method in Ecology*, Cambridge: Cambridge University Press.

SIJMONS, D. F. 1991. *Het casco-concept*, Ministerie van LNV, Utrecht.

SITARZ, D. (ed.) (1993). *Agenda 21: The Earth Summit Strategy to Save our Planet*, Boulder, Colo.: EarthPress.

SLEZKINE, Y. (1994). *Arctic Mirrors: Russia and the Small Peoples of the North*, Ithaca, NY: Cornell University Press.

SMITH, A. (1993). 'For all those who were Indian in a Former Life', in C. J. Adams (ed.), *Ecofeminism and the Sacred*, New York: Continuum, 168–71.

SMITH, C. A. (1984). 'Local History in Global Context: Social and Economic Transitions in Western Guatemala', *Comparative Studies In Society And History*, 26(2): 193–228.

SMITH, H. (1991). *The World's Religions: Our Great Wisdom Traditions*, San Francisco: Harper.

SMITH, R. Y. (1997). '*Hishuk ish ts'awalk*—All Things Are One: Traditional Ecological Knowledge and Forest Practices in Ahousaht First Nation's Traditional Territory, Clayoquot Sound, BC', MA Thesis, Trent University, Peterborough, Ont.

SMUTS, J. C. (1927). *Holism and Evolution*, London: Macmillan.

SNOW, D. A., and BENFORD, R. D. (1992). 'Master Frames and Cycles of Protest', in A. D. Morris and C. M. Mueller (eds.), *Frontiers in Social Movement Theory*, New Haven: Yale University Press, 133–55.

SONTHEIMER, S. (ed.) (1988), *Women and the Environment: A Reader, Crisis and Development in the Third World*, New York: Monthly Review Press.

SOROS, G. (1997). 'The Capitalist Threat', *The Atlantic Monthly*, 279.2 (Feb.): 45–58.

SPAEMANN, R. (1967). 'Genetisches zum Naturbegriff des 18. Jahrhunderts', *Archiv für Begriffsgeschichte*, 11: 59–74.

SPANGLER, D. (1993). 'Imagination, Gaia, and the Sacredness of the Earth', in F. Hull (ed.), *Earth & Spirit: The Spiritual Dimension of the Environmental Crisis*, New York: Continuum, 70–82.

SPOEHR, A. (1956). 'Cultural Differences in the Interpretation of Natural Resources', in Thomas (1956: 93–102).

SPRETNAK, C., and CAPRA, F. (1986). *Green Politics: The Global Promise*, rev. edn., Sante Fe: Bear and Co.

STARHAWK (1989). 'Feminist Earth-Based Spirituality and Ecofeminism', in J. Plant (ed.), *Healing the Wounds: The Promise of Ecofeminism*, Santa Cruz, Calif.: New Society Publishers, 174–85.

—— (1990). 'Power, Authority, and Mystery: Ecofeminism and Earth-Based Spirituality', in I. Diamond and G. F. Orenstein (eds.), *Reweaving the World: The Emergence of Ecofeminism*, San Francisco: Sierra Club Books.

SWARTZ, D. (1996). 'Jews, Jewish Texts, and Nature: A Brief History', in Gottlieb (1996: 87–103).

SWIDLER, A. (1986). 'Culture in Action: Symbols and Strategies', *American Sociological Review*, 51 (April): 273–86.

SZASZ, A. (1994). *EcoPopulism: Toxic Waste and the Movement for Environmental Justice*, Minneapolis: University of Minnesota Press.

TANDON, Y. (1993). 'Village Contradictions in Africa', in Sachs (1993:208–23).

TARROW, S. (1992). 'Mentalities, Political Cultures, and Collective Action Frames', in Morris (1992: 174–202).

TAYLOR, B. P. (1991). 'Environmental Ethics and Political Theory', *Polity*, 23: 567–83.

TAYLOR, B. R. (1995). 'Popular Ecological Resistance and Radical Environmentalism', in B. R. Taylor (ed.), *Ecological Resistance Movements: The Global Emergence of Radical and Popular Environmentalism*, Albany, NY: State University of New York Press, 334–54.

TAYLOR, C. (1975). *Hegel*, Cambridge: Cambridge University Press.

TAYLOR, D. (1992). 'Can the Environmental Movement Attract and Maintain the Support of Minorities?', in Bryant and Mohai (1992).

—— (1993). 'Environmentalism and the Politics of Inclusion', in Bullard (1993).

TAYLOR, P. J. (1988). 'Technocratic Optimism', *Journal of the History of Biology*, 21(2): 213–44.

—— (1990). 'Mapping Ecologists' Ecologies of Knowledge', *Philosophy of Science Association*, 2: 95–109.

—— (1992). 'Re/constructing Socio-Ecologies: System Dynamics Modeling of Nomadic Pastoralists in Sub-Saharan Africa', in A. Clarke and J. Fujimura (eds.), *The Right Tools For The Job: At Work In Twentieth-Century Life Sciences*, Princeton: Princeton University Press, 115–48.

—— (1995). 'Building on Construction: An Exploration of Heterogeneous Constructionism, Using an Analogy from Psychology and a Sketch from Socio-Economic Modeling', *Perspectives on Science*, 3(1): 66–98.

TAYLOR, P. J. (1997). 'Shifting Positions for Knowing and Intervening in the Cultural Politics of the Life Sciences', in P. J. Taylor, S. E. Halfon, and P. E. Edwards (eds.), *Changing Life: Genomes-Ecologies-Bodies-Commodities*, Minneapolis: University of Minnesota Press, 203–24.

—— (1999). 'Critical Tensions and Non-Standard Lessons from the "Tragedy of the Commons" ', in M. Maniates (ed.), *Teaching Global Environmental Politics As If Education Mattered*, forthcoming.

—— and BUTTEL, F. H. (1992). 'How do we Know we Have Global Environmental Problems? Science and the Globalization of Environmental Discourse', *Geoforum*, 23: 405–16.

—— and GARCÍA-BARRIOS, R. (1995). 'The Social Analysis of Ecological Change: From Systems to Intersecting Processes', *Social Science Information*, 34(1): 5–30.

—— (1997). 'Dynamics and Rhetorics of Socioenvironmental Change: Critical Perspectives on the Limits of Neo-Malthusian Environmentalism', *Advances in Human Ecology*, 6: 257–92.

—— and HAILA, Y. (1989). 'Mapping Workshops for Teaching Ecology', *Bulletin of the Ecological Society of America*, 70(2): 123–5.

THOMAS, W. L. (ed. 1956), *Man's Role in Changing the Face of the Earth*, Chicago: The University of Chicago Press.

THOMPSON, M. (1997a). 'Cultural Theory and Integrated Assessment', *Environmental Modelling and Assessment*, 2: 139–50.

—— (1997b). 'Re-writing the Precepts of Policy Analysis', in R. Ellis and M. Thompson (eds.), *Culture Matters* (Boulder, Colo.: West View Press, forthcoming), 203–16.

—— (1998). 'Style and Scale: Two Sources of Institutional Inappropriateness', in M. Goldman (ed.) *Privatizing Nature: Political Struggles for the Global Commons*, London: Pluto.

—— ELLIS, R., and WILDAVSKY, A. (1990). *Cultural Theory*, Boulder, Colo., and Oxford: West View Press.

—— and TRISOGLIO, A. (1997). 'Managing the Unmanageable', in L. A. Brooks and S. D. Vanderveer (eds) *Saving the Seas: Values, Scientists and International Governance*, College Park, Md.: Maryland Sea Grant College, 107–27.

—— WARBURTON, M., and HATLEY, T. (1986). *Uncertainty on a Himalayan Scale*, London: Ethnographica.

TIMM, R. E. (1993). 'The Ecological Fallout of Islamic Creation Theology', in M. E. Tucker and J. A. Grim (eds.), *Worldviews and Ecology*, Lewisburg, Pa.: Bucknell University Press, 83–95.

TOBIAS, M., MORRISON, J., and GRAY, B. (1995). *A Parliament of Souls: In Search of Global Spirituality*, San Francisco: KQED Books.

TODOROV, Z. (1984). *The Conquest of America*, New York: Harper Collins.

TORGERSON, D. (1995). 'The Uncertain Quest for Sustainability: Public Discourse and the Politics of Environmentalism', in Fischer and Black (1995: 3–20).

—— (1997). 'Policy Professionalism and the Voices of Dissent: The Case of Environmentalism', *Polity*, 29: 345–74.

—— (1999). *The Promise of Green Politics: Environmentalism and the Public Sphere*, Durham, NC: Duke University Press (forthcoming).

TREPL, L. (1983). 'Ökologie—eine grüne Leitwissenschaft?', *Kursbuch*, 74: 6–28.

TRICE, H. M. (1985). 'Rites and Ceremonials in Organizational Cultures', *Research in the Sociology of Organizations*, 4: 221–70.

TRZYNA, T. C. (1995). *A Sustainable World: Defining and Measuring Sustainable Development*, Berkeley: California Institute of Public Affairs.

TURNER, M. (1993). 'Overstocking the range: A critical analysis of the environmental science of Sahelian pastoralism', *Economic Geography*, 69(4): 402–21.

TURNER, T. (1995). *The Conserver Society*, London: Zed Books.

UCHITELLE, L. (1995). 'For Many, a Slower Climb up the Payroll Pecking Order', *New York Times*, Sunday 14 May, F.11.

VAN DER WINDT, H. (1995). *En dan: wat is natuur nog in dit land? Natuurbescherming in Nederland 1880–1990*, Amsterdam: Boom.

VAUGHAN, R. (1994). *The Arctic: A History*, Phoenix Mill, Gloucestershire: Alan Sutton.

VAYDA, A. P. (1996). *Methods and Explanations in the Study of Human Actions and their Environmental Effects*, Jakarta: Center for International Forestry Research.

VERA, F. W. M. (1992). 'Ecologische overwegingen', *Cahiers Bio-wetenschappen en Maatschap-pij*, 15(3): 15–23.

—— (1994). *Wagenings Universiteitsblad* (WUB), 6 Oct.

VERNANT, J.-P. (1991). *Mortals and Immortals: Collected Essays*, Princeton: Princeton University Press.

WACKERNAGEL, M., and REES, W. (1995). *Our Ecological Footprint: Reducing Human Impact on the Earth*, Gabriola Island (Canada): New Society Publishers.

WALDROP, M. (1992). *Complexity: The Emerging Science at the Edge of Order and Chaos*, New York: Simon and Schuster.

WALKER, B. G. (1988). *The Woman's Dictionary of Symbols & Sacred Objects*, San Francisco: Harper & Row.

WALL, D. (1994). *Green History: A Reader in Environmental Literature, Philosophy and Politics*, New York: Routledge.

WARING, M. (1988). *If Women Counted: A New Feminist Economics*, London: Macmillan.

WARREN, K. J. (ed.) (1994). *Ecological feminism*, New York: Routledge.

WEALE, A. (1992). *The New politics of Pollution*, Manchester: Manchester University Press.

WENZ, P. (1988). *Environmental Justice*, Albany, NY: State University of New York Press.

WESTMEN, W. E. (1978). 'How Much are Nature's Services Worth', *Science*, 197: 960–4.

WHITE, L., Jr. (1973). 'The Historical Roots of our Ecologic Crisis', in I. G. Barbour (ed.), *Western Man and Environmental Ethics: Attitudes toward Nature and Technology*, Reading, Mass.: Addison-Wesley, 18–30.

WHITEHEAD, A. N. (1925). *Science and the Modern World*, Cambridge: Cambridge University Press.

WIENS, J. A. (1996). 'Oil, Seabirds, and Science: The Effects of the Exxon Valdez Oil Spill', *BioScience*, 46: 587–97.

WILLIAMS, R. (1961). *The Long Revolution*, London: Chatto and Windus.

—— (1973). *The Country and the City*, London: Chatto and Windus.

—— (1989). *Resources of Hope*, London: Verso.

—— (1980). 'Ideas of Nature', in Raymond Williams, *Problems in Materialism and Culture*, London: Verso, 67–85.

WILHELM, R. (tr.) (1977). *The I Ching or Book of Changes*, Princeton: Princeton University Press.

WILSON, E. O. (1984). *Biophilia: The Human Bond with Other Species*, Cambridge, Mass.: Harvard University Press.

WITOSZEK, N. (1997). 'The Anti-Romantic Romantics; Nature, Knowledge, and Identity in Nineteenth-Century Norway', in T. Mikulás, R. Porter, and B. Gustafsson (eds.), *Nature and Society in Historical Context*, Cambridge: Cambridge University Press, 209–27.

WOMEN S INTERNATIONAL POLICY ACTION COMMITTEE (IPAC) (1992), *Official Report, World Women's Congress for a Healthy Planet*, Miami, Fla., 8–12 Nov. 1991, New York: Women's Environment and Development Organization (WEDO).

WORLD BANK (1992). *World Development Report 1992*, New York: Oxford University Press.

WORLD COMMISSION on ENVIRONMENT and DEVELOPMENT (1987). *Our Common Future*, New York: Oxford University Press.

WORSTER, D. (ed.) (1988). *The Ends of the Earth: Perspecitves on Modern Environmental History*, Cambridge: Cambridge University Press.

—— (1990). 'Ecology of Order and Chaos', *Environmental History Review*, 14(1–2) (Spring/Summer): 4–16.

—— (1992/4). *Nature's Economy: A History of Ecological Ideas*, Cambridge: Cambridge University Press.

WYNNE, B. (1994). 'Scientific Knowledge and the Global Environment', in M. Redclift and T. Benton (eds.), *Social Theory and the Global Environment*, London: Routledge, 169–89.

YALE SCHOOL OF FORESTRY and ENVIRONMENTAL STUDIES (1996). *Bulletin*, New Haven: Yale University.

YEARLEY, S. (1996). *Globalization, Environmentalism and Sociology*, London: Sage.

YOUNG, C. (1994). 'Clayoquot Silence: Who Will Speak for the Trees?', in H. Breen-Needham *et al.* (eds.), *Witness to Wilderness: The Clayoquot Sound Anthology*, Vancouver: Arsenal Pulp Press.

YOUNG, I. M. (1987). 'Impartiality and the Civic Public', in S. Benhabib and D. Cornell (eds.), *Feminism as Critique*, Minneapolis: University of Minnesota Press.

—— (1992). 'Communication and the Other: Beyond Deliberative Democracy', in S. Benhabib (ed.), *Democracy and Difference: Contesting the Boundaries of the Political*, Princeton: Princeton University Press.

ZIZEK, S. (1993). *Tarrying with the Negative: Kant, Hegel, and the Critique of Ideology*, Durham: Duke University Press.

ZWEERS, W. (1994). 'Radicalism or Historical Consciousness: On Breaks and Continuity in the Discussion of Basic Attitudes', in W. Zweers and J. J. Boersema (eds.), *Ecology, Technology and Culture*, Cambridge: The White Horse Press, 63–72.

INDEX

Note: major chapter references are in **bold** type

2042 INSO 23/3/7